THE

FOOTBALL

SPIDER WEB

How the Beautiful Game has Evolved

~A Journey through History~

1st Edition

Paperback ISBN: 9798682211081
Independently published by Amazon.com

Design and Typesetting by Ammandev Bajwa
Twitter & Instagram: @ammandev
YouTube Channel: 'Dev Bajwa'
LinkedIn: 'Dev Bajwa'

CONTENTS

'THE FAMILY MAN' 3

'TIT MEETS TAT' 21

'GOING TOO FAR' 33

'THE MASTER AT WORK' 45

'EL MAESTRO EN EL TRABAJO' 55

'I WENT TO AMSTERDAM ONCE ...' 73

'WHERE EVEN *IS* SOUTH AMERICA?' 81

'I'M NOT WEARING THESE!' 89

'THE HOOLIGAN'S GAME' 99

'MERGING THE STYLES' 113

'THE BIG IDEA' 123

'FOOTBALL'S GREATEST GLOW-UP' 133

'BREAKING FREE' 141

'THE FRENCH REVOLUTION' 149

'THE GALACTICOS' 165

'WELCOME TO 'CHELSKI'' 175

'MR. CONSISTENT' 193

'UNA CORTO SERIE DE EVENTOS DESAFORTUNADOS' 215

'THE SECOND COMING' 221

'PLEASE … I CAN CHANGE!' 235

'A GUIDE FOR WHAT *NOT* TO DO' 247

'WATCH AND LEARN' 261

'THE FALL OF A GIANT' 279

'MANCHESTER IS BLUE' 293

'THE RISE OF THE PHOENIX' 307

'WINNING BY KO' 319

'WHAT JUST HAPPENED?!' 329

'THE AGENT'S PLAYGROUND' 347

'LET'S TRY THIS AGAIN' 361

'KLOPP'S MERSEYSIDE REVOLUTION' 377

'LOOKING THROUGH THE CRYSTAL FOOT-BALL' 390

To Ms. Brown who helped me realise my love for writing, and to my Dad for introducing to me something worth writing about.

~ INTRODUCTION ~

The Journey Begins . . .

For those who truly embrace the game for what it is, it soon becomes apparent that football transcends the confines of a mere 'sport'.

You become personally affiliated with your team to the point where their triumphs and tribulations are your own, and there are few which can match football's reach and appeal when connecting with their audience. The international World Cup remains the most highly watched sporting competition on the globe each term that it appears, one of the game's elite stars in Cristiano Ronaldo ranks as the most influential athlete of his generation - with a chart-topping worldwide social media following to suit, and clubs as commercially visible as Manchester United or Real Madrid are among the most recognisable brands ever formed.

Personally, my appreciation for the game began very early on in my life and has since developed into something as in-depth as a *book* to get the message across! Now, I may not be an esteemed writer – or even a professional 'author' by definition, but I am a natural academic; someone who is addicted to learning and loves looking at things through a lens which is different to the convention. Some may call me a 'nerd' or a fully-fledged 'geek', though I prefer to use the term 'dedicated'. Therefore, my intention is for this novel to be seen as nothing less than a *dedication* to enciphering the key points in history which have defined the game that we can't live without.

Of course, I have my opinions and you will have yours, but let's approach this with an open mind, and then, who knows? You might even learn a thing or two.

~ 1 ~

'THE FAMILY MAN'
The King of the Dossier

I don't know about you, but for me, there are few things in this world that can match the excitement which surrounds a good weekend of football.

I suppose there's just something about two groups of bawdy lads kicking a ball around which gets our provincial juices pumping – actually, stick a cider in my hand and you're golden. Especially today, the game adopts a very high tempo, is massively hyped up and is played with a similar level of intensity throughout the world. But it wasn't always like that. In fact, as we will come to explore, the game has had to be transported through a myriad of changing times and influences to arrive at the what we recognise today. I suppose then, that it would be sensible to establish a timeline to work from.

I have chosen to begin our journey of reflection in the early 1970's. But before you get all 'you don't know anything' on me, allow me to say this: obviously, there are many important moments prior to this which have been very influential in the game's development as well, so my choice is not intended to render them insignificant. Far from it.

My reasoning is far more innocent: as we move into 2020, I thought '50' was a nice and round number to trace back with. Maths has never been my best subject but, 2020 − 50 = 1970, and it's only when I started researching this time's most historical moments that it proved to be a worthy choice.

For the want of sounding less and less like a typical millennial that knows nothing about 'the way things were', the 'mature' amongst you most likely look at the '70s game through rose-tinted spectacles … or spectacles of some kind, at least. I can almost hear you thinking aloud: 'sides were made of *real men'*, 'the game was just *different'*, 'what do you mean he's on three-hundred quid a *week*' blah-blah-blah.

In reality, and casting aside any generational bias, history shows us that football from around this time was insanely one-dimensional and … a little bit boring!

***

Particularly in England, most clubs employed that 'hoof the ball into the air and hope' approach which offered little by way of excitement or idiosyncrasy. Nowadays, the game is more fine-tuned, and its participants are divided by a series of systems emerging from dugouts and boardrooms the world over. But before their voices could be heard, fans had to settle for a usually direct and physical game plan, where even this decade's inaugural title winners were a case in point.

Although they aren't a typically forgiving bunch (the phrase 'Wenger Out' comes to mind), I do hope that any readers with an affinity to Arsenal Football Club will pardon my overlooking their achievements in the 1970/71 season. Though my reasoning is simple: their manager (Bertie Mee), while respected for his achievements, had relentlessly followed that battered old conventional tactic throughout the entire campaign. It went like this: crunch out your opponent's striker whenever they come near your penalty area, win the ball (legally or otherwise), poke it out to the midfield, ship it off to the wide men on the wings, cross the ball into the striker, and Bob will be your uncle. With that organised, and his team having possessed the competition's better players to carry this out on a weekly basis, it's no wonder that they won the title – when their adversaries were doing the same thing – only worse!

Quite frankly, if it were left up to them, the game may have continued at this level of predictability for a few more seasons, unless somebody was able to either: develop a better bunch of players to challenge them or, mercifully, introduce and implement a superior tactical style and nullify the method that was working too easily.

Luckily for us all, their closest competitors that season were Leeds United who, despite not winning the league, were planting the seeds of change. And playing the role of 'Chief Gardener' was an imposing, stern-faced character by the name of Donald Revie ... or 'Don' to his mates.

The term 'resolute' comes to mind when considering the early life and career of Don Revie; which I'd like to think he would have allowed me to call him. Born in between two World Wars, Revie was raised in the Northern UK county of

Middlesbrough – then a working class, metalworks and coal mining city struggling from the knock-on effects of the Great Depression in the United States – carrying over as the 'Great Slump' of the UK in the early 1930's.

Dubbed a "dismal town" by respected English novelist J.B. Priestley, his father (whose name was also 'Donald') was one of the many sufferers within the industrial heartlands.

In a period where work was hard to come by, any income had to be stretched, distorted and contorted in order to create a liveable environment for his wife and son; made all the more unbearable following the deeply unfortunate loss of Don's mother in 1939 - when her son was only twelve.

Revie - then a prepubescent lad angered by his old man's hardships – sought to escape the confines of the classroom in favour of a bricklaying apprenticeship to provide an additional income stream into the household. And after scoring a scheme with a local merchant (a friend of his dad's), his first day beckoned before an unwelcome radio announcement changed his plans … and everybody else's.

After UK Prime Minister Winston Churchill had declared war on Germany and their fearsome leader Adolf Hitler, a barbaric and deeply distressing six-year-long battle ensued before his tyrannical dictatorship was ended.

During this time, many of Don's age would either have been cooped up in a bomb shelter or shipped off to the countryside somewhere to find *Narnia*, instead, he stayed with his father in their family home in respect of that 'Keep Calm and Carry On' mentality. Then, once the war had ended and there was little left of the North East to keep your spirits up, through the creaking embers of his surroundings, a simple leather ball became a beacon of hope for a brighter post-War life for the 'Dons'; one where the young'un wouldn't have to lay a single brick.

Thus, began an eighteen-year-long senior football career, where Revie earned 450 appearances during stints in attack for: Leicester City, Hull City, Manchester City, Sunderland Athletic and, pointedly, Leeds United. Mind you, his eventual introduction to the Yorkshire side could've been a little rosier than it was.

Only two years prior to his arrival at the club in 1958 (which would turn out to be his final year as a player), the club had agreed to the sale of prolific striker John Charles to Turin powerhouses Juventus. The man once adored as 'The King' in his homeland exchanged his royal prefix for '*Il Gigante Buono*' in Italy (which loosely translates as 'The Good Giant' in Italian). And it was *Il Gigante's* departure which coincided with a dramatic drop in form for the remaining employees at Elland Road.

Contrasting the ecstasy of Leeds' promotion to England's top division in 1957 (thanks largely to Charles' goal-scoring record), Don had arrived just in time to enjoy one final season in the topflight before the club dropped back down into the Second Division at the end of the 1959/60 campaign.

By which point, at the age of 34, Don's weary war-hardened legs were no longer fit to compete in professional football, let alone one as physical and relentless as the domestic Second Division, and so he hung up his boots for good before Leeds's new campaign had even kicked off. However, as would come to be expected from Don Revie's impending managerial career, even his decision to retire (and the timing of it) was tactful and highly calculated on his part.

He'd adored the game and enjoyed a fine playing career but was by no means ready for a life of telling his offspring what a great player their 'Daddy' used to be. As far as he was concerned, there was still plenty more to do, just from a different vantage point. And frankly, his anally preparative and principal-like manner made a management role inevitable in theory, though the reality of his introduction into this line of work was unconventional at best.

Times were different to the exams-ridden process of what it takes to become a football manager today. And for those who have never been too bothered about what modern-day managers have to go through before being lambasted in the press and abused by their own supporters, it's a case of returning to the classroom – where domestic football associations offer a variety of courses aimed at honing and developing the skills presumedly required to succeed at the highest level.

In England, where the game is governed by the Football Association (the 'FA') you begin with the aptly named 'FA Level 1 in Coaching Football', through to the heralded 'FA Level 5 in Coaching Football' – more commonly known as a 'UEFA Pro License' - which gives the holder the opportunity to be hired on an international level within the EU … Brexit may mess this up a bit but the least said about that the better!

As you would imagine, this is a substantial undertaking for any coach to tackle in terms of the level of commitment and time that is required to get from Levels 1-5, notwithstanding the £4,000+ bill that the FA will shove through your letterbox once you get to Level 4. Luckily for Revie and many coaches around his era, he was able to benefit from an arrangement that is not too dissimilar to that of an unofficial apprenticeship under then-manager Jack Taylor – which is better than bricklaying, I imagine.

Though technically still employed as a footballer by Taylor, Revie's seniority soon invited a higher level of responsibility from the Gaffer on the pitch, where he often assumed the captain's duties and was accountable for directly translating his employer's wishes onto his teammates. Then, after having announced an overt interest in coaching, he soon struck up a healthy acquaintance with the manager – who'd in turn reward Don's *chutzpah* by allowing him to dish out the bibs in training sessions and chime in on the odd team talk here and there.

Eventually, the club's fall in form revealed Revie to be the most convenient and time-efficient successor to Taylor after he'd been sacked in the summer of 1961.

Now, regardless of how much he must've wanted to become a manager by this point in his career, this was a baptism of fire for even the most seasoned vet in his profession.

Not only was he tasked with restoring some of the pride lost in the Leeds crest, but he also had to manage his mates in the process! Lest we forget, it was practically yesterday when player Revie was just another name on the team sheet – lacing his boots up in the dressing room with the rest of the lads and taking the mickey out of the manager when his back was turned. And then suddenly, the jokes were going to be made without him and … *about him*. I tell you, better him than me!

So, you'd be forgiven for thinking that, once he was hired (a better term may be 'promoted'), he would be a little reticent in making any drastic changes to the setup - perhaps just ease your way in, learn the ropes and slowly see what might need changing … over a long period … and many cups of tea … perhaps a scone … or *scones* … plural.

But Don didn't do that. Oh no, instead he threw caution to the wind, and did what he felt was in the best interests of his club's long-term future.

Revie went above his station and set about changing the very foundations of Leeds United Football Club. For you see, as they fluttered between England's top two divisions over the past few years, Revie discovered flaws within the moral fabric of the club; where its lack of identity and sense of unity bred the fleeting form with which their fans became unwillingly accustomed to. And his solution, though 'radical' in terms of how it would be implemented, heeded closely to his simple, modest upbringing.

He was an old school man, from a working-class background - where the importance of family and togetherness formed the bedrock of his tight-knit community. Therefore, Leeds' disjointedness and inconsistency were the antithesis of what Revie considered 'normal' when he wound up there.

Growing up, Don came to respect the privilege that came with being a football player, and he felt that an injection of respect and humility was required to take the club forward. And by implementing an almost 'family-like' culture at 'work', Revie believed that the club stood a better chance of improving their togetherness and enjoying a more successful future together as a result

Before they knew it, everybody at the club – from the players to the cleaners – went from being disparate employees of 'Leeds United Football Club' to united members of the new 'Leeds family' – with Daddy Don acting as the sole patriarch.

It was a loving, yet revolutionary concept which bred a higher and more consistent level of performance during his revered tenure in charge of Leeds United. But don't let this fool you completely, just because this particular concept made sense and was successful, that's not to say that Don's managerial stint went *wholly* unblemished, and without the odd thing that either went wrong or couldn't be explained … not even by him!

For someone so exact and data-driven, the man did love a good ol' fashioned superstition. One of Revie's 'sons' in the technically gifted Johnny Giles offers up a typically straight-talking review of his manager's quirks: "He was unbelievably superstitious. Once, I had my boots in a brown paper bag and I had to go into the offices to see him and I put the boots on the desk, and we were talking for about 10 minutes and he said, 'What's that?' "'They're my boots'. [Revie said], 'Get them off the table quick!' Because it was bad luck apparently. I didn't know. It was bad luck apparently to have boots on the table. He was unbelievable with superstitions."

And even away from the dressing room talk, it's widely rumoured (a somewhat believable rumour, mind you) that even Leeds' *kit change* was inspired by another of Revie's questionable beliefs.

Prior to his appointment, they donned a more noticeable yellow and blue trim – a presumed link with their 'Peacocks' nickname. But only a year after his arrival, this name was binned in favour of the simpler 'Whites' which is a more direct representation of his proposed new outfit - which has stood the test of time to this day.

From that in-your-face yellow strip, they opted for a cleaner off-white colour with block navy blue lettering across the shoulders. Even their training gear followed the same pattern without any individual names – and only 'Leeds United' sprawled across their backs to hammer home that 'the team comes first' philosophy, that he worked so relentlessly to impose.

Presently, it's suggested that this transformation was made to mimic the appearance of Spanish titans Real Madrid – then a consistent favourite to pick up their domestic honours in a star-studded line-up headed by the most highly revered pair of strikers for their generation; Alfredo Di Stéfano and Ferenc Puskás.

Yet despite doing their best to look alike to the best team in Europe, this might be where much of the similarities end between the two outfits, because whereas the Madridians' mystique was formed upon their attractive and all-conquering playing style, Leeds were slowly earning themselves a reputation which wasn't as complimentary …

"Dirty Leeds,

Dirty Leeds,

Dirty Leeds,

Dirty … Leeds"

[Origins Unknown]

It all began following the Whites' table-topping Second Division side in the 1963-64 season, where they moved into England's top division the following year in a side underpinned by the club's 'hardman' partnership of Billy Bremner and Jack Charlton; men who would strike fear in even the most cold-hearted of opponents. Beginning with

Bremner, the fiery Scot was the midfield dynamo at the heart of Revie's plans.

His talents drew praise from the world over; the most glowing of which was imparted by Mr. Revie himself who believed that "no manager could wish for a greater leader or a greater player" and if he'd found himself in the trenches of war, he'd hope for Bremner by his side. Fitting then that his legacy has since been immortalised in a bronze statue outside of Elland Road – his footballing home for over 15 years! Whether the statue serves as a tribute to his legendary club status or acts as a physical representation of his on-pitch brutality is up for debate.

Backing Bremner, Englishman Jack Charlton spent his entire career in North Yorkshire, much to the chagrin of his brother Bobby who would go on to earn a knighthood for his services to football whilst covered in the red of Manchester United – who still remain one of Leeds' most bitter rivals as the other half of the 'Rose Derby'.

The Charltons supposedly had a rather tense relationship during this time, and the success enjoyed by the younger Sir Bobby was like waving a matador's cape in front of his raging relative, who was so desperate to rival his brother's trophy cabinet; that he'd joined forces with a *Scot* to stand a chance of doing so! *The nerve* (!)

Together, they set the standard against which any youngster or new signing would be measured. Technically gifted and physically imposing, they possessed a good amount of raw talent matched with the grit necessary to perform consistently.

Better still, with Charlton in the back line and Bremner sitting in front, much of the proverbial 'spine' of the squad was sorted without Revie having to do anything. Therefore, any transfer business need only be focused on the lad getting the goals for them – the 'fun' stuff.

With John Charles' departure leaving a lack of goals in his wake, much of Revie's early transfer business centred around getting another striker to follow in his footsteps. Early on, he opted for Bobby Collins – somebody who would go on to typify Leeds' more physical approach – in a £25,000 move from Everton. Though despite his experience, Collins did little to establish himself at the club, and set the tone for some of Revie's other acquisitions after him, including: ex-Middlesbrough man Alan Peacock and Don's own former Manchester City teammate Billy McAdams; who were both far too immobile and 'old-fashioned' to connect with Revie's new and more united philosophy.

Simply put, experienced players tend to stick with what they know rather than keep up with their manager's new-fangled ideas, so the best thing for Revie to do was to look on the opposite spectrum – away from the seasoned 'men' in the league, and onto younger kids whose game could be more easily moulded to fit Revie's exacting specifications. And for this, looking at the club's own academy proved a necessary and worthwhile exercise.

As much as any Leeds fan may be loath to admit, this whole 'give youth a chance' policy isn't theirs to claim. In fact, I might be burned at the stake for saying that this tactic looks like an homage to their fierce rivals in Manchester – whose foundational academic philosophy had begun some years earlier in 1958. However, where Leeds *opted* for this approach as an alternative to their failing transfer policy, Manchester United's reason was very different indeed.

In the early afternoon on the 6th February 1958, the club's first team and backroom staff were scheduled to take a flight home from Yugoslavia following a European Cup match against Red Star Belgrade, who they'd evidently bettered to secure a spot in that season's semi-finals.

It was a fixture plagued by an onslaught of wintery weather conditions which had unfortunately blown its way onto the runway of British European Airways Flight 609 prior to its scheduled take-off. Harrowing on-flight accounts reveal that the aircraft had stuttered on its first two take-off attempts, before its third had nose-dived onto the sludge-ridden tarmac from which it had tried to escape. The impact rippled throughout the plane – fortunately dislodging a number of passengers away from the main fuselage which had caught fire.

Many of those onboard, including the team's manager and captain in Matt Busby and Bobby Charlton had survived the ordeal, but the same couldn't be said for twenty-three of their colleagues and friends – including eight of the players who'd run out against Red Star the evening before; all of whose names have been etched into immortality in a well-kept mural on the East Side stand of United's home at Old Trafford.

A particularly tragic inclusion on the fatalities list was Dudley-born Duncan Edwards; cutting short a most promising career which already included 151 senior appearances and 18 caps for his national side by the age of 21. Acclaimed by many, including Bobby Charlton as "the only player who made [him] feel inferior", it is right then that his talent is forever remembered in its own right, via a statue standing proudly a stone's throw away from his childhood home.

Tenderly, the statue had arrived just in time to oversee a nearby United squad earn an unprecedented treble of European and domestic honours for the 1998/99 season, featuring a number of academy graduates who have not only elbowed their ways into the history of their club, but in doing so paid a great homage to the lives who set the precedent.

But before the glory days had the chance to grace their way over the hallowed turf at Old Trafford once again, Leeds had their own crop of youngsters to rave over – including the naturally skilful Eddie Gray and the larger than life Norman "bites yer legs" Hunter – a nickname popularised by many opposition managers in respect (or fear) of his no-nonsense playing style.

Another comes in the form of one of my personal favourites in attacking midfielder Peter Lorimer who became an ambassador for the theatrical and spectacular goal from his 'drifter' role in the squad and finally, the ever-dependable full-back Paul Reaney who would remarkably go on to rack up around 750 appearances for the club.

Then, with the youngsters holding their own in the First Division, it gave Revie some freedom to spend a little more frivolously when he did venture back into the world of buying other men for money.

Though I suspect few expected his presumptuous £53,000 deal to bring back fan's favourite John Charles from Juventus in 1962 – five years after he'd been sold - at the age of 31.

Looking back, I can see why the transfer would have made *some* sense, in spite of the fee. He was unquestionably talented as an out-and-out goal-scorer, highly experienced on both the domestic and European stage, and his existing legendary status was sure to get a few more bums in the seats at Elland Road. But as much as I hate to say it, it looked more like what we would refer to today as a 'marketing ploy' than anything else.

Leeds weren't in a position to invest so heavily in an ageing striker without at least having a business-focused reason for doing so. And the fact is that, despite being in the topflight for the first time under Revie's stewardship, his new-look squad had alienated a number of hid elder fans, so the signing of Charles went a long way in bringing some of the old guard back to the ground and give his youngsters a shot – if they're good enough for John Charles, then they'd be good enough for them, I guess!

Not surprisingly, the novelty had lasted for just a single season; where he struggled within a team whose system no longer suited his playing decisions – tallying up a mere 3 goals in 11 appearances.

But never mind, at least they got a tidy £17,000 profit a year later when he was resold to Italy, this time to the capital with AS Roma – which sort of hammers home my theory as to for why this deal happened in the first place. Whether I'm right or wrong, it was a sound and tidy investment for a single year's work.

Better still, much of that money went on to finance the procurement of the aforementioned midfielder Johnny Giles; whose career began in the wake of the Munich Air Disaster when he registered 99 appearances for a young and fearless Manchester United side. Then, realising that his game time looked limited in the shadows of Paddy Crerand, Nobby Stiles, Denis Law and Bobby Charlton in the new-look Red Devils side, the hard-nosed Irishman was persuaded by Revie to join his family up in Leeds.

383 appearances and 88 goals later suggest that this wasn't a half-bad choice. And I suspect that the Irishman much prefers to recall Revie's superstitious nonsense than a life on the bench over in Manchester.

Together, youth blended with experience to bring home the club's maiden top-tier domestic triumph with the Football League Cup trophy in 1968 against Arsenal, where an early Terry Cooper goal was protected by a resolute and tough defensive display from the Whites.

Thereafter, with mouths salivating and the success addiction forming, they followed this up with dividends after romping their way towards taking the 1968/69 English First Division trophy away from Bill Shankly's famous Liverpool side. And with that, the world saw the culmination of a frankly monolithic effort from Revie and Leeds United.

His familial philosophy worked a treat in completely renovating the club as they broke valiantly away from much of that cold and no-fun era which preceded their bubbly new father figure arriving on the scene. And in the space of just over five years, he'd transformed a provincial, disinterested Second Division side into title-winners and Cup-getters.

But with their ascent to fame came the undue criticism which often befalls a successful outfit from their lowly rivals.

In this case, it was Leeds' professional misconduct which, for many, had dulled the shine casting over their achievements. The styles of the mentioned Bremner, Charlton and Hunter were, while effective, alarmingly intimidating and brutishly physical – to a point where they placed unfavourably high in that season's disciplinary charts in such a way so as to evade governmental sanction, but frighten their rivals and attract condemnation from whoever they'd beaten … *literally*.

Nevertheless, remaining composed and dismissive of such criticism, Revie was largely able to bat away a lot of this reproach from his fellowship – denouncing it as coming from wounded battle-men who'd lost the war against his superior outfit, though there was one man whose opinion got under his skin more than any other.

A man whose outspokenness, by this point, had preceded any true managerial achievement, though would soon pose a worthy adversary to Don Revie and Leeds United.

In fact, it was the frequent battles between these two men which helped to further cement my decision to begin my timeline here, with their frequent duals of wit and derision precluding plenty of managerial rivalries which have since spawned since they left, not to mention the odd tactical implementation and piece of transfer business as some of the earlier signals of where the game would soon transport to.

So, in the white corner we have First Division champion, Mr. Don Revie and in the … other white … corner, we have an inexperienced Second Division manager named Brian Clough. Brian Howard Clough.

~ 2 ~

'TIT MEETS TAT'

Don Revie v Brian Clough

At this point, I feel it is my sworn duty to say that if you are looking to escape the confines of all these big words on a page and onto something more relatable, like a television screen or that of your new iPhone 13 Pro III-Oh-My-God-How-Can-I-Possibly-Live-Without-This … Max, then you'd be glad to hear that there is actually a *film* that you can watch, which provides an entertaining insight into Brian Clough's early career and his rivalry with Revie's Leeds. Though I urge you to approach it with a fistful of salt.

The film I'm referring to is *'The Damned United'*, in which Michael Sheen depicts a typically close-to-home interpretation of Brian Clough during his rise to prominence at Derby County (we'll get to that), and his ill-fated infamous 6 weeks in charge of Leeds United (oh, we'll *get to that*). Though my mentioned plea of caution is related to this film being based on David Peace's disgraced 'fact-based fictional' tale of the same name, published three years prior to the film's release. Now, on a normal day, Peace is a considered and educated writer whose work is as reliable as it is enjoyable. But perhaps he was tired when he wrote this one.

Personally, and after all that I've researched and watched of Brian Clough myself, I feel that even the film (which was supposedly meant to tone the book down) unwarrantedly focuses on his own personal misgivings, misguided as they may be, without accurately showing the savagery of the surroundings which may have ignited any 'emotional' behaviour.

And it seems as though I'm not the only one who feels this way. In fact, it's a surprise that a film adaptation was even made when you consider the sheer volume of dissenting reviews that it attracted, not least from Brian's wife.

Barbara Clough was outraged at Peace's fictional description of her husband, and vocally countered the book's depiction of a whiskey-riddled, cigarette-wielding Clough - who seemed to favour a swear word over basic communication – where her, more reliable, view is that her beloved husband needn't use such foul language given his aptitude for the spoken word. Also noting that he "barely drank … even in those days when he was a manager" when interviewed for a documentary with ITV.

Having said that, a lot of the book and film centred upon factual data which even Peace's words couldn't make inconclusive. Not least his pivotal partnership with ex-teammate-cum-partner-in-crime, Peter Taylor. Where, ironically, although the pair would go on to establish a very fond friendship and successful working partnership over their years together, they couldn't be any further apart during their playing days – quite *literally* given their positions.

Where Taylor eked out a living as an inscrutable figure between the sticks, Clough's existence was forged on his ability to stick a ball in between them. In fact, Clough was nothing short of a *prolific* goal-scorer in his day; whose record, by modern standards, would scarcely be matched by any of the top goal-scorers from the Premier League era (we'll get to that, too).

He slotted home 251 strikes in 274 appearances across shifts at both Middlesbrough and Sunderland, though an untimely physical clash in the First Division for the Black Cats is what ultimately ended his career far more prematurely than it ever deserved to be. You know, I find it crazy that his playing exploits aren't focused on a lot more than what they are, though perhaps it serves to highlight the weight behind his eventual managerial reputation, more than anything *deliberately* negative.

Injury aside, it was his time up in Sunderland where he first came into contact with second-choice stopper Peter Taylor, who described Clough as "an outstanding talent … from the moment he walked through the door"; though mind you, that's perhaps the nicest thing on record to be confessed between the pair.

At the time, the injury brought out a more insecure side of Clough which endeared himself to Taylor – who went from being a mere footballing comrade interested in his playing career, to a true friend fretting over his personal well-being, and whatever he was planning to do next once the floodlights had faded.

Naturally, it didn't take long before the duo exchanged their ideas on the game as a whole, i.e. what the game means to different footballing communities, and how it ought to be presented to them on the pitch. And one thing that struck a chord with both of them was their disdain for '*boring*' football.

They were proud men, from working-class backgrounds - where the game was as much a routine as it was a religion. Much like it remains today, it's a release from the mundane existence of one's upbringings for at least ninety minutes at a time. So, may the Lord damn anybody charged with not at least trying to make a spectacle of it.

To them, it was one thing to simply *win* a game of football and a whole other to win it '*well*' – where the desire for the former almost made the two mutually exclusive. And through a gulped beer here and a packet of crisps there, the duo endlessly theorised over their own approaches to the game and how, if ever given the opportunity, they would put their views into practise via a coaching role.

Ultimately, their vision was that football was a game that needed to be played on the ground and at a quick tempo - something they thought couldn't be achieved by being overly physical with air-born game plans. This therefore meant focusing on their team's wing-play, midfield dynamism and defensive ball-playing in order to thwart their typically conventional opposition. But before they could act upon this, they needed to hope that there was a boardroom somewhere in the country filled with executives who shared their sentiment.

They flogged their wares in any shop window that came into sight, and their succeeding legacy invites you to believe that there would be a line of suitors ready to ink their quill and obtain their signature, but you'd be wrong.

The pair were an unknown quantity by this point – simply joining a lengthy list of ex-players who knew nothing else but to succeed their playing career by telling others how to do theirs. But the fact that they came as a pair was their niche. Brian Clough's quick-witted persona and razor-sharp tongue made for a life on the front line as a manager, though its bite was provided by the quiet, tactical knowledge of somebody like Peter Taylor. Or as they put it – Brian would serve as the 'shop window', whilst Taylor would be the 'goods in the back'.

Even then, with their chances being around twice as good as many of their competitors, but they had to operate tactically, and with a sprinkle of humility if it was ever going to make a difference in their job search.

The reality was and still remains that no elite club or organisation in general would risk their immediate future on somebody who doesn't have the proven credentials to continue their good name. Therefore, the duo had to make the most out of whatever opportunity came along, regardless of where it might be or how significant the employers were – beggars can't be choosers, can they?

And after abusing their book of contacts and charming their ways into meeting rooms up and down the country, they caught a live one. Enthusiasm brimming and ideas at the ready, their first managerial voyage began in earnest; with Clough and Taylor installed as first team manager and assistant manager respectively, at rural club, Hartlepools United … yes, *plural*.

Personally, I'd only ever heard of this club due to their association with current iconic *Sky Sports* presenter Jeff Stelling. And even then, I'd recognised them as the singular '*Hartlepool* United' - such a millennial, ain't I?!

Well, apparently, the pluralistic form was to recognise the two existing clubs from Hartlepool ('West' and 'Old') that had joined financial forces to prevent expulsion from their Football League for administrative mis-management. But unfortunately for them, the issues had persisted on into the early '70s, where the 'Old' Hartlepool side of the club was let go for the greater good, and the new 'Hartlepool United' name has lasted ever since.

Pop culture reference incoming: this situation makes me think of Justin Timberlake's performance of 'Sean Parker' in the film '*The Social Network*', where he encourages a young Mark Zuckerberg to remove the 'The' from his first website name; as the simpler '*Facebook*' was a "cleaner" alternative.

Though come to think of it, perhaps 'clean' isn't the most fitting word to describe the state of their new workplace by the time Clough and Taylor were shoved through the door.

The club's hierarchy were overjoyed with their appointment, but the lads' new workplace left a lot to be desired. The dishevelled squad languished in the English Third Division, and their home at County Park was awash with numerous issues that the pair picked up on immediately when they joined – with Taylor's own memoir highlighting their toilets, pitch surface and dilapidated stands as particular points of criticism. And if that's what the mild-mannered Taylor thought of it, the mind wanders on to consider what Cloughie's more poetic rendition would be like.

In its best state, it was a clobbered old group of bricks and mortar forming a series of elevated junctures that encased a battered, overgrown turf with the corner flag being its most pristine fixture. But where most may see all of these as part of a sullen overview for a role they wouldn't bother taking on, it was their steppingstone to prove how dedicated they were to further their career and realise their dreams.

Naturally, they mucked in and helped to turn the fortunes of the club in the right direction throughout their stay, until their financial issues reared its ugly head in a way in which a lick of paint couldn't fix.

So much of their funds had been wrapped up in stadium repairs and regulatory changes, that it left a rather minimal amount with which to reinvest in the playing squad. And although Clough had possessed an ordained turn of phrase required to inject a bit of oomph into whatever team he had, Taylor's desire to explore the transfer market could never be realised so long as these issues persisted. Therefore, sensing an irreconcilable difference in the near future, whatever 'charm' the club possessed at the beginning had worn too thin for Taylor without any retail therapy to offset it, and in 1967 – two years into the job – they were on the search once again. Yet despite the impediment seemingly caused by leaving their first job so soon after taking it on, it had at least introduced them into the world of football management.

Meaning that, all of a sudden, their next pursuit wasn't a case of pleading: 'give us a chance, we promise we won't let you down', for now they had some demonstrable experience to add gravitas to their presentation. And more importantly, they could aim a little higher than Hartlepools, with a couple of years and solid references now etched onto their CV.

Barely a month had passed before their formidable shadows cast over the doors of the Baseball Ground – the long-term home of Derby County Football Club, as their next stopping point. Rooted in the Second Division and without a major honour to their name for the past 30 years, the duo had it all to do to turn their fortunes around, but at least they had a cleaner slate to work from … in its most *literal* sense.

County's running operations were a lot smoother than what the lads had experienced over at Hartlepools. Granted, it wasn't exactly a cathedral of contemporary architecture, but at least everything was affixed, painted and in place without them needing to lend a hand in any of that. It was a bigger club, a *richer* club, and more critically, one that was graced with the love of a community not too dissimilar from the ones both Clough and Taylor had been brought up in themselves.

Referring to that other clump of words you read through earlier to get here, their arrival and impending task in Derby somewhat resembles that of Revie's at Leeds.

Derby and Leeds were both provincial clubs, headed by forward-thinking chairmen that were crying out for innovative managers to drive their beloved team forward for the benefit of their hard-to-please sets of supporters – and they both dressed in white! *How embarrassing!*

Having said that, where Revie's accomplishments at Leeds were predicated on their fledgling academy prospects, Derby's facilities were nowhere near as advanced to yield a similar result. And like most, only ever included any of their graduates in a first team line-up through necessity as opposed to choice. Ergo, Derby's hopes relied heavily on a synergy between Clough's coaching skill and Taylor's scouting acumen.

Mercifully, Taylor was given a fair budget to play around with to bolster the squad. And given his close relationship with the manager, he knew precisely the type of players that cater best to his personal style, *and* of which possessed the playing attributes required to propel Derby to where they needed to be.

The seas of change came and went as Derby retained only *four* of their most-played starting eleven from the previous season, and among their new recruits were Messrs John McGovern and John O'Hare, an inseparable twosome who would go on to make nearly 450 appearances between them across 6 years at The Baseball Ground.

Of the two, McGovern appeared as a fresh-faced eighteen-year-old tasked with injecting some enthusiasm into the midfield while the slower, more cumbersome O'Hare was employed up-front for his positional sense and raw scoring ability.

After relieving themselves of £27,500 for the two of them, the board seemed content with their new managers' relatively subtle pieces of business, as their potential looked to justify the investment given their presumed long-term futures. However, Clough did attract *some* criticism when his slap-dash recruitment policy extended to the backroom staff – reportedly sacking the chief scout and recruitment analyst with Taylor earmarked to absorb their duties. And his inscrutable nature didn't go down too well when his questionable antics raised further suspicion.

In fairness to Clough, altering *his* backroom staff generally falls under the jurisdiction of the manager, and his seemingly long-term and sensible recruitment strategy had so far done well to quell any suspicion that he wasn't acting in the best interests of the club. Though I suppose following this up by splashing another £5,000 on ageing sweeper Dave Mackay, days before his 34th birthday, left a lot to be desired; and all too much to be explained.

By comparison, *investments* into the likes of McGovern and O'Hare were seen as much safer outlays for the Derby board to get their minds around. To them: should the lads come good and fulfil their first team potential, then happy days, but if not, then at least they might've been young enough to command a high-enough amount to recoup a significant portion of their initial investment. All of which posed an antithetical proposition to that of signing Mackay – who was four years older than his manager!

Nevertheless, Clough persisted with the transfer under Taylor's sacrosanct recommendation, and it would turn out to be one of the most inspired pieces of business in the club's history.

True, Mackay was a downright nasty piece of work to encounter on the pitch at times - like a salivating terrier looking to get his ball back whenever the opposition attackers played around with it. He was ruthless in the tackle and savagely unapologetic about it, but above all, he was an experienced and deceptively gifted ball-carrier; who set a strong example for any of the young'uns to live up to.

And poignantly, his value to the side had earned a deserved FWA (Football Writers' Association) Player of the Season award for the 1967/68 campaign; primarily for his consistent performances and relentless work ethic. Not too bad for a withering veteran eh? Though I think he'd prefer the term 'wounded'.

***

Soon enough, Derby found themselves crowned champions of the Second Division and anointed with top division football in Clough's and Taylor's second season in charge. Then, in the two subsequent seasons following their ascent, the club achieved respectable 4th and 9th-place finishes to establish themselves in the top-flight before they met for a particularly clamorous encounter with champions, Leeds United in 1972.

The 4-0 thrashing handed to Derby at Elland Road wasn't the primary source of the ignominy which followed. That courtesy derives from Revie's post-match interview, where he denounced the Midlands team's ability as being lacking in every department compared to his 'sons'.

Now you see, Brian Clough was the kind of man who could start an argument in an empty room, which was known to anybody who had the pleasure of working with him, but to Revie, he would've simply been *another* manager to defeat. So his review, while it may have ignited a disparagement between himself and Clough, was largely unintentional and doesn't hide the fact that his side had comprehensively defeated Derby. Therefore, it was going to take a major investment on County's part if they were ever going to close the gap, and boy did Clough know it.

As he preferred his teams to play the ball out from the back, it seemed sensible to set their sights on a defender confident and able enough to bring the ball forward and add another dimension to their build-up play. Nowadays, this is a common feature of a modern centre-half but was a novel attribute that only the top-quality defenders were able to exhibit.

As a result, Taylor found it difficult to match up these qualities with his tried-and-tested 'diamond-in-the-rough' recruitment policy. Instead, it was Derby's first opportunity to make a real splash in the transfer market which supposedly satisfied the managers on two fronts: i) that they actually *needed* this type of signing to benefit the squad and ii) splashing the cash is a sure-fire to get noticed by your rivals.

Plus, with the concept of a transfer window not coming into fruition until the next millennium, there was nothing preventing Derby from instantly homing in on their primary target; who was none other than the 'Prince of the North' Colin Todd.

A man who takes my vote as one of the most forward-thinking central defenders to ever be given real license to express himself on the domestic stage. Even if it did ruffle a few feathers to get the deal over the line.

~ 3 ~

'GOING TOO FAR'

Presented by Brian Clough

The managers had first come across the centre-back as an emerging youngster up in Sunderland – a club with a recognised tradition for promoting their youth products as often as they can. By contrast to Mackay (as the whole comparative edition to the new-boy's talents), Todd was thirteen years his junior when Derby's interest was made public, and his presumed longevity contributed heavily to Sunderland's £170,000 asking price – more than 30 times the price they had 'shelled out' for ol' Dave.

Even so, Todd proved a more than worthy investment. Partnered with the no-nonsense frames of Dave Mackay and Roy McFarland (another of Clough's more modest recruits), his composure on the ball and vision through the middle of the park enabled a more aesthetic build-up play, whilst his positional capability relieved pressure on his own goal. And this increased confidence and swagger in defence helped greatly to elevate Derby from a mid-table prospect into potential title contenders.

With him at the back, the squad in front of him were given greater license to express themselves, and Derby laid siege to opposition defences before being crowned unexpected champions of the English First Division in the 1971-72 season, with much of their gameplay made up of that 'pretty' brand of football imposed by their new-look squad.

Much like their 'nemeses', the pair had transformed a provincial club from mediocre Football League participants into First Division champions; forever cementing themselves into the competition's history in the process. Which unfortunately, was a fact which wasn't lost on Brian Clough, whose new-found confidence was beginning to aggravate his simpler employers.

Never one to run away from the headlines, the initial ill-feeling sprouted from one of Clough's early infamous media appearances. Ironically enough, the man didn't even swear or anything, instead, it concerned that bleedin' Todd transfer, and Clough's complicated relationship with the truth.

Long before Clough and Taylor appeared on the scene, the club lived a modest, hand-to-mouth existence; perpetually recycling whatever money was brought in via gate receipts, television broadcast agreements and competition pay-outs back through in order to finance player wages, stadium improvements and transfer fees. So, you would think that the sheer volume of new recruitment expenses would annoy their frugal board in itself.

But that wasn't the case; as they were largely signed under the consensus of the managers *and* the board – to jointly satisfy the coaches justifiable desire for higher quality livestock without putting too much of a strain on their superiors' bank balance in the process. By contrast, Mackay's and Todd's signings were decidedly more arbitrary than those around them, and the latter's was finalised in direct contempt of the chairman's wishes – the king of frugal financiers, Sam Longson.

'Uncle Sam', as I'm sure he would *not* like me to call him, was Derby through and through, and wanted nothing else but to help them achieve something worthwhile. Though after a childhood of watching his beloved Rams yo-yo up and down the divisions, Longson's leadership was centred upon merely rooting their place in the Football League. And as far as he was concerned, his ideal manager would come in, steady the ship and (hopefully) give the fans a good time while doing it, though he was wrong to assume that somebody like Clough would rest easy at that level.

To be fair to Longson, and under the presumption that Clough was on his best behaviour during the interview process, he can be forgiven for not foreseeing the ferocity of his manager's ambition, and I imagine it didn't matter all that much so long as the team was performing well, and a respect for the owner was preserved. And thus, we arrive at the issue of the manager's many televisual appearances.

Now, Brian Clough's affinity with the media wasn't a problem *in itself*. In fact, as far as Longson was concerned, televising his employee's charm and charisma seeks only to breed a positive image for the club he represents. But under such circumstances, the last thing you'd want is for your head coach to bring up anything which needn't be explored by the press; who are more concerned with arranging an eye-grabbing headline than providing a thoughtful article. And, like most would, Derby's chairman *really* didn't want the club's financial issue made public – something which is a highly charged and personal matter to consider. Though, unfortunately for everybody involved, Clough couldn't resist the urge to goad the press when he made public his intent to pursue Todd's record-breaking transfer, nor could he do it without poking a bit of fun at his 'stingy' board.

To begin with, he is filmed categorically refuting his interest in signing Todd due to his price tag; a reflection of what I presume he was conveying to the board at the same time. Then, of his own volition, he retracts this and commits a record-breaking fee to secure him; all the while his employers are just as blind to his truer intentions as the rest of us.

In doing so, while he may have had a little giggle to himself in the camera's blind spot, he had inadvertently mocked his chairman's financial insecurities and blurred the lines between who was in ultimate control of the club. Sure, Clough may have been in charge of how his team played, but he wasn't using his own money to bolster it; he was using Longson's. And using the media to create this confusion was never going to end well; especially since Longson himself was among the viewers.

But even then, the TV opps came few and far between during the off-season, and the new campaign gave the two authority figures a chance to start afresh. After all, we're only human and are all capable of making the odd petulant mistake here and there. The important thing is to *learn* from them and stick them in the past. So … did he? Did Clough see the errors in his ways and approach the next year in a more mature fashion? Erm. No, no … he didn't.

Despite the 1972/73 season not being their most prolific on home soil, a combination of form and fortune bought Derby a ticket to the UEFA European Cup semi-finals in April 1973, eventually losing out to Italian champions, Juventus.

Now, considering the pedigree of their opponents, it was a more than graceful exit, and in fact, Derby can consider themselves somewhat unlucky to not reach the final. Plus, given how highly charged these situations can be, a part of me wants to be sympathetic towards Clough's emotional post-match press meet-up. But no amount of editing can disguise what was a completely abhorrent and dishonourable showing from the Derby boss.

In a blatant attempt to side-line his own team's shortcomings, Clough searched far and wide to decipher a more favourable way of explaining what just transpired. He could have focused on their missed chances. He could have *even* suggested that the Italians had God on their side. But him launching a political tirade against the Italian Second World War effort is not only completely inaccurate, but it's distasteful, highly offensive and made him look like a petulant loser who will stop at nothing to preserve his ego in the eyes of defeat.

And then things got worse when he provided a summary on Leeds' rebound title win in their absence – one which not only attacked their brutish tactical style, but also the very organisation who seemed to allow it without sanction; the English Football Association ('the FA').

Just a Quick One:

Each footballing nation has their own board of governance that decide over how they want the game to be played, and arbitrarily dish out whatever disciplinary action they deem necessary to preserve the sanctity of the game they are in charge of. Plus, back in these days, members of such associations would be closely affiliated with some of their country's bigger club owners – so as to presumably ensure a synergy between them and their biggest exploits to ensure they don't fall out of line.

So, as you would expect, taking shots at them (and their business operation) doesn't bode well for one's long-term future in English football - especially when your own employer is buddied up with the board!

As expected, Longson didn't take well to Clough's persistent outspokenness against his friends, and further club sanctions followed in a bid to quell his manager's perversion for the extreme - sanctions which weren't met in the way with which they were intended to be, and instead ignited a game for which the winner's medal would be dished out to whoever went too far. A gold star is in offer, if you can guess who did that first.

Apparently believing that things at Derby could only get better *without* Longson, Clough sought to indirectly remove the businessman from his *own board*!

Crazier still, both he and Taylor believed that the best way of doing so was to submit a formal letter of resignation; in a bid to arise some insecurity with the wider board that their chairman had presumably forced his most successful managers to do the unthinkable. But instead, it had revealed just *how* inflated their nouveau-successful employees had become.

Then, despite a host of misinformed dissent among the Derby fans hinting at a positive ending, their managers' resignations were accepted and actioned with immediate effect. And any idea of a retraction was soon dispelled once their previous employers had selected a newly retired and fully qualified Dave Mackay as their successor.

As for the discarded, Clough and Taylor's bruised reputations had done little to detract a whole host of bended-knee proposals, with the most intriguing of prospects appearing on the South Coast with Third Division side, Brighton & Hove Albion – where ambitious owner Mike Bamber rewarded the pair with an all-expenses-paid trip to Mallorca upon signing.

Though what was intended to be a period of sun-filled respite for the new Seasiders, soon turned into one of anticipation and disbelief once they were able to translate the local news broadcast.

Nowadays, national jobs are viewed quite distastefully - like a poisoned chalice that few distinguished managers would want to touch for fear of tarnishing their club reputation. But believe it or not, there was once a time where an offer was as good as the Queen tapping that sword over your shoulders herself; a feeling that would soon be experienced by the one and only … Don Revie. Thus, freeing up his coveted position at Elland Road.

Leeds United were off the back of a near 30-game unbeaten run in their bid to dethrone Shankly's Liverpool by the end of the 1973/74 season. And simply put, not only does it take a manager of serious quality to reach such a feat, but arguably an even more remarkable one to improve on it.

Shankly himself looked a reasonable contender for the task at hand, though his immediate contract extension at Liverpool rebuffed any early interest. So, I guess it was time for Plan B … or, more like Plans C & T. Yes … *them*!

Forgiving their prior contempt for 'Daddy Don', the pair were arguably the highest calibre of management available on the staff market at the time, and it was presumed that the Derby learning curve would do much to curb any premature indiscretion in their new home. Though this was all under the caveat that the pair joined as a twosome; and that one of them hadn't gotten too high off of that South Coast air to say 'no'. As it happened, an 'intoxicated' Taylor had rejected Leeds' advances in exchange for seeing out his commitments to Brighton, thus initiating a 'Ross and Rachel'-type 'break' on his nuptials with Clough, as they went to pursue divergent paths. And of the two, I reckon only one of them has more regrets than the other …

Now look, there is an infinite amount of text available on the subject of Clough's lonely tenure at Leeds, so for the sake of our bedtime schedules, I'm going to summarise it all in the briefest way possible.

Here we go:

[*inhale*]

Clough loses his first competitive match as manager – the 1974 Charity Shield against Liverpool – following a bloody altercation between star man Billy Bremner and Reds ace Kevin Keegan. Bremner is suspended for six weeks; leading Clough to raid his former club for some squad depth. Thus, alienating his existing squad and causing a mutiny which attributed to one of Leeds' worst top-flight starts in history. A start which, not even after Bremner's return from suspension, called for Clough's head before Autumn.

[*exhale*]

And if you think that my summary ended too abruptly and/or quickly then you'd be right, but I'd be damned if you thought it was anything other than accurate. But you don't need me to tell you that; as ITV were on hand to give Clough the opportunity to tell you himself!

With every respectable news coverer vying for Clough's appearance to share his story, the Freeview outlet were able to orchestrate one of the most extraordinary televised sports interviews of all time. You see, typically, the person answering the questions is accompanied by none other than the person asking them – making for a calm setting within which the subject can feel comfortable enough to bear all matters of interest. Anything other than this can raise a tension which proves palpable through the camera's eye; making for a nervy and decidedly *uncomfortable* viewing experience.

Though I guess this was what ITV wanted, for they had somehow been able to arrange for a separate interviewee to sit alongside Clough during his moment of infamy. And his 'partner' was none other than the very man who he'd sought to replace in the first instance. That's right! Placed no more than a metre apart from each other was Brian Clough and *Don Revie* – with one looking decidedly more smug than the other.

Not surprisingly, it made for great television – with Revie lambasting Clough's lack of paternal care for his ex-players and Clough himself asserting this very existing connection as the reason for why he struggled to establish one of his own. It's an intriguing cat-and-mouse scenario with Clough escaping Revie's claws at every corner, and in retrospect, it appears as though this entire sordid affair proved paramount in Clough's later managerial career; one which led to a reconnaissance mission with Peter Taylor and a glory-soaked empire over at Nottingham Forest.

Yet away from all the overt testimonies that have since adorned their successes, both Clough's and Revie's own particular stories align in ways which reveal their trail-blazing pathways into the worlds of club identity transformation and media presentation.

For you see, beyond merely squiggling tactics on a whiteboard and shouting incoherently from the touchline, both managers were willing to step out of all recognisable comfort zones to stamp their authority on their workplaces. And indeed, Liverpool's Bill Shankly is a more than worthy inclusion into this conversation, as well.

Gone seemed to be the days of managers tentatively entering a role for fear of ruining whatever was there, and in came an era where ambitious coaches would stride into their new offices to form a legacy that would be indelible upon their departure. Together, they had all connected with their glory-hungry sets of supporters, and set about doing whatever it took to appease their hunger – even if it meant upsetting the apple cart to do so!

Not to mention their frequent media attendances (perhaps more so aimed at Clough here, than anybody else), which brought an entirely different dimension to what was a usually mundane and predictable sports piece.

Before, a simple interview would be a cumbersome 'Q&A' format met with a political non-answer by way of conclusion. But now, it became a snippet of airtime through which confident managers could communicate how they *really* felt; to give the fans something to talk about when they were bored, and perhaps even something to feel hopeful about when times looked bleak. And it's a system used throughout the footballing world today, as the worlds of social media and 'clickbait' headlines have seemed to only inflate narratives like these.

Then you had the brief, yet encapsulating Clough-Revie rivalry, which further heightened the game's appeal to a more mainstream audience. Sure, it'll take a while to indoctrinate a general non-sports fan into the world of football, but who doesn't like a bit of reality-show-like drama to sink their teeth into? *Exactly*!

So, all in all, there's certainly a lot to be thankful for in recounting the stories of Revie, Clough and Taylor, though perhaps where they all faltered was addressing the way the game was actually *played*.

Even at the best of times, the game of football (certainly in England) wasn't an undertaking for the sport's purists, and even some of our mentioned steps into the modern world looked like largely isolated incidents; in a league where one's likelihood of winning was dictated by their selection's ability to beat their opponent's at their own game. For example, when Leeds had Billy Bremner, Derby had Dave Mackay, Peter Lorimer - Alan Hinton, Mick Jones - John McGovern … and the list goes on.

Thus, as a dedicated supporter, watching such similar outings was a bit like eating the same chocolate treat over and over again as dessert – it's still chocolate … but variety feeds the soul. So, if the game's future was ever going to brighten up, things needed to diversify. The game needed *variety*.

And thankfully, a modest-looking Dutchman was on hand to provide exactly that.

~ 4 ~

'THE MASTER AT WORK'

Shh … don't disturb him!

Whether these discussions take place in the poshest of boardrooms or the dingiest of dive bars, opinions will continue to diverge on who earns the right to be called the 'greatest football player of all time'. And in my opinion, it's a question that will never be answered; as it an inherently flawed one to ask.

For me, the blanket term 'greatest' is one that's far too open to interpretation and allows for every participant to tag it in front of whatever attribute they deem important enough to warrant the overall title. For example, I may think that a player's goal tally is the 'greatest' thing that one can build, where you may believe that their natural skill or dedication to the game takes precedent over that – so whoever we each deem to be the 'best example' of our own allocated fields; will more than likely adopt our selection for being 'the greatest ever'.

But as I've just demonstrated, these are narrow-minded choices driven by personal ideals — neither of which is required to accurately determine the answer to such an objective question. As a result, I tend to opt for a more *specific* line of questioning to arrive at more *reasoned* conclusions.

For example, I believe the 'most naturally gifted player' award is a toss-up between Lionel Messi and Diego Maradona, and the 'greatest goal-scorer of all time' is a very tight contest between Ronaldo de Rosario de Lima (A.K.A. 'The Brazilian Ronaldo') and Thierry Henry. However, where I can side in favour with more than one candidate for either of the mentioned categories, there is one category which can only conclude with a single answer, but for the sake of democracy, let me ask you:

Who do you believe is the most **significant** player to ever play the game of football?

Someone who transformed the game more than any other, and is most responsible for providing its truest form of beauty and grace; which has since been best adopted into the modern era? I know it's quite an imposing question, but really, the answer is simple.

The answer is Dutch maestro, **Johan Cruyff**.

Born fortuitously close to the AFC Ajax stadium — home to the biggest football club in Holland - it seemed as if the east-Amsterdam outfit was always going to be a part of young Johan's destiny. And so it came to be once a budding scout named Jany van Der Veen, had formalised an unconditional offer for the schoolboy to join the club's academy.

Now *ideally*, any kid looking to make a name for themselves in an academy as prestigious as Ajax's, will at least have a sturdy pair of boots and a fitted kit within which to make a long-lasting impression upon their coaches. But Johan wasn't in this kind of position back then. He was a modest lad, from a working-class background and was therefore fighting somewhat of an uphill battle against his more fortunate peers; whose own back gardens and bedroom closets were far more wholesome and sophisticated to whatever he would've grown accustomed to. Though where most may have been intimidated at the thought of starting things off from a square behind their competitors, it proved a source of inspiration for a youngster who had a fate to realise.

Plus, when your only option to play the game involves mucking about with your mates on some battered old patch of grass with a half-inflated ball, you're unconsciously playing at a more advanced level to those whose fortunate background afforded better equipment and playing conditions. For example, to them, it was a lot easier to freely play the ball on the ground (and at pace), as they could trust the surface and its elements to guide it to where it's supposed to go.

Though Johan's typical setting was far too erratic for this to be reliable for him, thereby innately developing his own technical qualities in manipulating the ball and creating space for it to be received in order to have the same effect; which allowed him to stand out from the crowd once he was given a break on that luscious turf at the academy. And all under the watchful eye of first team coach, and pioneering strategist; Rinus Michels. Later honoured as an Officer of the Order of Orange-Nassau in 1988 for his services to football,

Michels enjoyed a fine one-club playing career at Ajax before swapping his boots for the tactics board, though his eventual reunion with the capital outfit had to wait until 1965 – by which point, their esteemed hierarchy were charmed to find out more about some of his avant-garde systems deployed in the lower leagues.

More specifically, whilst at the respectably lesser 'Amsterdamsche Football Club' (stationed a neck rotation away from his old employers), there appeared to be a palpable disdain for that 'kick the ball up and batter your opponents on its way down' policy; where the Dutchman instead encouraged a method in which his players' own footballing intelligence and team spirit made for a more calculated, reliable and *aesthetic* game-plan. And true to form, Michels had reportedly been equally as passionate about communicating his envisaged brand of the game in his preliminary meet-up with Ajax, in which his hypothesis for a team *controlling* the game (as opposed to allowing its variables to control them), had struck a particular chord with his glory-and-efficiency- obsessed interviewers.

Also, this 'controlling the match' idea wasn't even a case of attracting the game's most sought after talents in order to make it effective. Instead, it was a simple series of algorithms centred upon his side being able to maximise their use of the space around them; capable of being effective for any group that are merely conscious to what the game requires of them.

Practically, this would involve stretching and narrowing the team's formation when necessary; to either expand on their attacking movement or constrict the opponents' own freedom when having to defend. And like I say, you don't need the greatest team in the world to be capable of doing this … but it sure doesn't hurt to have a darn good one to hand!

That Ajax squad – with attacking midfielder Johan Neeskens and defensive stalwart Ruud Krol to name a couple – were the ideal subjects for Michels' innovations; not to mention the plethora of Dutch national stars available to him throughout the club ranks, and a spattering of youth starlets making a name for themselves from the academy setup. Including some awkward looking 'Cruyff' kid whose name had become as common as a tulip on their coaches' mouths.

Johan came along and ***revolutionised everything***
… he [was] the expression of our identity [and]
brought us a style of football we love.''

– Vic Buckingham (Cruyff's first senior Ajax coach)

Right okay, let's all take a deep breath together and expel it slowly, for the time has come for me to actually describe what Johan Cruyff was like as a professional football player. I'll do my best to keep it brief though every fibre of my being wants me to do the opposite. So how about we keep it to a simple word? Does that sound okay? Well, in that case, the man was absolutely *magnificent*.

Like most sporting icons, he was the first one into a training session, the last one to leave, and even made a point of sharpening his tools during his 'downtime' just so to get ahead of the grade whenever class restarted. And Michels wasted little time in promoting this extra-credited seventeen-year-old to the first team setup, and even less time thereafter in deploying him as their prime creative asset in the final third.

Upon joining, Cruyff's arrival had signalled a merciful end to your dependable four in defence, four in midfield and two up-top arrangement, with the simple reason being that he was wholly incapable of fitting into such a rigid structure.

Thus, despite being branded as a 'striker', he was given license by the manager to *feel* the vibe of the game and allow it to dictate wherever he would end up; often dropping unconventionally deep when sensing pressure, then using his wider vantage point to seek out a journey through on goal. In doing so, Cruyff would often vacate a purely advanced striker's post, and eventually took up a more permanent residence in that proverbial 'hole' behind your typical front line; a precursor to what we commonly refer to now as a 'False 9' role.

***

But despite all of this new position stuff, getting the best out of him required an entirely new system for the rest of the squad as well — so that everybody could complement each other's movement, and flow more intravenously together with an enigmatic Cruyff popping up wherever he felt like doing so.

What they needed was to have a means of supporting their mobile False 9 in the wider areas, whilst being supplied by a midfield gang who could divvy up one another's defensive and attacking duties to suit the ambiance of the game. All the while backed by a group of defenders where even the full backs were allowed to roam a lot more freely than what they were used to.

And what they ended up with was *another* incept for something which is more common today than a bad haircut or questionable 'Tweet' – the dynamic 4-3-3. Then, in stepped the *real* genius of Michels; and for why his version of this ideology has since proven to be one of its most heralded forms since the game's invention.

Not only did he alter his squad's general organisation, but he also cracked the whip on their mindset to increase its effectiveness. To put it plainly, Michels believed that your average 4-4-2-like formation encouraged each player to be selfish; where each player knew what they had to do and stuck to doing just that, especially when it wasn't commonplace to interchange your responsibilities for the good of team. Michels took a different view.

Here's How it Worked …

Suppose the player in front of or behind you (e.g. a centre back in relation to a central midfielder) finds themselves outnumbered or out of position, then you would be *obligated* to take up whatever position had just been vacated / left vulnerable.

Whilst there, you carry out your 'new role' until the original man reassumes their station; all the while that same shifting process has happened for your old position. And around and around we go. Like a merry-go-round of technically gifted 'helpers' who adhere to whatever role the game forced them to perform. In doing so, not only had it broadened the individual skillsets of those elected to play for

Michels, but it had improved the overall *totality* and well-roundedness of the team's game plan. Now it just needed a name, and as every expecting parent will tell you, sometimes it's best to just keep everything as wholesome and simple as possible when making such a pivotal decision, and thus 'Total Football' was introduced to the world as the shining beacon of change for which it proved to be.

'Totaalvoetbal' as it's known at home, took very little time to prove effective for Michels' Cruyff-led band; with the 1970/71 season earning Ajax an unprecedented level of success on home and continental soil.

After only narrowly missing out on the league ('Eredivisie') title, they picked up the Dutch Cup *en route* to an unstoppable European road trip; rounded off by a restrained 2-0 score line against hapless Greek champions, Panathinaikos in the final. And to make things even more momentous for them, the stage was set in one of the most fabled settings in world football – Wembley Stadium, *and* Panathinaikos themselves were managed by the legendary ex-*'Blancos'* front man Ferenc Puskas; thus serving as an almost poetic rendition of the man (who was largely responsible for Real Madrid's own mystique on the global stage) passing the baton onto Cruyff and co. as a form of 'blessing' for the new era of football domination we were all yet to witness.

Staggeringly, Ajax found themselves in *another* European Cup final fixture the very next season, this time against stronger opponents in Inter Milan - an equally significant match-up where the 'dinosaurs' of Italian football (more on that later) were run ragged by Ajax's totality in all areas. And, forming another notch in the storybook, history repeated itself with Johan Cruyff scoring both of the goals to ensure that the iconic 'big-eared' trophy remained in Amsterdam. I'm not even sure how it's possible to form a 'legacy' in a couple of years, but here we have just that.

Over two seasons, the world now had no choice but to watch in awe as Ajax single-handedly brought the game into technicolour. And just in case this wasn't enough for any of you cynics out there, they one-upped their European triumph with a cross-Atlantic victory in the Intercontinental Cup over two legs in Argentina versus Independiente … and *then* in the European Super Cup against Rangers a few months later! I feel feverish.

Then by 1971, their top performer had earned a much-deserved Ballon D'Or accolade for playing his part – an award which crowns its keeper as 'the best player in the world' for that year. A truly monumental effort on his part.

Oh, Right! …

There's something I forgot to mention here which may surprise you, and it's that the second triumph against Inter Milan was achieved *without* the guidance of Rinus Michels.

Up until this match-up, the 'Dutch Dumbledore' had garnered plenty of alluring offers from abroad and found a four-year deal to manage Spain's FC Barcelona too good to turn down; a fate which would soon befall the very protégé he'd been most loathed to have to leave behind!

~ 5 ~

'EL MAESTRO EN EL TRABAJO'

Cruyff's Spanish Escapade

Although there isn't really much to back this up, I personally believe that Cruyff's decision to join Barcelona (particularly ahead of fellow suitors Real Madrid) has a lot to do with where the clubs were at the time – and his drive to achieve a more outstanding feat with the relatively unconventional choice.

Though a more obvious reason for wanting to sign for them was the chance to reignite the successes he enjoyed back home with Rinus Michels – and on an even grander stage.

To them, Ajax can be seen as an introductory period within which to freely experiment their new methods to see if they worked or not, and after realising its power, Barcelona presented the opportunity to challenge their ideas against comparatively stronger opposition, with the hope of attracting an even greater level of acclaim and notoriety. It certainly wasn't the easiest of tasks to sink your teeth into, and their reunion was pivotal to their chances of seeing it through.

Six million guilders (the currency used by the Dutch prior to the Euro in 2002) was what it took to relocate Cruyff from the canals of Amsterdam to the cauldron of Catalunya; aptly translating into the highest ever fee committed for the services of a football player at around $2 million. Even then, fellow legend Franz Beckenbauer denounces any suggestion that the fee was too high for the Dutchman; believing that even a figure in the *billions* would represent good value for somebody as talented as Johan.

Penny for your thoughts, Franz …

"When players like [Gareth] Bale and [Cristiano] Ronaldo are worth around €100 million, Johan [Cruyff] would go in the billions … and that's okay!"

— Franz Beckenbauer

And while the annuls of sports history is rife with similar testimonies to his ability, it particularly means a lot coming from a former player of Beckenbauer's esteem; where his summary escapes any awe-based sentiments from your average soccer fan or journalist, and allows us all an authentic, first-hand interpretation of somebody who he believes deserves this kind of description.

A tremendous 5-0 showing away at the Santiago Bernabéu stadium against Real Madrid, soon put to rest most immediate worries that Barca had over-spent on their latest recruit, and even fewer still once it proved a mere footnote in a string of world-class performances that earned the club that season's 'La Liga' title – their first top-flight domestic honour for over 13 years.

Then, almost evidential by this point, Cruyff's influence had snagged home another European Cup by the summer of 1974; thus, inspiring his manager to continue their trajectory with another big-money move for somebody his protégé had already become very familiar with.

Johan Neeskens – better known as *Johan Segon* (Johan the 2nd) to most, became Barcelona's latest procurement from the Dutch capital, and took very little time in proving his worth to his new Spanish comrades.

A disgustingly underrated playmaker for his time, he was as fleet-footed as they come, more direct than a new divorcee and had the vision of a crow when searching for the correct pass to play. And while he may not have possessed Cruyff's natural leadership qualities and adorning aura, he was almost equally as effective in providing the fluidity for which Ajax's forward play became known; especially when attacking from the wider areas.

After signing, the pair picked up where they left off, and amassed 283 appearances with roughly 83 goals between them across all competitions, over another trophy-laden three-year period for them and their trusted manager. Though rumblings of some political instability behind the scenes at the club, were threatening to wreak havoc upon the dynasty they had aimed to preserve.

Here's where things get political …

FC Barcelona, though technically a Spanish resident, are based within the self-governing city of Catalunya – which (by this point) had been attempting to break free from the wider authority of the country in a bid to become a sovereign state in of themselves.

So, since the club had proven central to much of the city's welfare once erected, their own hierarchy's intentions were often made to mirror those of the state within which they're based. And it was widely reported that having an 'unconnectable' Dutchman in charge (as opposed to 'one of their own'), didn't align with what was believed to be beneficial for the residents of Catalunya.

Therefore, under the impending threat of being forced out of the club, Michels embarked on a perceptive FTC-like venture to take over the Netherlands national squad for the 1974 World Cup in the club's off-season – all authorised under the pretence that he would return to Barcelona come the tournament's end, and that it would hopefully serve to quell some of the needless attention that had garnered his wonderful stint in charge. Though he was powerless to resist that 'we need to talk' episode with the Barca board, once his side forfeited the title to Real Madrid the next season; promptly resigning as their Head Coach on his own terms as opposed to having theirs being presented to him.

Without him, the club endured two perilous spells under Hennes Weisweiller and Laureano Ruiz in a single season – which was largely spent by the board appreciating what they had before it was gone. And after a hearty helping of humble pie, Michels was laughably reinstated in the Camp Nou dugout as one of their top earners on a two-year 'extension' package – only to be forced out *again* through the board's patience-less and autocratic tendencies to impose upon his station as manager. An altogether disgraceful way of treating one of the game's most innovative patrons.

He was a legendary servant to the club, and I dread to think that Michels himself held any regrets about his time in Spain. It certainly didn't end in the way that he would've liked but, at the root of it all, he was the victim of the club's own innate struggles and was still able to achieve an unprecedented level of success for them under his own invention; one that has formed the basis of their footballing philosophy ever since.

Plus, when you team together all of his achievements as a coach, there are very few whose CV will command the respect that his does, and even fewer who can claim to have affected the game as positively as he did – the man even won FIFA's Coach of the Century Award in 1999, for crying out loud!

All things considered, I really don't think that there's anything left to say about him from our end, though I hope his former employers would have better words in the tank if the topic ever came up.

**

Lo and behold, Cruyff followed his *sensei* out the door at the earliest opportunity, where the sands of time forced his hand into making a decision which I'm sure he'd love to take back.

By this point, Johan had reached the grand old age of thirty; where (like many of our game's mid-life favourites) his stock had plummeted further than one of Jamie Oliver's restaurants. Though 'fortunately' for Cruyff, he had another thing going for him, in that he was equally as talented on the pitch, as he was a *marketable* asset away from it. And if there's one sporting nation which knows how to properly deal with a marketable asset, it's the United States of America.

> "A brand for a company is like a reputation for a person. You earn reputation by trying to do the hard things well."
>
> – Jeff Bezos

The USA is the birthplace of advertising and promotion, and has since become home to many industry front-runners whenever they've joined the party. For instance, the world had 'performing arts' so they made *Broadway*, the world had film / TV and up sprang Hollywood. So, when sport became the new fix on the corner, they embarked on creating enterprises suitable to the growing allure of each one. They somehow turned the game of rounders into the revenue machine that is Major League Baseball and their version of 'football' (where they use their hands) became the ground-breaking NFL brand – both of which are as much a spectacle to behold as they are identifiable as brands.

However, in these cases, the US took their time in fully understanding the products *and* their audience. They knew what drew a theatregoer to their seat and what baseball fans wanted the game experience to be like. But as we will come to discuss later on in its own dedicated section, they had a whitewash approach which failed to acknowledge the fine-tuned aspects required to bring the game of football to life.

Between the ages of 30 and 33, Cruyff turned out for the Los Angeles Aztecs and Washington Diplomats, but soon realised that, barring he and a few other fellow foreign imports, America's 'North American Soccer League' wasn't at a high-enough calibre for him to stick it out there for longer than he did. And though he enjoyed a higher quality of life in the States, there was more to be done within the continent he'd deserted three years earlier.

Sure enough, with his fitness levels restored and his drive greater than ever, Johan charmed his way into a brief Spanish stop-over in Levante before earning an unlikely return to his boyhood club.

It should have been a renaissance for the ages – 'the prodigal son returning home', 'the boy who came good giving back to his roots', 'Ajax, what light through yonder window breaks!' and all that wholesome stuff. But things were different this time round, and there was a monumental misunderstanding as to what his role would be when joining for the second time.

Whether he wanted to accept it or not, he simply wasn't the peak Johan Cruyff that had left almost a decade earlier. He was slower, less physical and far less able to keep up with the cyclical development of the very academy that he'd blossomed from; which had undergone quite the revolution in his absence.

Without the likes of Neeskens and Cruyff to weigh in, Ajax had little option but to rely on their younger cohort as they looked to maintain the club's newly inflated status. And with the dutiful Frank Rijkaard and goal-grabbing Marco van Basten leading the charge, the club were reticent in allowing Cruyff's reunion to disturb their progress.

So, instead of playing week-in, week-out (as I'm sure he would've anticipated), his role was reduced to that of an 'impact player'; expected to chime in when necessary to pass on his expertise to the next generation. And although this may have seemed a mutually beneficial arrangement for both player and club at the time, things became a lot stickier once his modest two-year hand-out had expired. Right then, let's spill some tea.

Upon his return, Cruyff played roughly 40 times and contributed to an average of a goal every other game within this timeframe. He proved that he was still physically fit for his age, had a lot to offer in terms of his leadership and experience, and remained very determined to do his best for the club he loved. Having said that, the numbers I've just mentioned admittedly seesaw in its majority toward his first season - where his second campaign lacked below his unerringly high standards.

Therefore, sensing a further decline on the cards, the Ajax board had determined that his recent form wasn't deserving of a contract extension; and made a fateful error in failing to take into account Cruyff's legendary status at the club when sharing their intentions.

In his memoir '*My Turn*', Johan recalls never having really sat down for a negotiation with the board about his future once his contract was up. Instead, his frequent inquiries for a meeting were tossed aside in favour of a silence which alienated their now-vengeful ex-starlet, which made for another (*very* intriguing) crossroads moment for the Dutchman.

Back a couple of pages ago, even the most die-hard Ajax fan wouldn't have begrudged Cruyff's earlier decision to move to Barcelona; as it wasn't much a 'slap in the face' to his old employers, as it was an exclusive desire to earn a stand-alone achievement with a new one. The two didn't overlap much.

But fast forward to here, and he had a trio of immediate options on the table with their own insecurities and consequences to consider:

1. Does he stick it out with Ajax and negotiate further in the hope of signing a new contract?
2. Does he hang up his boots entirely and maybe look to follow Michels' footsteps into coaching? Or;
3. Does he join another club in an attempt to prove to Ajax how stupid they were to let him go?

Erm … yeah … *that* one.

With the 'American Dream' idea done and regretted, and other emerging competitions appearing equally unstable, lower tier La Liga and Eredivisie sides looked the more viable destinations for the veteran, before one of the bigger fish threw their hat into the ring.

Now, as an occupational hazard, every football team has a rival which either develops geographically between the fans or through being close, fierce competitors over time. Imagine then how severe a rivalry becomes when you have an element of both. Well, this was and remains to be the case between AFC Ajax and local haters Feyenoord; Johan's latest offeror.

In what can only be described as an effort to irritate their enemy, Feyenoord launched a dastardly plan to prise Ajax's prodigal son away from Amsterdam and, buoyed by an evident lack of loyalty on the board's part, Cruyff returned the favour! He joined in the summer of 1983 and, having meshed in quickly with Feyenoord's own learners, guided them to a domestic league title and a personal Dutch Footballer of the Year award in that single season. In footballing terms, it was a bit like getting together with your ex's best friend and giving them the wedding which their former partner had been hammering on about … and then inviting that friend to officiate it. 'Savage' isn't even the word.

Juicier still, Johan had decided to retire once his point was made, thus, ending his career one year older and two accolades richer than the folks at Ajax had ever thought possible. And emotions aside, it was an appropriately theatrical way to end a career like his and acts as another example of the level of performance which became commonplace throughout his time on the grass. In fact, now seems a good time to do a cheeky recap of the man. And who better to provide one than the bloke who facilitated it all …

> He seemed like a **conductor** directing a symphony orchestra. It was as if Cruyff was helping his colleagues to realize an approximate rendering on the field to match the sublime vision in his mind of how the space ought to be ordered."
>
> - Rinus Michels

With the curtain falling on Johan's playing time, a coaching career was a given, and if anything, he was in an even better position to spruce up his mentor's work.

For all of his accomplishments, Michels had very itchy feet as a manager - moving around more times than a rally car on a dirt track. And because of this, much of his success was preserved in an hourglass - enjoyed briefly before the sands of time signalled the start of a new venture.

On the other hand, notwithstanding his American escapade, Cruyff tended to see things further to the end; which is what every potential employer likes to see.

Not to mention, he had first-hand experience in seeing how different players (i.e. his teammates) react to that 'Total Football' idea – whose reviews could be used to tweak it here and there to bring the best out of whoever he would end up managing. And after having learnt from their prior indiscretions, Ajax couldn't afford to have lightning strike twice – promptly installing Cruyff as their new manager with a few agreed expectations in place.

Namely, that he would superimpose an identity on the club that would stand the test of time; best achieved by future-proofing their academy and funnelling club revenue away from transfer business and back into its infrastructure. He signed off happily on all of these demands and, true to form, he overachieved.

Being the boss, he was free to employ what he believed to be a *fuller* version of the 'Total Football' philosophy. Where, having found some inflexibility in Michels' version, Cruyff took a more literal interpretation to spread the system's plasticity throughout the entire line-up – where *all* of the defensive players (including the goalkeeper) would be indoctrinated into that 'you scratch my back, I scratch yours' arrangement. But for that to work, Cruyff's troops had to line up in a different way.

This time, instead of having two resolute central defenders supported by wide men on either side, he would deploy three conscientious defenders to operate freely across the back line - constantly interchanging positions to better their chances in crowding out the opposing attackers. Then, he would deploy that spare defender further forward as a 'defensive midfielder', to sit stably in behind more expressive teammates, who would behave in a similar way to what they would've done under Michels. Altogether, this innovative change invented yet *another* formation that has grown more common over time; the 3-4-3.

Testament to his new style's guile and fluidity, his side managed an average positive goal difference of 25 strikes to their closest rival over each of his next three seasons in Holland - earning 2 garnishing Dutch Cups and a European Cup Winner's Cup in the process. All of which paid a fitting homage to his former manager, whilst simultaneously adhering to his superior's expectations upon signing; hence the fast-tracked developments of Rijkaard, Danny Blind, van Basten and Dennis Bergkamp to name a few.

With his contract up for discussion once more in 1988, it was time that Ajax let their son fly the nest for good, and into the welcoming arms of the very people who gave him his first abroad assignment all those years ago. What a coincidence!

And with his feet planted firmly in the footsteps of his predecessor, a bright-eyed Cruyff willingly signed for FC Barcelona on an initial four-year-contract to become their latest Head Coach. But unfortunately for him, they still hadn't got their act together. Not by a long shot.

The club were stranded in debt, playing badly and hadn't experienced anywhere near the success that he'd brought them on the pitch. So, his instalment wasn't as much a total recognition of his managerial ability, as it was in hope of instilling a sense of reprieve via his icon status as a player.

Whatever the true reason, he needed to change a lot of things if he ever hoped to be successful in Catalunya, but only in ways with which the rewards could be reaped very quickly –

so that he didn't anger their trigger-happy board or attract unwelcome attention from the press.

So strategically, he first looked to strengthen his squad by testing the quality of the club's *La Masia* academy, and soon happened upon a defensive midfielder who looked to possess the qualities required to exceed in his 'Total Football' adaptation, and after giving the youngster early chances to impress for the first team, writing the words 'Pep' and 'Guardiola' would prove a rather repetitive process in the Camp Nou dressing room.

Then, shortly after locating Guardiola, Cruyff went to the transfer market to find someone in defence who could back the Spaniard and become a consistent performer in that mobile back three. And given his strict search requirements, it only made sense that his target would be somebody who proved their worth in that same system at Ajax.

Ronald Koeman was his man, and he soon proved to be somewhat of a fan's favourite in the years to come. In fact, unless you're Bobby Moore or Franz Beckenbauer, defenders don't tend to attract the level of acclaim that Koeman did during his Barca stint. But being able to fire home a set-piece when you're not heading them in yourself is always a decent way of endearing yourself to the fans.

Moving into the more 'exciting' areas, the signings got a little flashier - to the point where it completely ignored the club's debt problems and stuck Cruyff's own job on the line if they didn't perform. In hindsight, he needn't have worried much about his first major signing in Michael Laudrup who, having struggled the previous season at Juventus, had nothing to lose by the time he posed in front of the cameras with a Blaugrana shirt in 1989.

A startlingly composed playmaker forged in the mould of his manager, he was ideal to have in behind the front trio – a line which was in need of some serious renovation of its own. And beginning his DIY task on the wings, ol' man Cruyff got a little nostalgic on us.

Throughout his career, the nation of Hungary went from being one of the most revered talent producers on the planet, to a mere footnote in the times of yesteryear – and Johan seemed hell bent on writing another chapter. In his search, the Dutchman spread his scouting network throughout the country in the hope of finding somebody fit to carry the legacy left by Kocsis, Hidegkuti, Puskas and the like.

Sure enough, a pattern soon began to emerge with his team homing in on a gruff young man patrolling the flanks at CSKA Sofia. And after seeing the lad play with his own eyes, barely a blink had overcome them before signing off on a 3 million Euro cheque to secure the services of Hristo Stoichkov.

This was a mighty big risk. Stoichkov was a completely different proposition to the 'safer' transactions that managers tended to make – especially those whose moves were under as much scrutiny as Johan's at the time. But he knows better than most, that if you stand a chance of being a championship-winning side, you need to possess that little something different which opposing teams will struggle to counter.

You need an *enigma*.

'ENIGMA'

noun

a person or thing that is mysterious or difficult to understand.

In a sporting sense, these types of players don't necessarily have to be the most talented, but they offer a variety to their team's game plan which can be switched on whenever the situation calls for it. A good example outside of football would be Dennis Rodman in that famous all-stars Chicago Bulls NBA team in the early 1990's. In that team, you had Michael Jordan and Scottie Pippen who deservedly attract much of the attention for the Bulls' five-time-championship mystique. But Rodman, with his spray-painted hair, exuberant personality and explosive tendencies gave them an *added* dimension - putting more butts on the seats and causing more problems for the opposition than they'd accounted for with the more 'obvious' performers.

This was Stoichkov – while the other lads stuck to the script, he went rogue. Granted, his hair remained far more stable than his NBA link, though he was the guy Cruyff would employ to go beyond the call of duty and, more often than not, the Bulgarian was more than up to the task.

With the 'Rodman role' sorted, Cruyff needed his Michael Jordan - his main man. An argument can be made to say that he already had this in Laudrup, but sport is a fickle business. In Basketball, it's about whoever throws the most points, in the NFL, whoever runs the most touchdowns and in football, goals are the order of the day. And by this admission, Cruyff's chief operative was Romário - one of the greatest goal scorers to ever strike a ball.

Self-ordained as the 'man of a thousand goals', Romário was quite an unfathomable figure; whose scoring ability looked more divinely ordained than incessantly improved on. In fact, as many of his teammates will confirm, he wasn't the most dedicated trainer in the world and, but for his blessed metabolism, his waistline may have evidenced his poorer lifestyle choices.

Nevertheless, he remained in shape long enough to retain his spot in the squad and continued to turn up for them when called upon. Purchased after a near goal-per-game ratio in the Netherlands with PSV Eindhoven, he linked up with Laudrup and Stoichkov to spearhead Cruyff's 'Dream Team'. Together, they won four La Liga titles in a row between 1991 and 1995 - with a European Cup triumph thrown in for good measure in 1992. But as I have been trying to say to you since the words 'Johan' and 'Cruyff' were first typed down, his legacy exceeds far beyond the mere number of trophies he was able to win.

The 'Dutch Way' first imposed by Michels had been personified, perfected and popularised by Johan as a player *and* as a manager, where his version was even more effective and long-lasting than its predecessor. In doing so, he not only gave rise to one of the most forward-thinking formations for his *own* sides, but the wider footballing community had also taken note of his innovations.

Managers everywhere had begun searching for their own ways to one-up his theory – and all to varying degrees of success. Though one in particular opted for a more obvious imitation than most, and it's a journey which brings us back to the British shores. Over there, a struggling English manager was looking for a way to get his side scoring goals again, and like we all did, he liked what he saw from that mid-to-late '70s Ajax team.

So, in what would become the first official adaptation of European tactics in the English game, we venture away from the 'local agriculture' of Amsterdam and onto the modest estate of Ipswich Town Football Club, where a budding manager by the name of Bobby Robson had some work to do.

~ 6 ~

'I WENT TO AMSTERDAM ONCE …'

… Can't remember much!

The managerial story of Sir Bobby Robson (knighted for his services to the English game in 2002) is one that attracts a very high level of esteem throughout the footballing community. So much so, that even after his passing from a long cancer battle in 2009, stories continue to flood in over his infectious personality and overwhelming enthusiasm for the sport he served for so long. Though that's not to say that his entire career went unscathed. Actually, far from it.

When an interest in coaching creeped in following a more than adequate midfield playing career, he was instructed by a confidante at the FA to undertake a minimum-level coaching qualification before some on-the-job training would hopefully open up a door to a manager's office. Fortunately for him (depending on how you look at this), his most recent employers were in no position to be picky when searching for a new coach to see out their season;

thus, offering Robson a fateful caretaker position from January 1968 until the term's end.

An affluent club placed delicately beside the River Thames in West London, his maiden voyage with Fulham Football Club proved to be a choppy one - with the team lying at the foot of the First Division with a mere 16 points from 24 games by the time it was offered to him, and the rookie found the task too much to handle before overseeing their relegation to the league below.

Thereafter adopting a 'the only way is up' mantra, Robson looked to put that ignominy behind him and soldier on to re-raise the club from the depths that they'd fallen to under his stewardship, but he would quickly learn just how fickle the world of football can be – especially when you're on the losing end.

He was sacked in November the same year – roughly eleven months from taking on the job and less than a quarter of the way into the new season in the Second Division. And to make matters even worse, the announcement of his departure in the local news reel was just as big a surprise to him as anybody else!

The story goes that, although he may have had an inkling that the future wasn't as bright as it could be, its stormy confirmation came when Robson picked up the local newspaper on the way to work; only to discover a 'Robson Sacked' headline as a reason to make a 'U'-turn. Luckily for us all, Robson licked his wounds, got down to the job centre and soon found a home away from home at Ipswich Town. There, he developed a strong working relationship with chairman John Cobbold – a man who held the purse strings quite tightly during his fabled tenure there.

In line with this, Robson was basically made to work with what he had until some outsider cash injection (or divine intervention) would provide grounds for an acquisition or two with which to treat his predictable roster; though it was this precise consistency which had earned them a gradual promotion pass to the First Division in 1972. After which, they eked out a largely meagre existence in the promised land before a couple of over-performing seasons thrusted them into the public eye. Though few were prepared for their unlikely FA Cup Final fixture against Arsenal in 1978 - and even fewer were ready for the outcome.

The odds were highly stacked against Ipswich, with many expecting Arsenal's fresher attacking talents to exploit Town's withering defensive components. But they hadn't accounted for Robson's unerring qualities in man-management, which made for a dogged, determined display from his side. And after they'd managed a strike of their own with less than fifteen minutes on the clock, they may as well have cancelled the game there and then – for there was no way that Arsenal were going to get through. Indeed, 1-0 was how it ended, and the loyal Ipswich support were greeted to a triumph which their devotion had earned.

But it seemed to be the peak of anything they would be able to accomplish in the near future; unless things began to change around them. Even looking back at Town's starting line-up, many of their sell-by dates were approaching far sooner than anything to suggest an improvement to Ipswich's fiscal situation.

And to make matters worse, Messrs Clough & Taylor's headline-grabbing deals from the same time (now at Nottingham Forest), were among a number of those which had begun to inflate the domestic transfer market; then the only realistic avenue available to bring new lads in through the doors of somewhere like Portman Road. But you know how sometimes you pray for one thing, and the Gods above reward us in a way that we may not expect? Well, have a read of this …

Following a series of government referendums and frivolous debate, England had finally gained admission to the European Union (the 'EU') in 1975. And before you sigh and lodge this book somewhere you'll never find it, let me assure you that I haven't any interest whatsoever in exploring the complexities of the UK's involvement in the Union, nor do I wish to take up any more time in your day in considering that *Brexit* b******.

Instead, I'm here to explain how this initial membership helped to shape the timeline upon which this book is based, and that has an awful lot to do with the European transfer market.

As one of many outsider doctrines enshrined within the EU's foundations, The Treaty of Rome [1957] proposed to establish a 'European Economic Community' – where all countries inducted into the Union would wilfully loosen their domestic borders in order to allow the 'free movement of trade' across them.

In simpler terms, its principles were to allow one person working in one section of this territory, to move freely into a position of employment within another area of the territory – with there being nothing in place to restrict something like this from taking place and, consequently, anything that is considered to be a restriction here would be 'unlawful' and up for review under Europe's supra-national law courts.

Therefore, in a footballing sense, it meant that foreign players were now under just as much consideration to foreign clubs as any of their domestic options would have been, and the rule still applies today as a sacrosanct principle of the EU.

Altering the EU Football Economy

Now, I don't mean to get all 'I studied Economics in school' on your behind, but I'm going to just for a little bit. Opening up the borders to foreign talent represented an influx of higher football player supply in the transfer market. Thus, higher supply with a consistent level of demand leads to wider options and more competitive pricing. To you and me, it means cheaper (and better) choices for our teams to buy a greater array of players.

It was a major step in a more inclusive direction for the European continent – and a rather far cry from the war-torn disparities which plagued them a few decades before this. In fact, there was even a time in the 1930's where Herbert Chapman was strongly forbidden from bringing in an Austrian goalkeeper to his Arsenal side; to the point where he was officially sanctioned by the UK government as a reminder to preserve their national borders. So, it was a welcome development on these moral grounds.

Though more to the point at hand, this movement expanded the horizons of English football to include a now more attainable crop of players from across key territories in Europe – ones who embraced and celebrated football as much as they did e.g. France, Italy and more poignantly, the birthplace of Total Football in Holland. The latter of which proved an insatiable prospect for long-term admirer, Mr. Robson.

No time was wasted once there arose an opportunity to use Ipswich's FA Cup prestige and England's new economic standing to lure a couple of Dutchmen into Portman Road. And with the side's midriff looking a little worse for ware, the manager began by bringing in Arnold Mühren - a cultured and delicate right-sided central midfielder, who added a much-needed layer of flair to Robson's single-minded Ipswich team.

Then, after proving his worth to the side early on, Cobbold afforded Robson the opportunity to double up on his initial investment; akin to what Michels was able to do with Barcelona beforehand.

According to Mühren himself, he was personally enlisted to decide on Ipswich's next signing; with the hope of embodying a similar game to his own for the want of bettering their midfield output. And ex-FC Twente teammate Frans Thijssen stood out as the obvious choice.

Given their prior affiliation to one another, Thijssen took to Ipswich like a duck to water - where he and his mate 'Arnie' helped to establish a kind of football which aided heavily in a UEFA Cup win in 1981 against AZ Alkmaar over two legs - with Thijssen scoring the pick of the goals with a long-range volley in the first, and Mühren arguably being the Blues' stand-out performer across the fixture.

Funny how things work out ...

So ... Holland become this epicentre for the world's new brand of exciting and expressive football, they then inspire a British manager who, after the EU borders lower, brings in a couple of Dutchmen to his rustic British side, and they aid heavily in securing their new employers' first international trophy … *against a Dutch team*!

Remarkable.

Of the two, despite Thijssen arguably being the more talented, it was Mühren who would go on to own the better CV – continuing his British fling with a triplet of anniversaries in Manchester United colours before retiring back home a decorated hero. Meanwhile, Thijssen would flirt around with a few different clubs in Holland and the US before ending life as a relatively globetrotter. Though let's not get bogged down in this idea of 'who made their parents prouder' because together, they helped to make a very important point.

For British football in particular, their successes had become an in-your-face example of what can be achieved for a club that was willing to uproot from what's comfortable and venture into the unknown. Especially in this new socio-economic background of harmony and union, there really was no telling the level of triumph one may experience if they picked a route like this – something Keith Burkinshaw was ready and willing to test in the extreme.

~ 7 ~

'WHERE EVEN *IS* SOUTH AMERICA?'

Somewhere 'South', I'd imagine . . .

Formally, where the de-restricted movement of trade across the 'EEC' allowed the UK transfer market to be more inclusive of its European neighbours, the same did not (and still doesn't) apply to transactions concerning those beyond Europe.

Therefore, suppose if you wanted to acquire a player from another continent, a lot more work was needed behind the scenes to get something like this signed off. But since we've just been going on about Holland's various European conquests, why are we even having this discussion?

Well, it just so happens that while the Dutchmen were painting the game orange with their 'Total Football' concept, there was a fleeting yet irreversible moment where it was unseated. Not by perhaps the most 'efficient' of techniques as far as 'getting results' go, but by one which was on par (if not greater) in terms of pure, unadulterated entertainment value.

In less cryptic terms, while the likes of Robson and co. were courted by the Cruyff Revolution that gradually claimed the majority of the decade, the 1978 World Cup was of particular allure to Keith Burkinshaw - one which he intended to act upon in an even more obvious manner than Robson did with his choice.

Hosted within the noisy, ticker-tape-littered stadiums of Argentina, the inhibit flair of South American football was on show for all to see. Even through the grainy, sort-of-technicoloured footage available to us through our frequently smacked, cinder-block-type television boxes, it was clear to see the happiness and guile with which the game was played in this area of the world. Even more so when you consider that Argentina went on to win the bloody thing against our fabled Netherlands squad!

Watching from afar, Burkinshaw was hooked from the get-go, and decided to capitalise on the competition's success by poaching a few of their star players for his own. Though it proved to be a far more laborious undertaking than history gives credit for.

At the time, he was a struggling manager for Tottenham Hotspur – who were sat comfortably in the middle of England's top tier, and looked better off sticking to the status quo than they were attracting some South American play-things to come and join them, particularly with the likes of Liverpool, Manchester United and Leeds hovering about. But Burkinshaw didn't see things like that. Granted, the mentioned teams did indeed dwarf his in terms of their affluence, domestic prestige and relative allure, but these aren't the only things which will attract somebody to join a football team

We touched on this briefly with the Cruyff-Barcelona decision a few swipes ago, but this is an even better example of the point I was trying to make back then.

Consider this …

A highly talented footballer is the industry's equivalent of somebody who is simply very good at their job. And should there arise an opportunity to hog them for yourselves then, more often than not, a hoard of potential suitors will gather on the scene quicker than some skimpy-dressed women in an old *Lynx* advert.

Thereafter, once a fee has been agreed between the two sets of employers, it comes down to how the player themselves actually *feel* about moving to a new club; and their own personal reasoning behind making that ultimate decision. Some go for the colder, tried-and-tested 'bigger team means more money' option. Though others opt for a place where they can see themselves having the greatest impact; where outright prestige of one choice is replaced by the potential and *vision* of another. So, it's up to those in Burkinshaw's position to sell these players that vision, when attracting them to their club. And I tell you what, it had to have been a presentation from the Gods given who his targets were.

With his extraordinary sales patter at the ready, the ambitious Burkinshaw saw no reason not to target the very best of the World Cup-winning Argentina side; promptly homing in on playmaker, Osvaldo ("Ossie") Ardiles and tricky forward, Ricardo ("Ricky") Villa. Yeah … Anglicising names was just a *thing* back then. 'Different times', I suppose

sigh

***

The two were reportedly inseparable throughout their time with the national squad, and their friendship morphed into a twin-level telepathy on the pitch – with Ardiles navigating the murky waters of the midfield to supply the clinical Villa in attack. So, unsurprisingly, with their mastery evident to anybody with a TV screen or access to a nearby pub, a plethora of suitors came calling for the pair – with the majority of the plaudits being aimed in little Ardiles' direction.

In his own words, 'Ossie' himself admits his favour towards the offers from Spain, Italy and France at the time, with England further from the spectrum than the chain of events would suggest. Though this is where Burkinshaw comes in; whose thoughtful proposal to the Argentine formed the bedrock of his Spurs journey. For not only did he re-assure Ardiles of his intentions to become the 'main man' for the Lilywhites, but he'd also recognised a few issues which could hinder his time in London, and set about making them far more manageable for him.

Although the Falklands War (which cemented the ill-feel between the two nations) would begin some four years after Ardiles' signature, the two hadn't had the greatest of relationships as far as their national football teams were concerned. In fact, but for Geoff Hurst's controversial winner against the Germans in the final, that 1966 England World Cup triumph may have been overshadowed by their quarter-final outing against the Latin stars.

Where, despite the Lions running out as worthy 1-0 victors, the game's temperament within those ninety minutes had carried over after the final whistle had been blown - with England manager Alf Ramsey refusing to allow his players to trade shirts with their fallen enemies in retaliation for their dishonourable behaviour. And given the nations' estranged existence after the tournament, much of that ill feeling remained even by the time Spurs had declared some interest in Ardiles some twelve years later. But do you know what makes you feel a little better in such circumstances? Going through them with your buddy!

To sweeten the deal, Burkinshaw also threw in an offer for Villa to join the club at the same time; a proposal which wasn't matched by any of the continent's big wigs who were only interested in Ardiles. In doing so, it helped to embed either star into an otherwise unfamiliar setting, and allowed their innate partnership to shine through any personal insecurities they had about relocating to England – especially given that Villa was promised as much first team football as Ardiles. Sure, they may have been £750,000 worse off after the deal, but I reckon it was worth it.

Then, after a series of intensive language courses and regular bonding exercises with their new teammates, the pair had earned 'cult hero' status within their second year at White Hart Lane; with many of their stand-out moments coming in the Cup competitions over domestic form; most notably in one of two FA Cup triumphs against Manchester City, where Villa provided us all with a moment which typified the very reason for why Burkinshaw had decided to sanction this kind of deal.

Deep into the second half, the static-ridden footage of the time reveals a slender, full-bearded Villa picking up the ball at the edge of the opponent's penalty area. Then, opposed by more defenders than a *Land Rover* showroom, he sets off on a meandering journey edging closer to his target point in the City goalmouth. On his way, the ball remains glued to his right foot – dancing its way through a dizzying myriad of Sky-Blue shirts – before slotting home clinically to the goalkeeper's right. A deceptively beautiful attempt from a man as tall and seemingly unkept as Ricardo Villa, and one that would prove to be his swansong outing for the North London, before life as a globe-trotter took hold.

Meanwhile, Ossie (now fully settled under the arm of his friend) took to North London like barely anybody had expected, and remained at the club long after Villa had departed. During which time, his escapeless charm and boyish persona endeared himself to every Lillywhite in the city, and even earned him a managerial stint at the club shortly after retiring; which perhaps explains why his legacy at Spurs lingers on a little deeper than the man who joined him.

But much like Mühren and Thijssen before them, let's not split hairs between these two lads. They came as a pair and, together, they had helped to broaden our eyes *even* further to what those comparable Dutchmen had managed to do over at Ipswich.

Therefore, as a *quartet*, they had breached the seemingly impenetrable wall that guarded this lacklustre form of football that had been adored thus far in England. And looking back, their individual trail-blazing successes have formed the basis of the cultural diversity which adorns the British game today; where the current inclusion of European talents can thank the pioneering Robson Dutch duo, and the wider interest in South American football can tip their hats off to Burkinshaw's boys. But having said that, no matter how well they played or how impactful they became, it wasn't a fair reflection on some of the game's more 'lowly' patrons; who were being personally affected by a lot of the behind-the-scenes politics creeping into the game's structure. Namely, the archaic procedures respected by the immoveable authorities' responses to bringing the sport into the modern world - something which the owners of Kettering Town are probably still annoyed about to this day.

~ 8 ~

'I'M NOT WEARING THESE!'
Unless you pay me

Nowadays, having an obscure sponsor's name scribed across a footballer's chest is like its own equivalent to having the fabled 'verified' blue tick on your *Twitter* account – to be considered a 'somebody', you *have* to have one.

And where the likes of *Twitter* and *Instagram* seek to bestow this honour solely upon those whose relevance translates into a significant number of followers, it really isn't much different to how it's applied in the world of sport. The only tangible difference being that there's only one 'type' of verification afforded to social media influencers, whereas heaps of sponsors have flocked to the footballing scene over the years; each with their own expectations and motives for doing so.

As a general rule of thumb, there is often a positive correlation between a club's reputation and the calibre of sponsor that they can attract – hence why a brand as resourceful as Chevrolet would prefer to opt for a club as popular as Manchester United. But away from this, the decision could be more about company/brand affiliation than pure monetary gain.

Using the example of Chevrolet, perhaps it's no coincidence that it is the favoured choice of United's American owners – and the same can probably be said of Etihad Airways' association with the Abu-Dhabi-funded Manchester City. But as these powerhouses duel in this endless joust of 'my sponsor is bigger than your sponsor', history traces this evolution back to a delightfully more modest form.

But before I go on …

Have you ever heard of the 'Mandela Effect'?

It's where your mind supposedly conjures up an inaccurate recollection of something common, though you are *absolutely* sure that your incorrect memory is more correct than any official information could convince you otherwise.

Its eponymy apparently derives from the misconception that, during his lengthy prison stay after his activist efforts in an Apartheid-torn South Africa, Nelson Mandela had passed away whilst incarcerated. I'd never personally understood why *this* fallacy was considered believable enough to attribute the overall theory to it; given his forthcoming presidency and enforced counter-Apartheid policies. But regardless of my astounding knowledge, the name stands, and the theory lingers onto more accepted examples.

Including:

'the vanishing tail' of *Curious George* (i.e. the fact that he never had one), the air-freshener *'Febreze'* only being spelled with a single 'e' despite its pronunciation, the lack of monocle on the face of the '*Monopoly* Man' and many more!

Accordingly, the 'Mandela Effect' applies to the area of football sponsorship among its vast collection of relatives – where it is believed that Liverpool, then one of the most dominant forces in world football, were the first club to conceive of the idea when striking up a deal with Japanese conglomerate, *Hitachi*, to brandish their logo during the 1979/80 season.

However, in this case, I shall forgive the unbending minds of those who stand by this 'fact', as Liverpool did it on a much bigger stage than anybody before them – much like how the inception of the 'moonwalk' dance is credited to Michael Jackson for his televised *Motown* performance, despite the fact that he himself adopted the move from *Shalimar's* Jeffrey Daniel who birthed the iconic move on *Soul Train*.

Here, it was Michael's adaptation which gave the move its notoriety and Liverpool's dominance which made the corporate move more obvious and exemplary. Nevertheless, MJ did not *create* the moonwalk, and nor did Liverpool *invent* the concept of sponsoring a football outfit – for that honour belongs to 'The Doog'; once the enigmatic chairman of Kettering Town Football Club.

Now languishing in or around the 6th tier of English football, most people surrounding the club must curse their luck that the pioneering actions of Dougan failed to materialise into little more than an interesting footnote in football's commercial history … or indeed a short interlude in some book written by a law graduate. Though this may be because of just how subtle their actions were, and how remarkably quickly they were shut down. Having struck up a deal with local business 'Kettering Tyres', a 'four figure sum' was promised to the club in return for emblazoning a simple letter 'T' after the word 'Kettering' which was already across the first team shirt. Where, to your average spectator, and indeed the loyal fans of Kettering Town, the use of the letter 'T' could easily be viewed as both representing their own club's initials as much as their association with Kettering Tyres.

But even something as withheld as this didn't escape the gaze of the 'we like things the way they are' Football Association, who continued to forbid any of their clubs from advertising another brand which may seek to take the attention away from football.

And without a UK legal precedent as a foundation to change anything, The FA saw fit to fine Kettering Town £1,000 for their little 'indiscretion' which, considering the fact that their endeavours had reportedly earned them a similar figured amount from the start, looked more like a deterrent for future behaviour than a proportionate response to the offence.

Though luckily for Kettering, a similar occurrence from *another* country had given them basis for an appeal under the new EU regulatory framework; where they could take their matter beyond the domestic legal system and into Europe's – whose ruling would be superimposed on the original decision if there were grounds for it to be overturned.

For this, we journey to Germany and lower league club Braunschweiger Turn-und Sportverein Eintracht von 1895 e.V., more commonly referred to as 'Eintracht Braunschweiger' - say that three times fast.

In 1973 – three years prior to Dougan's case – Braunschweiger opted for a more overt commercial approach to club kit sponsorship. By contrast to the local Kettering deal, the German club threw caution to the wind and directly incorporated one of the country's biggest brands into their company directive. Was it a local brand? No. Was it a sporting brand? No! Was it even a brand which promoted football in a positive manner? Not really!

Cheekily, they approached *Jägermeister*, a well-known alcohol company derived from a region far distant to the stadium which now bore its name. And here, given the drink's popularity in the country, they intended to lambast their crest across their new partners in a way that poor old 'Kettering Tyres' could only dream of.

After the kits were done, their logo extended throughout the stadium's advertising hoardings, club merchandise and there were even talks of incorporating it into the name of the club … though they probably ran out of space for that one.

And the price for all this subtlety? A handsome 100,000 Deutschmarks; which would have roughly amounted to over 40 times the amount which the FA had considered too gruesome for Dougan's Kettering to receive. Talk about 'gaining a perspective'!

Braunschweiger's deal not only continued but went unscathed; with the reason being delightfully progressive for its time. It was agreed that their enterprise was fairly reflective of the industry that they were in, and they were allowed to keep their investment on the belief that it would be re-cycled it in any way which would benefit the club; something which the German FA would have wanted to encourage but couldn't actively enforce. So, when you pair up this reasoning with Dougan's actions, you have a match. He struck a deal which, at its heart, was proposed for the benefit of the club he loved; not for some egotistical/nonfootballing reason which sought to bring the game into disrepute, and even if this example wasn't considered enough to back Dougan's appeal on its own, it helps very much that he was backed by a lot of influential people on home soil.

In particular, Bolton Wanderers and Derby County became vocal patrons for Dougan's innovation, whilst critically informing Dougan to see some error in his ways. For you see, sometimes, simply 'being right' isn't enough to get the outcome you're looking for. In such circumstances, it's about pandering to the powers that be to ensure that they take your actions in the way you intend them to take them; hopefully before following up with the actions you envisaged at the start. Therefore, perhaps flaunting your new ideas on a league game day before even getting a sense of how the 'suits' may respond, is not a good way of being heard in the tone with which you intend to be.

'Pop Culture' Reference incoming ...

In a way, it reminds me of Katniss Everdeen in *The Hunger Games,* where she defiantly holds her three fingers aloft as a symbol to promote peace and solidarity among her audience. Though what she deems to be a passive symbol of respect, becomes misconstrued by her longing-for-hope audience and stern-faced authority figures. Subsequently, her *Mockingjay* image is wholly rejected as representative of a much-despised rebellion which is sought to be destroyed by the very organisation it threatens.

So, imagine that situation with an institution as old-fashioned as the FA ... and bang! A substantial fine acts as their equivalent to starting a *Quarter Quell* - you really should read these books if you haven't already, they're fantastic! They even have film adaptations if you're bored of all this 'wordy' stuff.

Nevertheless, you can't change the past and Dougan had to contend with the fact that he should have handled things very differently in context, but at least he had some new friends by his side to aid his appeal process. The hierarchy at Bolton and Derby were far more seasoned in the art of top-league procedure than Kettering's make-do chairman, and together, their efforts formed an official application to the domestic authorities which argued the case for corporate sponsorship in football; citing the German precedent and the game's ever-changing commercial landscape as the basis for their case.

And after a long year-and-a-half of persistent negotiations, hard-headed stances and correspondence getting 'lost in the post', the FA granted their application and has since welcomed the commercial world into their cocooned industry.

But as far as 'The Doog' was concerned, the chronicles of history seem to have forgotten his outstanding contribution to the sport, and instead tend to focus more on his polarising life choices after leaving football. Though when we tunnel our vision purely into his influence on the game, there can be no denying that his pioneering influence forms one of many points which better explain the monolithic commercial power which the sport has become today.

However, just to throw another spanner in the works, and much to the dismay of Liverpool and other top-flight clubs who followed Kettering's example, broadcasting regulations on showing sponsored teams were *even more* stringent than those of the FA. Which is something I could never personally understand given the state of football media at the time.

With league football's schedule restricted to a single time slot on the BBC (3pm on a Saturday afternoon), there wasn't much scope to show many games live, and instead matches were often broadcasted via a highlights reel once they had time to be edited, analysed and presented back. So, it's not like there was even that much airtime to be given to a club with some obscure name ironed onto their fronts. But I suppose this is the BBC we're talking about – often marked as the antithesis of liberality and the patron-saint of correctness and order. And meshing the worlds of sport and commercialism seemed to be an unwanted influence on a game whose fans were typically as old-fashioned as they were.

They therefore banned the broadcast of any club matches (even as highlights) where there was an 'advertising message' displayed by any of the competing teams.

I mean, does this count? Really? A message to me, is more like a call to action or something which describes the thing it's advertising - not the mere appearance of the advert itself. For example, pressing on a 'Red Bull' logo doesn't give me much of a message unless I attach one to it, though 'it gives you wiiiiings' encourages me to think differently.

Eventually, the broadcasters saw the errors in ways like these and eventually abolished this archaic reasoning by 1983, where kits have since been littered with sponsors wherever there arose space to have one; representing another step that we were moving into a defining age for the business side of the game; which was advancing just as quickly as its technical side.

So, all things considered, things looked pretty much set, didn't they? The game was becoming a lot nicer to watch, certain personalities were boosting the sport's mainstream interest and its embrace of modern change suggested that richer (and more efficient) days were on the horizon. But what about actually *attending* the games?

More specifically, who you're sitting next to, how the atmosphere makes you feel, the level of security at the ready, the state of the stadium and anything else to that effect. Well, a word more favourable than 'horrific' is a deceptive summary to any of these questions.

And indeed, before the English game (and most of Europe's) could truly grasp its on-pitch and behind-the-scenes developments, they all had to muck in and deal with what went on in the stands; to make the game feel accessible and safe enough to be fully enjoyed by its attendees and accepted by the greater mainstream audience.

If only they'd acted more quickly than they did ...

~ 9 ~

'THE HOOLIGAN'S GAME'
Some of Football's Darkest Days

I must warn you, this is going to be a pretty heavy chapter to stick with, so how about we start things lightly by learning a little something about the author? Yeah? Okay, well …

One of the things that you will see highlighted and underlined several times in my bucket list is my desire to visit a number of football stadiums from around the world; stemming from my unashamed 'glory-hunting' childhood when it came to watching foreign football. And I'm lucky enough to say that I popped my soul-searching cherry with a trip to watch A.C. Milan in December 2019, within their monolithic 'San Siro' stadium.

An imposing façade reinforced by a series of concrete spiral structures to form a makeshift exit trail, had greeted my initial enthusiasm upon breaching its fabled doors. Thereafter, a distinct lack of modern influence burned a lactic-induced fatigue into my thighs as I lumbered my way up its endless route to wherever my ticket said I'd needed to go.

Further and further I climbed – air thinning with each passing moment – until mercifully, a gateway opened to reveal a bright green turf, a sea of red and black shirts and a deafening Italian chorus of appreciation from the other fans in attendance; like some opening into a *Rossoneri* 'VIP' section in heaven.

Offensively, the game that I was privileged to watch was a bore nil-nil draw between the 10th placed Milan and the 12th placed Sassuolo – with little other than a VAR-removed goal to give the expecting home supporters anything to cheer for.

Nonetheless, the experience as a whole was one to saviour; and has only served to boost my mentioned desire to chalk off a few other worthy stadia from that pesky bucket list. And yet, as I was recalling my vacation to family and friends; as unashamedly as anyone who's been on a trip that they refuse to shut up about, the general reception was one of concern.

As an Anglo-Indian man, I (among many others) have been on the receiving end of racially fuelled verbal and (at times) physical abuse throughout various points in my life. Thankfully, they have failed to leave a lasting imprint on how I view future experiences, though it remains strong in the mind of most people I associate with. Especially so for my parents who couldn't have been much overjoyed at the prospect of feeding their offspring to the 'hooligans' of continental football; and even more so considering that racism and general violence in the game is by no means a foregone conclusion.

Though as I say, my various journeys to Old Trafford, Stamford Bridge, Anfield and Wembley to name a few have never once given me much cause for concern in this area. However, this isn't down to some *obligation* inherently respected by the supporters in attendance, but more so the evolutionary result of conscious efforts to make up for the sins of the past.

The 1980's marked a change in UK governance, where the new appointees were shamelessly overt in their disdain for the poor state of English football. Where, without actually *saying* the words, they had denounced the game's fans as 'lowly degenerates' who spend their Saturday afternoons picking their noses, hurling indiscriminate abuse and sparking physical altercations for the sake of 'supporting their club'.

Now, whilst I remain politically aware in my daily life, I find the general area of UK politics to be a myriad of convoluted nonsense which portrays our country in a way that I don't resonate with. And I imagine my current sensibilities (or lack thereof) would extend to Thatcher's government also. But even I must concede that, when it comes to the matter of football fan culture around this period, they did have a point.

Although it was great to see certain proud, working-class sides 'come good' for their football-loving community, their pantheons of prayer weren't exactly architectural masterpieces. In fact, most boardrooms (even at the highest level of the game) were so caught up in the headlines of big-name signings and filling their dust-ridden trophy cabinet, that a blatantly insufficient level of attention was given to preserving their home and controlling the behaviour of their visitors. Some to a more harrowing degree of negligence than others.

Saturday, 11th May 1985 is a match-day which will remain long in the memory of anybody associated with Bradford

City Football Club for what happened during that game's interval.

Today, that 'half-time' signal begins a fifteen-minute respite with the odd fan competition thrown in to keep those immovable fans entertained while their lads got a talking-to, but at Valley Parade in the mid-'80s (like with all other lower English League clubs), it was a slap-and-dash, ten-minute free-for-all for those who needed to tend to their stomach or bowels and act accordingly – only to be greeted by sub-par bathroom facilities, unhygienic food stalls and putrid smells which accompanied the pair of them.

And often neighbouring either of their choices were mountains of empty crisp packets, disposable teacups and personal litter; inattentively growing in size as the game continued to its close. However, on this particular day, its presence proved far more destructive than an irritation of the nose or a sore of the eye, especially when it came into contact with a nearby smoker's half-lit cigarette. Once the union was made, the sheer volume of rubbish cascading the stadium served as kindling for the devastating fire which ensued; shortly engulfing the main stand of the Valley Parade after starting, with the blustery conditions of the day serving to accelerate its impact.

It was a truly harrowing ordeal which scarcely matches your worst fears if you haven't seen any pictures from the incident to add to your presumptions, and acting commentator John Helm can never be blamed for failing to find the correct words to match the situation; much like I'm struggling to do so now.

The flames roared on in the early minutes of the second half and encased over 7,000 fans at the venue; 50 of whom weren't among the luckier ones who managed to live to tell the tale. And all resulting from a single person not disposing of their cigarette carefully enough, and the shameful state of a ground which transformed their action into much more than some nonchalant mistake.

A Tribute to our Fellow Fans ...

Before I go on, allow me to express my most sincere condolences to those affected by this appalling event, and indeed for the others who will be referenced in a later incident of similar tragedy. We can all empathise as much as we can and do our best to share in the disdain at the chain of events which led to this happening, but at its heart, fellow football fans like you and I set out to watch their beloved team play – the highlight of their week – and were never able to return.

The nature of their deaths was public, vile, unexplained and reported with a sheer lack of decency towards their humanity.

The tragedies had each indiscriminately claimed the lives of men, women and children alike, and ought never be forgotten regardless of where the game advances to - much like how it won't ever be for those personally affected by them.

All we can hope for now is that their loved ones have found solace and that their souls rest in peace.

To make matters even worse, as the world of football mourned the awful tragedy which took place that day, it soon dawned on the nation's right-wing leaders that poor stadium housekeeping wasn't the *only* plague befalling what they'd already considered to be a 'ne'er-do-well's sport'; a title which instead attaches itself to the conscious actions of rival fans than the unintentional action of one.

Not too dissimilar to how gangs would align themselves based on locality as cause for wreaking indiscriminate havoc on opposing areas, football history is littered with infamous groups of rival factions who channelled their hatred directly onto the opposition - with stadiums' surrounding roads and drinking establishments often acting as the arenas for such altercations to take place. Correspondingly, with England boasting one of the largest football league setups around, it's no wonder that it's been 'awarded' with the highest number of factions across Europe in recent years.

From Aldershot Town's 'Company' firm to Chelsea FC's 'Head-Hunters', the list bulged to a point where it raised even greater suspicion from Baroness Thatcher's government; though not enough to be called into action before another, deeply harrowing, tragedy affected a domestic establishment.

A mere *two weeks* after the Bradford City fire's casualties were identified, England's Liverpool and Italy's Juventus met at a neutral venue to finalise the 1985 European Cup campaign, at the Heysel Stadium in Belgium.

Solemnly, the 60,000-capacity stadium was not fit for use, and in an alternatively destructive way to what we explored with Valley Parade. Years of misuse had taken its toll on the arena, to the point where it's a wonder as to how the place even stood on its own two legs for that long, let alone be deemed practical enough to host that season's most watched and coveted fixture; with two of the most proud and fiery sets of supporters threatening to lock horns before kick-off.

As is common with matches played at 'neutral' venues (i.e. a stadium which isn't home to any of the competing clubs), both sides are accredited with an equal number of spots for their fans to attend, with an emptied space forming an invisible barrier between the two clans at whatever end of the stadium that they end up converging at. And more often than not, you'll see a healthy line of policemen at the divide to ensure that things don't get out of hand in that interim.

Though here, with around 2,000 opposing fans actively goading each other at either end of the invisible line between them, no real amount of police resistance could have prevented the inevitable collision once tensions had finally boiled over.

Before you knew it, foresight remained dormant for every Liverpool fan which laid siege to the retreating Juventus clan. And my next few words are only to be taken towards those *actively* involved in the impending Heysel tragedy; and should not be considered as reflective as my thoughts towards to 20,000-or-so law-abiding fans in attendance that evening.

To those who did indeed elect to forego any human decency in their search for blood, I can't even find the words to describe what I think about it. It was a senseless act of violence which had no place in a street war, let alone the sanctity of a football match. Worse still, the resulting reality of the casualties' demise adjudged to have been stimulated by their own fans' disturbance of the whittling Heysel ground, is almost too inconceivable to imagine.

In their bid to retreat from what was objectively seen as the *true* source of immediate danger, a significant number of Juventus fans sought for the security seemingly provided by the backing wall of their most nearby stand. But little did they know that this crumbling affixture was held up by a decaying support structure which was threatening to give way at the earliest sign of distress. And so, it did.

Thirty-nine fans (mostly of Juventus) were pronounced dead at the scene, with fourteen Reds found guilty of voluntary manslaughter in the second degree, punishable by up to five years' imprisonment by the English criminal legal system, for playing their part in this unspeakable catastrophe.

But do you know what makes this even worse than it already was? After it had happened. After the bodies had been cleared and the inquest began. The game still went ahead. I mean … if *ever* there was something which showed football to be a callous, brutish sport, then this was it; not just for the senseless actions of the attendees, but for the insensitive and heartless response to having it happen.

Sure, it was completely unprecedented, and maybe the officials simply didn't know how to handle the hangover of calling off a European Cup Final. But that's no excuse, and the game should never have gone ahead. Plain and simple.

When the news filtered back to the Prime Minister's headquarters, Mrs. Thatcher had little choice but to respond to the tragedy, and despite a lot of her emotional reactions being well-founded, I don't think that they were particularly helpful in preventing future tragedies from taking place.

Like many did, she fixated on her condemnation for those who attributed to the incident, and whilst nothing ought to detract from the deplorable actions of those explicitly attempting to harm their counterpart, it wasn't the operating cause for the deaths that had resulted from the altercation on the terraces.

There was little evidence to suggest that the concrete structure gave way *purely* under the intense strain placed upon it in the build-up to the game. For instance, nobody had directly attacked the stadium itself, and when isolated, it simply didn't appear stable enough to withstand much further general ware, or even perhaps the average crowd movements during a game as emotional and congested as a European Cup Final.

So, to blame the fans entirely was a very short-sighted indictment which more spoke of the Baroness' hatred for football than it did for her desire to improve anything which was shaming it. And none more so than her blind acceptance to the resulting five-year-ban imposed upon all English clubs from participating in European competition. As such, any lessons learned from the Heysel disaster were never used in ways that they should have been at the time i.e. as a direct instruction for domestic clubs to take preventative action on their own homes, before their issues prove equally as destructive for their own fans.

***

After the Heysel incident, Thatcher's government soon set up a war-cabinet-like approach to assessing any trends to help better understand fan behaviour. Though a palpable bias towards seeking a means upon which to disregard the sport undermined much of whatever point they were trying to make; as recognised by a powerful dissenting voice within their own ranks!

Serving as the country's Home Secretary, seasoned politician Douglas Hurd refused to accept this *prima facie* interpretation of how his government approached the footballing sphere, and instead argued that football's 'hooliganism' culture had derived from a myriad of deeper-rooted societies that simply converged upon the popularity of the game; and not directly resulting from it.

Quite rightly, he pointed out that "punks and skinheads" which ran rife in the football community "inherited a long tradition" and that the concept of drunken mob violence "goes back centuries". He also directly pointed to the impact of excessive drinking *and* lack of stadium maintenance and policing as reasons for why fans could become unruly; where the former removes one's inhibitions to behave correctly and the latter provides little restraint to hold them back if things escalate.

He also opposed the government's proposal to enforce a 'rural riot squad' which would be deployed to react to any instances of hooliganism at football matches; sensing that it would incite a 'caged animal' effect that would reverse any positive intentions of them being there as a restraint. His preference was for tougher licensing laws, quicker prosecutions, exemplary sentences, and improved policing procedures. And history wishes that either his voice was louder to be heard, or was protracted to an audience who were open to hearing it …

By 1989, the English game had gone four years of continental isolation which, to the closed-minded, is four long years of fans turning their hatred on one another without any European 'reprieve', but for the 'woke' ones (like Hurd) with a vague idea of what goes on behind the scenes, that's four *long* years of continued strain being put on stadiums that were whittling further as the seasons went on. Unfortunately, Hillsborough was a case in point.

On April 15th, 1989 a fixture between Liverpool and Nottingham Forest in that season's FA Cup semi-final revealed the shortcomings of the Hillsborough stadium, and to cataclysmic effect for those in attendance.

A mixture of overcrowding and police negligence led to an unorderly file of excess Liverpool supporters making their way to the stands; thereby overwhelming the crumbling stadium structure in a not too dissimilar fashion from the Heysel tragedy almost half a decade before it. However, this time, there were nearly one thousand injuries to account for with ninety-six Liverpool supporters unable to walk away from the scene.

In its aftermath, and right up until a stand-alone inquiry by the Hillsborough Independent Panel in 2012, culpability was (once again) placed firmly at the feet of the fans themselves; as yet another indictment of the shameful actions that going to a football game was believed to incite.

But luckily for us all, and in particular for the families of those who've since been exonerated from any criminal involvement in the tragedy, Lord Justice Taylor had launched an earlier official inquiry into why the Hillsborough Stadium had fallen in the way that it had; which not only paved a way forward for getting to the 'true source' of *this* disaster, but also in officialising any by-the-way concerns for how the game was being handled in England, *and* directly specifying a number of stellar ideas for how the game should develop for the better.

It remains a sophisticated work which formed the foundation for a completely renovated league structure;

which ensured that all participating clubs adhered to a sea of regulations aimed at making a football match a safer place to be. And it would be a major English First Division club's Vice Chairman's interpretation of it, that would take Taylor's insightful findings, and mould them into a new brand of football which formed the foundation of the very league that we all recognise today.

But for now, why don't we see what our European brethren got up to while the UK sorted themselves out? Word on the streets is that they weren't doing too badly at all.

~ 10 ~

'MERGING THE STYLES'
The Italian Job

In the game's illustrious history, very few have been able to reach a 'galactic' status for their particular era. But among the elite, you have the original great Real Madrid side of the '60s (the one with Di Stefano and Puskas), the Ajax/Barcelona sides of the '70s (as mentioned earlier) and Arrigo Sacchi's Dutch-inspired A.C. Milan side from the '80s; which was a spell that almost didn't happen given the fickle state of Italian football at the time.

In more times than we can count, football has proven to be a game that is marshalled by those who are often too proud to accept anything new. Especially at an elder boardroom level, once something becomes traditional to their side, it can prove to be very difficult indeed to get them singing a different tune; particularly so when their *modus operandi* had proven so steady and successful to begin with, and has formed an allegiance of support with their fan-base that is greatly dependent on this recognition and consistency.

Of course, this all depends on how malleable the individuals are and how willing they are to subject their club to change, though you'll be pressed to find an institution more immovable than the *Rossoneri*.

Their fans are no-nonsense, volatile, highly passionate and hold a deep sense of connection to their club. And over their proud history, the fans have been spoiled by continuous and unrelenting success; especially on the domestic stage and particularly within the timeline through which this book is journeying. But with great success, comes great expectation, and with *that*, comes a deeper-rooted tendency to stick with what's recognised for fear of upsetting the status quo.

Imagine this …

You are an author publishing your first book. You've poured your heart and soul into this thing and can only pray that people enjoy reading your work just as much as you've enjoyed making it (relatable, much!). Then, once it's out there, it exceeds all expectations; I'm talking 'Number 1 selling book' across all major global bookstores, getting added to Oprah's Book Club after being invited onto her show to talk about it, and the Queen of England calling it 'lit' … on Instagram … *live*.

Then, once the dust settles, and you're understandably overjoyed by how well it's done, you're inspired to write a few sequels. Now, let me ask you this: How do you think your mood changes in regard to how you expect your new work to be received, given how well the first one was? And if you stay grounded enough to have your expectations unaffected the first time, then at what point along these many points of 'good launches' does your thought process begin to change?

‾   Where you go from thinking 'I hope this does well', to 'I hope this does as well as the last one', to 'this better be up to par with the last two', to 'when is Oprah going to call?' And it's a similar evolution of thinking that's adopted by many a top-level football team whenever their comparable successes arrive.

In the case of A.C. Milan, they begin by winning a couple of titles here and there, and are overcome with the pure joy of having won *those* titles, then their following successes slowly take them across that bridge from humility to expectation. And once anyone (leave alone a high-strung football organization) makes that voyage, it's very hard to alter the pattern of play that was largely responsible for bringing you to where you are.

Therefore, by the time a fresh-faced Arrigo Sacchi appeared in the shadow of the San Siro - ideas in mind and notebook in hand - the club were *already* steeped in a very proud heritage; and were fixed to an 'if it ain't broke, don't fix it' mantra.

But Sacchi didn't get that memo. Either that or he garnished it with salt and pepper, consumed it whole and … presented it back. Because a combination of hard-nosed decisions and fortuitous timing enabled this man to completely change the face of A.C. Milan forever. To the point where much of my own personal admiration for the club traces back to his time in Italy.

Arriving at the San Siro in 1987 to steady the ship after a short-lived few months under Fabio Capello, then-promising

Parma coach Sacchi appeared a relatively surprising appointment; whose track record seemed to oppose what Milan were searching for upon Capello's departure.

Though this very lack of expectation appeared to work in Arrigo's favour, where he had almost nothing to lose and everything to gain; and could therefore afford to be far more expressive and experimental than he would otherwise have been without this freedom. Especially given that the Italian's affinity with *Totaalvoetbal* formed the basis of his intended changes at the club – and was particularly difficult to implement given not only his new supporter's antithesis for 'going against the grain', but the innately defensive-based customs adhered to by Italian football at the time.

But here's where Sacchi's genius comes to the fore, for his plan was the merge the two worlds together to create an unstoppable footballing entity – polymerising a 'typically' Italian defence with that beautifully elegant Dutch attack.

Bellisima!

In implementing his plan, Sacchi soon realised that his Dutch effect would have to arrive out of the transfer market, but was fortunate enough to have a rather enviable selection of Italian defenders at the ready to form his side's backbone; including the legendary Franco Baresi, Alessandro Costacurta and Mauro Tossotti, with a young Paolo Maldini quietly peering his head around the corner.

And if that wasn't enough, then there was also a competent defensive midfielder by the name of Carlo Ancelotti which helped to further ease his manager's defensive concerns; by solidly adopting that 'Guardiola' role in a deeper midfield position. So now, together with his ambitious chairman's desire to see out his plan, Sacchi was able to focus the lion's share of his attention (and a significant financial outlay) on his team's fire-power – beginning with a prodigious forward inspired by that 'Cruyff' fellow who keeps popping up in conversation – Marco van Basten.

133 appearances and 128 goals. That is an average of 0.96 goals per game and a rough amount of around 22 goals across 6 seasons at Ajax. And even after a sequence of career-threatening injuries (without which he would arguably be deemed the most efficient striker of all time), he still slotted home 90 strikes from 147 games after moving to Italy. An absolute goal-machine – and a clear indication that Sacchi was 'on to something' with his Dutch incorporation, hence why he didn't stop there.

Sure, most would be content with splashing out over €1 million on one of the most coveted strikers on the planet, but Milan needed a midfielder. And as it turned out, Ajax weren't the only club in Europe capable of breeding livestock worthy of selling on for a profit, in fact they weren't the only club in *Holland* to make a living off the back of it!

Close competitive rivals PSV Eindhoven were slowly beginning to develop a delightful crop of their own talent to rival that pesky Ajax lot. Recent years have seen the likes of Boudewijn ('Bolo') Zenden, Park Ji-Sung, Ruud van Nistelrooy and Memphis Depay rise to the top of their respective squads before seeking pastures new; and back here, their most prized 'for-sale' item was Ruud Gullit; a dynamic midfield powerhouse proudly displayed in PSV's show window with an eye-water €6 million price tag dangling off his finger. Even then, an absolute *bargain*.

He was a complete colossus of a player who possessed absolutely everything required to be successful in his position. He was tall, imposing, confident, calm on the ball and oozed complete and utter quality with every touch of it. He may as well have massaged the bloody thing; he was so graceful. And to add a grand ol' cherry atop this absurd arrangement, he was coming to Milan to link up with his Dutch teammate, Marco van Basten - somebody who understood his game-play and would benefit strongly from having a like-minded man in behind him. But even once the pair of them were signed, there was *still* something missing. Now, this is just greedy!

It seems almost criminal to call this an 'issue', but the knit pickers among the Milan ranks had spotted a slight imbalance within their midfield. As Ancelotti reached his prime years, a tendency to venture into the attacking areas came with it. And although this didn't happen very often, it encouraged the Italian giants to plug that gap before it became a more evident problem. Now, I doubt that Sacchi had a direct line to Bobby Robson, but clearly, great minds think alike.

For he deployed the same tactic Robson had done when the Ipswich man was looking for Mühren's midfield partner a decade earlier; by asking Mühren himself. So, Sacchi did the same thing. To make sure his next addition was absolutely right for Gullit and van Basten, he simply asked Gullit and van Basten. And much like Mühren did with Thijssen, they suggested their mate Frank … Frank Rijkaard.

***

And there we have it. One of world football's greatest ever trios was created, and one of the very few which accommodated more than one area of the pitch. Gullit: the aggressor in the middle, van Basten: the finisher up top and Rijkaard: the protector at the back.

Sacchi is quoted in saying that "great clubs have one thing in common … they owned the pitch and they owned the ball". And following that 'Total Football'-inspired ideology, the lads went on to claim the domestic title (the *Schudetto*) in Sacchi's first season - ending a turbulent 9-year drought without one. The *Supercoppa Italiana* soon followed and European glory was on the horizon, though that would have to wait until the new season.

It's simple …

'Total Football' = European Cup wins

Maths.

Having basked in their glory on home soil, they entered the 1988/89 European campaign with a tangible level of swagger and mystique, before carving out an unstoppable route to the Final.

Ironically, the Camp Nou (Cruyff's ex-yard) was the setting for *Il Rossoneri's* first European Cup final under their new regime. Though it wasn't so much the 4-0 thrashing of Romania's Steaua Bucureşti in that match which is the key talking point of that competition, instead I think its most pivotal moment came in the semi-final; where they romped towards a 6-1 aggregate win over the mighty Real Madrid.

I find it strangely poignant that two of the most significant points in football tactical history comes at the fall of Madrid. If I were a poet, I'd say that it was a personification of how new concepts can combine with daring figures to topple an organisation which stands as the authority against which all innovations should be tested. I like that actually, let's stick with that!

The Milan side then followed up their initial European Cup win by retaining the title in the following campaign - further cementing Arrigo Sacchi and his bandy group of recruits into the history of their restored club, as well as laying down a marker for how future Milan generations would be judged.

> "The only way you can build a side is by getting players who speak the same language and can play a team game. I often quote what Michelangelo said: 'The spirit guides the hand."
>
> – Arrigo Sacchi

Soon after they did the double, the squad soon reverted to type; Van Basten's injury issues were catching up with him, Ruud Gullit had left the club by 1993 and Rijkaard decided to return home to Ajax once Sacchi himself had been courted for the Italian national job in 1991.

Though their legacies at the club remain as indelible as ever, where despite A.C. Milan retaining their place among Europe's elite for decades to come, I would argue that *this* Milan side are unparalleled in terms of the *way* they won football matches and the innovation and creativity it took to build them in the first place. *Grazie mille,* Sacchi and ors.

Milan's line-up changed exponentially over the next few years after welcoming the re-arrival of Fabio Capello; who returned a more seasoned pro far removed from the enigmatic figure who'd left the club before Sacchi arrived. Bygones were bygones, and Capello helped to bring yet another highly successful period of dominance for the club in Italy; utilising their fledgling academy and domestic prospects to maintain their mystique at home.

But I doubt that this would've been as accessible to Capello but for Sacchi restoring Milan to the mantle from which they were falling. And there's no way that Sacchi himself could've achieved that without the brilliance of his Dutchmen, who themselves may not have been the forces they were if not for the influence of Johan Cruyff (both as a philosopher and direct coach), *who ALSO* may not have gotten so far without the brilliance of Rinus Michels.

The evolution is there, people!

But now we come to a *Back to the Future II*-like point where the timeline completely skews off into an alternate dimension. As far as 'being the best' is concerned, we've mainly been discussing the times when the Italians and Spaniards had to re-develop their institutions to accommodate for this new style of football that was coming to the fore.

Whether it was Sacchi's Milan or Cruyff's Barcelona, they were each the dominant forces in their hometowns as well as on the European stage, with very little opposition coming from the further corners of Europe. In descending order, It was Italy on top, Spain as the runners-up, a sprinkle of Germany to make it interesting and *the rest* picking up a 'thanks for trying' medal on their way out. And let's not forget, English clubs were still banned from competing in international club competitions because they couldn't get their act together, so they were falling even further behind the pack as they raced away.

To make things even worse for them, the mentioned Italian and Spanish clubs only saw their prestige grow as they hoovered up those continental honours. So, just as much as every fan wanted to watch them, pretty much every footballer wanted to play for them, and England was at risk of being left behind by their own men whose ambitions had shifted.

Being a footballer is still a 'job' after all, and being involved in a big Italian or Spanish club often implied: better working conditions, a better brand of football, probably a higher salary and a lowered likelihood that some wrong'un would put his cigarette out on your cheek when you came to take a throw-in.

So, in order to 'Keep up with the Joneses', English football needed to plan something big for their European return. Ideally, something like a global commercial empire with a sophisticated marketing and financial business plan, that they could arrange to have broadcasted through the most advanced network available to the furthest corners of the globe.

If only, right?

~ 11 ~

'THE BIG IDEA'
Hmm ... interesting ...

If I'm being honest, although 'European fever' (as I'm now going to call it) became a prevalent issue when English football was off-screen, the epidemic long precedes our timeline.

Denis Law and Jordan Charles swapped the North West for Napoli and Juventus respectively in the '60s, Kevin Keegan calmed post-war relations with a stop-over in Germany with Hannover in the late '70s and *Walker's Crips* ambassador Gary Lineker became an honorary Catalan after a positive showing after the 1986 World Cup. For some, it was great to see some of our homegrown lads flying their flags abroad, but from their departed clubs' perspective, the business ramifications were sizable and, at times, crippling.

As much as the purists would like you to forget this, there's no escaping the fact that the running of a football club is a complete business enterprise founded on a peculiar model. Namely, that it merges a number of different industries which directly impact one-another into a single mainframe.

Media, Legal, Financial, Retail, you name it and your beloved club is probably involved with that sector. And all of these are predicated on the success that your team has on the pitch; where their playing well directly correlates to the success of the arms we'd mentioned earlier.

So, it gives you a brief idea as to how impactful losing your best player can be – a fear which grew further into a reality as the years without European football persisted.

Though thankfully, not every major club 'big wig' was sitting idly by to allow this inevitability to wash over them, and in fact, a select few key executives banded together to form a strategy to combat the potential effects that could have resulted from being banned. This group of merry men included: David Dein heading up the Gunners, Everton's Philip Carter, Noel White of Liverpool, Martin Edwards at Manchester United and Tottenham Hotspur's Irving Scholar.

From the outside looking in, they form little more than a classy-looking quintet of wealthy businessmen who like to argue about football over a glass of scotch, when in reality, they were the linchpins of the clubs that had formed English Football's original 'Big 5' - the country's most successful and powerful club sides. And given their standings in the domestic football community, they were best placed to act upon many of the issues we've considered so far in a bid to reclaim their international standing in the sport, and to birth a cleaner, longer-lasting image for the domestic game.

History traces this thought process back to an anxious meeting in the summer of 1986, where the mentioned 'Big 5' laboured despondently over the issues that were threatening to bring them down. Namely, lost revenue from international competition (and its adorning broadcasting deals), reduced interest in their sides by consequence of not being as visible as their competitors, and in particular, a really annoying homegrown agreement which inherently limited their opportunity to make up for whatever revenue they'd now lost.

As agreed by the Football Association, any residuary income from the BBC (who had long been acting as their primary broadcaster) during the ban, would be fairly split throughout all clubs registered under the English Football League. From their view, it was a way to promote fairness and equality between their clubs, though it clearly wasn't representative of who they'd ought to thank for bringing in the money in the first place.

Under this set-up, a club who were actually *on television* would earn the same (if not a very similar amount) to those who could only *dream* about being on television. This angered the 'Big 5' - whose clubs were primarily responsible for bringing in televisual income - to a point where a new broadcasting revenue model became one of the focal points for the executives' many meetings to come; and their resulting idea for changing this routine didn't sit well with the Association which implemented it.

Instead of highlighting their concerns with the FA and seeking to find an improvement on their existing deal, the group looked to completely distance themselves from the rest of the competition and set up a new league with its own unique, proportionate broadcasting system.

This proposal would then be put forward to the other 'higher-level' clubs in the First Division who would decide their fate for themselves – either join them and be rich or stay where they are and keep their mouths shut. The audacity! *I love it!*

The thing is though, from a purely business standpoint … they weren't necessarily in the wrong for doing this. All they wanted was for their teams and all others to directly benefit from a media arrangement which better reflected their standings as clubs; and not allowing others to 'mooch off' of those who are in a better position than they were. However, where there was some substance to their argument, it was posed in a way which looked nothing short of a power-play to the Association.

Moreover, the FA has prided itself for many years on ensuring the survival of all clubs registered to them, so when these fancy-dressed seniors challenged them with a business model that focused on nothing but themselves, it's no wonder to me that their initial pitch was hung out to dry.

Looking back, it might be fair to say that things would've gone a little smoother had they better understood who they were talking to. Their ideas were radical but not totally unreasonable, and had they presented their case a little more compassionately to their authority, then it may have been taken in the way that they would've liked.

Remember, their idea wasn't just for *them* to switch up from convention, for it also meant leaving their ex-members to essentially fend for themselves; while almost all of the commercial attention followed them on their new venture. In turn, this could lead to a potentially damning lack of demand for lower-league competition and a chasm of talent forming between the new league and theirs.

It was a big deal. And one which didn't call for a stern-faced presentation nor a callous delivery. A 'softer sell' was required here, and perhaps a little brown-nosing along the way to get the signature they needed. The Execs understood this, and promptly returned to the FA headquarters with a much more careful and considered proposal. I call it: 'Getting our Way 2.0'.

For a long while, another harrowing indictment of the English game was its floundering national side. Even at the time of writing, journalists and bar-drinkers alike marvel at the success of the World Cup-winning team in 1966 as if it were yesterday. Of course, they were an exceptional side and deserve the respect they're given, though none have since come anywhere near reliving those heights by the time these 'Big 5' meetings were arranged.

Therefore, in order to appease the Association, they decided to go on the charm offensive; as if their radical changes were directly seeking to aid the development of the England National Team. The idea was that, if they were to branch out and expand away from the confines of the Football League, not only would the clubs *themselves* be able to benefit from the untapped riches coming in from broadcasting, partnerships and other commercial enterprises, but the money would be recycled into developing their own homegrown talent, and any overseas acquisitions would inevitably improve the standard of the British players around them. 'Intriguing …', thought the FA.

Even more so when the next two World Cups came into view. Beginning with a Sir Bobby Robson-led quarter final journey in Mexico, 1986, which ended rather controversially against old foes Argentina. This time, against the backdrop of the Falklands War and with a prime-time Diego Maradona staring back at them … with his hand held aloft. 'The tale of two goals' as it's known on the streetz.

For the first, he's pictured running head-first into England's defence in his typically fearless style, before the ball ricocheted away from him and was hoisted high into the air by defender, Steve Hodge. The clearance looked set to fall directly into 'keeper Peter Shilton's grasp who rose high to meet it, only to be beaten by the flailing arm of Maradona to spank the ball into the net and wheel away in celebration.

"Surely it hit the hand of Maradona" squealed the commentator. Though I'm sure that all other viewers with an English relative close by chose a few other words to express their sentiments. Then came that *other* goal.

The stocky forward picks up the ball near the centre-circle and only has one journey in mind. The next second, he sets sail towards the England net - jinking past four oncoming defenders on his route - before having the composure to slide the ball delicately around Shilton to finish in an empty net. It was a fantastic display, no denying that. But there's no excusing the shadiness of his opener; at least, not in Robson's eyes.

When asked to comment on the first goal, Sir Bobby simply responded with the rhetorical: "Maradona handled the ball, didn't he?", only to be greeted by a deafening silence which added gravitas to his statement. He then famously denounced Maradona's 'Hand of God' christening with a more apt interpretation; that 'it was the Hand of a Rascal!'

Well, whatever you call it, that same hand wrapped its clammy self around the World Cup trophy a week later, and England had little choice but to sit idly by and complain. But was that such a bad thing?

Hear me out!

Although Maradona's opener proved to be a pivotal turning point in the match, there's technically nothing which can prove that England would have won without it. And considering how brilliant his second goal was, what's to suggest that he (or any of his teammates) wouldn't be able to switch it on again to claim the more respectable victory for themselves anyway?

So, assuming this, if you absolutely *had to* be taken out of a competition, then uniting against a common enemy - where the wider football audience sides with you - isn't a bad way to go about it. Even to this day, many condemn Maradona's actions in that game and it clouds their consequential win - with England being viewed as the 'unfortunate lot' who 'didn't deserve to lose' as opposed to being 'sore losers' who 'don't deserve to feel the way that they do'.

Therefore, while it may have been an acrimonious exit, it was a good showing from the lads; and a positive way to kick off a forthcoming half-decade of isolation. And it served to add some much-needed weight behind the 'Big 5's presentation to the FA; where the patriotic focus of their revised mission statement struck a chord with the organisation, that had just seen their treasured side knocked out on somebody else's terms. And then came *Italia 90* – arguably the country's most significant international outing since their '66 win.

Also driven by Robson with some 'Gascoigne' lad to fret over, the latter's 'big game' persona served his country well to guide them to a semi-final opportunity against West Germany – where the baby-faced Geordie tapped into our more dormant emotions.

With the game undecided mid-way through the second half, a stricken German is seen rolling around on the floor with little 'Gazza' looking mightily guilty beside him. Contesting a 50-50 loose ball, the Englishman's enthusiasm took over; clattering his stocky right boot into the leg of his opponent after having completely missed its target. A booking, therefore, being a more than appropriate consequence for this indiscretion.

Quite often, a caution from the referee wouldn't have much of an impact beyond the game in which it's issued, but given that it wasn't the first that Gazza had amassed in the competition, receiving another meant that he would be suspended from the Final; something the emotional recipient struggled to deal with.

Lips quivered all over the world when they saw his reaction, and the night went from bad to much worse as England were promptly knocked out on penalties; with a surprisingly tame effort from 'Psycho' Stuart Peace sealing their fate. It's your classic 'if only' story which, once the tears had subsided, helped to attract some much-needed positive media attention for the English game from abroad.

Among the viewers were, of course, the 'Big 5' who now had even greater ammunition for their latest presentation to the FA. I mean, given their prediction to improve the calibre of homegrown English players, perhaps their prospectus could have them going all the way at some point! They'd come pretty close over the past two World Cups, so maybe *this* could be the final element to lifting it once again. It hasn't happened yet, but it's a nice idea!

Not only this, but their continuous negotiations with the FA had evolved by this point to incorporate Lord Justice Taylor's in-depth report following the Hillsborough disaster. So now, what began as a proposed breakaway for income purposes, had evolved to a set of principles aimed at completely revitalising the English game – both in practicality *and* in image. All that was left was to formalise the league's rules, media arrangements, founding members and Taylor-induced regulations. Oh yeah, and it needed a name … with the 'FA' in it somewhere because 'pinky promises' ought never be broken.

~ 12 ~

'FOOTBALL'S GREATEST GLOW-UP'

... and I thought mine was good!

Explaining all of the nuances and decision-making that went into creating the 'FA Premier League' is a pretty tough task, and for this reason, I've got to show a lot of respect to Joshua Robinson and Jonathan Clegg for their own novel: '*The Club*'.

The pair of them go into a perverse level of detail about the Premier League and how it went from being an idea written on a napkin to the global powerhouse as recognised today. For the purpose of this edition, I'm going to do my best to go through the key points which are poignant to my own narrative, though if you wish to find out more about the League and each of its initial conspirators, then please do check it out. Great read.

Of the 'Big 5', arguably their most influential member was David Dein; who helped to establish a clearer blueprint for this invention than any other. Not only had he been a major patron for the Taylor report and enforced regulatory action on any clubs applying to be a part of the ' FA Premier League', but he had also completely revitalised the league's marketing strategy; inspired by a fortuitous sporting holiday across the United States.

I've said this before and I'll say it again because Mr. Dein would agree, the United States of America is the birthplace and front-runner in the world of advertising. And whilst visiting various NFL and MLB events in the States, the Arsenal Vice Chairman was overcome by the shamelessness with which the sports' franchises promoted themselves. So, Dein thought it was necessary to take a few leaves out of their book in order to make this new league's content more sellable to a mainstream audience.

For them, it wasn't a case of simply 'going to a match' and 'supporting your team'. It was far more than that. It was about going for an experience that cannot be matched anywhere in the world. A place where you can escape your monotonous surroundings to have all of your primeval sporting desires satisfied; for however long the spectacle was scheduled to last.

There's deafening music resonating from the speaker systems, cheerleaders and fireworks aplenty as the soldiers take their position for the national anthem, and even coordinated staff members to dish out free face paints and souvenirs for the youngsters in the crowd.

Plus, even if you weren't in attendance at a particular game, there were *plenty* of options for you to support from home - and not just through a brief highlights package either. Sports media is an untamed beast in the States, and it came to be that their extended programming schedule incorporated a more in-depth and insightful viewing experience for those at home. I'm talking tactical boards, live debates, pre-and-post-match interviews. The works. And all of this proved palpable in providing Dean with some empirical evidence as to what this new league could look like if they adapted these ideas to suit the British sporting scene, now it was a case of putting everything he saw into action.

Having officialised their ideas in *The Founder Members Agreement* in 1991, it was put forward to the other top-flight clubs to gauge their initial interest to join the new setup. Soon enough, they had twenty-two players at the table for the inaugural FA Premier League season (later reduced to twenty to ease the fixture schedule).

From this point on, Dein and co. were ready to get right into the thick of it all, beginning with the very thing that led them to wanting to break away from the Football League in the first place - a complete stand-alone broadcasting arrangement with a new, qualitative income structure. And for those who copped their seats early enough, they were present to oversee and influence the league's new broadcasting auction.

With the new season set to kick off in August 1992, the 'new founding fathers' met up with their brethren in the summer to see what their 'new income flow' would look like in practise i.e. who would show their content, how much they'd pay for it and who would get what for their televisual appearances.

It soon became a two-horse race between ITV, represented by respected TV personality Greg Dyke, and BSkyB; owned by infamous mogul Rupert Murdoch. As seems typical by the latter, it was a controversial late bid from the media tycoon which earned the rights for Sky; beating their competition out the water with a deal worth £300+ million over five years (from 1992-1997), with the option for renewal which takes any change in value into consideration after the term has ended.

With this, full package games were removed from your ordinary TV license, leaving only BBC's *'Match of the Day'* highlights package untouched. But now, if you wanted to watch Premier League football, you had to pay *another* subscription for the privilege. But don't you worry, this money generated from this arrangement meant that fan's ticket prices largely stayed around the same level, so if you didn't want to pay for that subscription package, you could always just go to a game. And our friend Mr. Dein had us covered on that one.

As briefly mentioned, under this new regime, present fans benefited directly from the findings in the Taylor Report. Stadiums became fully seated, regularly maintained, appropriately staffed and most were freshly painted to keep up their appearance. Dein had even committed the new members to up the toilet and catering facilities which fans would frequent during their now *fifteen*-minute half-time respite. All in all, massive credit must go out to Mr. Dein for acknowledging what was truly important in our game, and similarly to our new 'founders' for helping to implement them for the benefit of their supporters.

***

On television, a football match became a highly sophisticated affair, where programming began and lasted long before and after the actual game went on air. Prior to kick-off, Sky established a presentation panel which laboured over the points which your average pub-goer would debate, and they spent a similar period after the game analysing the bits and pieces worth talking about.

It was a smorgasbord of well-groomed presenters and raw football brains coming together to thrash out their opinions. And the two seesawed well together to ensure that it was an easy-to-watch programme. When the game's on, an ever-changing commentary line-up explains the things that the picture won't - a picture in itself that was far more crisp and clearer than it had ever been before. I reckon they must have cleaned the lens or something as well. Classy!

Each club was also given creative control over how to get their fans amped up for the game. Whether it be a firework display, a cheerleader routine or an up-beat song on the PA system, that was up to them - all a part of making it an experience catered towards their own fans; both pleasing them and providing that 'home game' advantage all the same. With these little tweaks, the Premier League became completely incomparable with its dwindling ancestor, and its introduction lived up to all expectations.

The 1992/93 season kicked off with a bang; and retained that level of entertainment through to the end. Manchester United were crowned the inaugural champions despite losing the first ever Premier League fixture against Sheffield United - something I'm sure Brian Deane refuses to shut up about, and thus began a quick, spearheaded journey to the top of the world football ladder for the competition. Gone were the days of crumbling stadiums, slapdash technologies and multiple fan arrests, and in came an era of architectural reinforcement, thoughtful resource investment and only a couple arrests … if that! And we haven't even spoken about the football on show.

As eventual winners, Manchester United attracted a lot of attention on their route to the top, namely for their habit of never letting up on their opponents. Their Old Trafford stadium became a fortress preserved by the men in red who wouldn't dare let anybody disrespect them. And their knack for scoring a goal against the run of play or with time against them became a pivotal mechanism in their overall success … *and* in the season afterwards!

The key behind their triumph? Well, a lot of you will purely mention their manager, Sir Alex Ferguson; the most decorated British manager in the history of the game. Perhaps. Some of you may reference their emerging academy stars, the 'Class of '92'. Could be. But without the continental influence in the squad, I doubt that its balance and spirit would have carried in the way that it had.

In goal, United could rely on 'Great Dane' Peter Schmeichel; purchased from Brøndby IF in Denmark prior to the season's opener. Who was not only as tall as he was broad, but was also deceptively quick for a big guy. His saves were unconventional, he possessed very little fear and had little issue with ensuring that his voice was heard by his teammates.

At full anger and to the untrained eye, it looked like they took his straitjacket off too early, but don't let that fool you. Peter Schmeichel was a leader in that side whose instructions were always useful for his fellow troops - particularly for the pimple-faced lads coming to the fore in front of him.

Then you look at the other end of the pitch and you had Andrei Kanchelskis; one of United's most underrated wingers in their history. If you're talking about being direct and forward-thinking, then whether you like it or not, you're talking about Kanchelskis. Born into a Lithuanian culture within the Soviet-led Ukraine, the promised land of the Premier League was just as alien to him as any of the United fans were to their new winger. Very few knew what to expect when he popped on the United jersey with all those letters on the back, but by the time they gathered their thoughts, he was already pacing his way down the right flank. Out of sight, out of mind.

His game was simple - take on possession, switch on the afterburners and slap the ball in towards the striker; a task which he completed with a tennis player's level of precision throughout his early years in England. Plus, in terms of his influence on the dressing room (and much like the team's goalkeeper), he was a professional individual whose impact wore off positively on the new crop coming in.

An altogether sturdy piece of business from the Red Devils and yet another example of what can be achieved by introducing some foreign flair to a domestic side. Then, buoyed by their international success stories, Ferguson opted to add yet another 'outsider' to his eventual title-winners ... and a really, *really* important one at that. Eric Cantona.

Nonchalantly stolen from fierce rivals Leeds United during the first half of the 1992/93 season, few were too sure on how signing Cantona would work out for Sir Alex. The media made no small point in mentioning Cantona's supposedly burnt bridges at Elland Road, with many outlets suggesting that his stereotypical 'French ways' were beginning to irk his proud, old-school employers. How much of this can be substantiated is a tough one to call, but in real time, it genuinely doesn't matter.

Eric Cantona is not your *typical* player; therefore, he mustn't be treated in a typical way. We've gone over this, so

I dare not labour this point for much longer but ... Cruyff? Villa? Gascoigne? They weren't 'typical' either. In Cantona's case, he was simply the man you'd give the ball to, wait for his decision on what to do next, and act accordingly. No questions asked. And don't look him directly in the eye, either.

With the mercurial Frenchman on their books, United stormed their way to another Premier League title a year into its era; and in an even more comprehensive style than before. Thereby proving (once again) to the British elite that European migration was the way forward!

Though in hindsight, where they made European transfer business looked quite easy, it was an option for which its easiness often correlated to whatever teams were involved – where the 'lesser' the side you were, the tougher it might have been to finance transfers like these. However, things were set to get a whole lot easier across the board thanks to some unassuming Belgian lad, who knew a little bit about how the law worked.

~ 13 ~

'BREAKING FREE'
The Chronicles of Jean-Marc Bosman

Don't be fooled by the headlines, transfers are *not* an easy thing to pull off. They require a number of different mechanisms working in tandem together and towards the same goal. And if one of those are: out of sync, aligned awkwardly or missing altogether; then the entire operation could fall through as a result.

The process looks a little something like this:

You begin by identifying your chosen target then, just like you would in any retail store when you spot something of your taste, you check to see what the price is. This is usually done by asking the player's club or, more recently, through their representative. Once that's clearer, you go home to confer over the proposed price and launch your initial bid given the information you've gathered. After which, a back-and-forth negotiation often ensues unless you got it right the first time.

Later, once you've agreed on a fee together and how to pay it, it's all about getting the player on side. Ideally, they're as equally happy at the prospect of joining, as the club is of purchasing them. For when this happens, discussing their wage requirements, bonus schemes and additional contract clauses are a simple business, otherwise it can be a very sensitive arrangement with business taking over pleasure.

Assuming the first option, the player then goes for a medical; which tests their cardiovascular vitals and analyses any existing injury history that the new club should be aware of. *Then*, you sign a mountain of regulatory paperwork for the Association you're aligned with, which officially 'registers' the player to their new squad. And finally, a new shirt is printed, a number is given, and pictures are taken for the press release. Maybe a press conference is called before your debut game if you're really good.

That's a lot, isn't it? For one piece of business. But this is only when you're negotiating between two domestic clubs, so it gets even more strenuous when you're arranging a purchase between two different countries.

A lot of what we went through is very time-sensitive; where prolonging one stage can have negative knock-on effects for the next stages e.g. if you take ages haggling over a transfer fee, it might imply to the player that you aren't all that serious about them, so why would they want to consider personal terms? Plus, when you're negotiating with foreign clubs, you have to contend with things beyond your control that will invariably screw up your timeline anyway. Time zones being one thing.

You launch a bid via email (or pigeon, whatever) and you might not be able to decide on a final fee until a few days later - all the while the player might get unsettled and doesn't know how to feel about the perceived delay. There could also be a cultural issue. As ever when negotiating a business transaction, you've got to be very careful that your typical ways don't tread on the toes of the other party. And we haven't even spoken about the potential language issue.

Should you overcomplicate a clause or speak out of turn at some point, then you may have scuppered the deal with the slip of a tongue. It's not like you could *WhatsApp* them and say, 'sorry, that was my brother', 'cause the damage is probably done by this point. And most importantly, it would be the *clubs* in charge of everything we've just mentioned – with the player subservient to whatever was going on around them - something that a certain Jean-Marc Bosman knows all too well.

In 1990, the then-RFC Liège midfielder had seen out his two-year contract with the Belgian outfit. At which point, following a sub-par attempt from his current club to renew the deal at roughly 25% of its original value, in came French club Dunkerque looking for his signature.

I hope you'll agree that this should have been a very simple situation to deal with; Liège decided that he wasn't worth offering a contract, but Dunkerque did. 'One man's trash' and all that malarkey. He should therefore be the driver behind deciding where he wants to go … right?

Well, talks soon broke down between the two clubs when Liège refused to bulk from their €500,000 valuation of Bosman. This amount was rejected by Dunkerque as they felt it wasn't reflective of his demand in the market nor the value of his now-expired contract. In response, Liège argued that their valuation was a sum of all expenses incurred by their club while he was employed - like training, physio and other operational costs.

I mean ... that's a bit like you wanting to change jobs after your salary gets halved, and yet your employer maintains the right to charge your future employer for the cost of your uniform and lunches over the past year. How would you respond? Kick up a fuss? Cut up those uniforms? Call them some names? Well, Bosman was far too dignified for that. He backed himself, stuck to his moral guns, and attempted to single-handedly arrange the transfer to Dunkerque by himself. It was at this moment, that things became weirdly complicated, but all towards the greater good.

Time for some EU Lawyer-isms ...

All we need to concern ourselves with here is the establishment of the European Union, which was referenced earlier. More specifically, that pesky (yet delightful) 'Free Movement of Trade' article from the Treaty of Rome. Bosman (representing himself) took Liège to court, arguing that their complicating his move to Dunkerque by asking for a fee despite being out of contract, acted as an *unlawful restriction to trade* within the EU.

Remember, he was no longer *contracted* to Liège and did not receive a salary from them, so therefore shouldn't have his future left to their discretion without said contract being valid. He argued that, once your contract is up with a club and it hasn't been renewed, the only person who ought to dictate the future of the player is the player themselves. Logical, right? Well, remember, this is the world of football we're talking about here - where common sense takes a little longer to sink in.

It ultimately took five long and insufferable years of investigation and referrals which led a jaded Bosman through the doors of the European Courts of Justice and, armed with a well-thought-out argument against Liège along with a positive mission statement for how things should be dealt with in the future, he won his case.

His reward was two-fold: 150,000 Euros by way of compensation and a 'rule' named after him; one that would go on to transform the football landscape beyond recognition. I mean, if merely entering the EU had opened up the doors to foreign football migration, the 'Bosman ruling' had smashed it down with a machete.

When the gavel was lowered in the court, players suddenly became free to dictate their own careers as 'free agents' whenever they weren't tied down to a contract, and 'player power' has since become the phenomenon which shapes almost everything you understand about the current transfer market.

The entire recipe of a transfer had changed; with both clubs fully aware that the player's imminent freedom could drastically alter the original terms of the agreement. For you see, the impending threat of the player's departure on a free move to anybody *he* chooses (as opposed to the club arranging between themselves), shifted the balance of power onto the player and away from either club. To the point where contracts had to improve in the player's favour to ensure it didn't get to that stage.

Let's get hypothetical ...

There is an above-average player who is on a contract with one year remaining at his current club. Now, in a pre-Bosman world, his value may drop somewhat, but any potential club may be put off by the fact that his club still reserves the right to receive a fee, but in this post-Bosman dimension, suitors would arrive in their drones; knowing full-well that they could isolate their target, flash a bit of cash in his face and walk away with their hands cupping his hip. In situations like these, it's clear to see that your player's market valuation slides off a cliff as they edge closer to their expiration date, but it's a completely differently story at the opposing end of the spectrum.

Instead, let's presume that this player has something like five years left on their contract and isn't at risk of being lost for free anytime soon, well then now it's time to hike up their transfer value as the threat of losing your investment isn't as imminent. Before, a player could hear of some interest and say 'I want to join them, let's arrange something fair for everyone', but now the club will say 'No, you have X amount of years on your contract, let's resume this conversation when we're further down the line'.

And let's be honest, although big-money deals still do happen for the reasons I've mentioned and have their own exciting aspects to it, the real *juicy* stuff comes when players end up leaving on a free transfer. There really is nothing quite like it: the dread, the uncertainty, the speculation and the revelation. It's gripping … and oh so frequent! Don't believe me? Well then, let's play a little game. Not like *Saw*, so quit worrying.

Get yourselves a piece of paper from somewhere (not on the inside cover here, thank you very much!), get your pencil ready and write down some notable Bosman signings since the rule was made official in 1995. Any high-profile ones that you can think of. And for those who couldn't be arsed, here are some that I know:

Steve McManaman – Liverpool to Real Madrid [1999]
Ronaldinho – Grêmio to Paris Saint-Germain [2001]
Robert Lewandowski – Dortmund to FC Bayern [2014]
Andrea Pirlo – A.C. Milan to Juventus [2011]
Sol Campbell – Tottenham Hotspur to Arsenal [2001]
Edgar Davids – AFC Ajax to A.C. Milan [1996]
Gianluca Vialli – Juventus to Chelsea [1996]
Miroslav Klose – FC Bayern to Lazio [2011]
Henrik Larsson – Celtic to FC Barcelona [2004]
Phillip Cocu – PSV Eindhoven to FC Barcelona [1998]
Gary McAllister – Coventry City to Liverpool [2000]
Michael Ballack – FC Bayern to Chelsea [2006]
Esteban Cambiasso – Real Madrid to Inter Milan [2004]
Cambiasso again - Inter Milan to Leicester City [2014]
Edwin van der Sar – AFC Ajax to Juventus [1999]
Cafu – A.S. Roma to A.C. Milan [2003]
Michael Owen – Newcastle to Manchester United [2009]
Javier Saviola – FC Barcelona to Real Madrid [2007]
Roberto Baggio – A.C. Milan to Bologna [1997]
David Silva – Manchester City to Real Sociedad [2020]

I really could go on forever here as I find something incredibly intriguing about the world of football transfers, especially with the special ingredient of the Bosman ruling. And in case you didn't notice, I am talking about some pretty big names here, which doesn't even begin to illustrate the sheer volume of just how many moves have directly benefited from this.

It gave players their freedom and has since allowed the world of football as a whole to be more accessible, inclusive and exciting to watch. All of a sudden, the game's greatest talents were far more readily available to countries and leagues which they might never have previously considered, and if there was ever a competition and club which embraced this idea more than any other, it was most certainly the FA Premier League and David Dein's beloved Arsenal.

~ 14 ~

'THE FRENCH REVOLUTION'
J'adore ... la Gunners

Arsenal Football Club endured a topsy-turvy start to life in the Premier League. In the early stages, they were guided by a shameless, old-school manager in George Graham, who favoured that fiery, strong-willed, 'my way or the highway' approach to management. Still, he was highly regarded among his peers and attracted a trophy cabinet fit enough to illustrate that. Though unfortunately for him and ignoring his First Division feats, history will remember something a lot less savoury about his time at the club; and that is the shadiness of his dismissal.

To understand why he was fired requires a little bit of context as to what the role of a football agent is in a transfer negotiation. Nowadays, it's a generally structured affair where agents are the driving force from point A ('the bid') to point B ('the signature'), after which not only are their clients rewarded with a signing-on fee, but they themselves are compensated rather handsomely in the form of an agent's fee – more on that later.

The FA's recommendation has since been for the agent to receive no more than a net 7% commission from their client's deal, though some agents' close relationship with their client suggests that paying them more than this might increase your chances of getting the deal done. So, it soon became commonplace to pay representatives beyond that 7% line; in a bid to not only get a particular arrangement over the line, but to equally sweeten your relationship with them in view of conducting future business. A sort of 'remember that time when …' relationship.

However, as Graham and Arsenal would come to find out, the situation could work both ways depending on who you were dealing with as a representative. Not only could the club ask to be thrusted up the pecking order for an agent's list with whom they were in cahoots with (allegedly), but the agent could also flip the script on them; and strong-arm the club into conducting earlier business on their terms should they wish to retain that positive, long-term relationship. After all, who were they going to run off to and tell? This was all illicit business!

In either of these instances, there's usually some money changing hands. And whoever wants the deal to happen will often be the party withdrawing the cash, ready to hand it off to whoever is responsible for putting their wishes into action. We call these types of payments, 'bungs'.

They were whole cash payments, and, like an 'Old Western' flick, they were commonly found in brown packages with a note stapled on the inside - so-styled that the cleaners wouldn't mess around with it and the recipients knew what they were in for by opening it. It was a different world back then, and this was so common that it doesn't even bear thinking about how many times this has happened to managers, players, agents and even top-level executives, though times were beginning to catch up with George Graham. Talk about, 'bad luck'!

It was widely suspected that he was partial to the occasional cash offering, though there was very little evidence to pin directly against him. That is, until one glaringly obvious case of 'please sign my client, I'll make it worth your while' came to fruition. Ironically, I suspect that one of the reasons contributing to Graham's investigation was down to the fact that he was far too good in the transfer market to make such an obvious blunder; without something fishy going on behind the scenes to explain it.

When you're signing future club legends like David Seaman and Ian Wright for next to nothing from neighbouring London clubs, to go and sign two lads from Scandinavia for almost double the price throws a major red flag in the air.

The first of these was John Jensen – somehow the most successful of the pair. In fairness to him, he did score the European Championship-winning goal for Denmark in 1992, but other than that, he had a largely average career. As it happened, he did not possess the technical ability to compete with the likes of Ray Parlour, Paul Merson and Anders Limpar in Arsenal's midfield, and was soon isolated as a result. The second of the two, Pal Lydersen's legacy deserves nothing more than half a sentence to illustrate what he brought to the club.

Further investigation revealed that both players had been represented by 'super-agent' Rune Hauge - I prefix the word 'super' to his name as, away from this Danish debacle, he also represented Peter Schmeichel, Ole Gunnar Solskjær and Morten Gamst Pedersen to name a few over his decorated agency career; each of whom have since earned regal status for their respective Premier League clubs. So, overpaying for a couple of his clients looks to me (and everyone else) that maybe it was a way of keeping him sweet given who else he could be hiding in his back pocket.

Finally, in 1994 - a couple of years after the signings took place (cheers, justice!) - George Graham admitted to the FA to receiving an illegal payment believed to be around £425,000 to sign both of Hauge's clients for Arsenal, and the governing body were quick to ban him from all football-related matters for one year - following his inevitable axe from Arsenal.

Succeeding Graham came the militant Bruce Rioch who, having been seasoned by a good few seasons as manager of Bolton Wanderers, was largely believed to be a short-term arrangement to steady the Gunners ship; while the chairman sought after its true captain.

A shopping list of Europe's most elite names were linked with the job, yet Mr. Dein decided to use his depth of contacts to find a more unconventional choice. He physically searched far and wide before his ventures took him to, of all places, Japan! There, he would come to learn about the radical techniques employed by Nagoya Grampus Eight's cultured head coach … *Arsène Wenger*.

A brief glance back at the glittering career of Wenger at Arsenal will not only justify Dein's decision, but rank it as one of the most shrewd acquisitions in football managerial history. After beginning as an apprentice at Cannes and enduring a baptism of fire in keeping Nancy in France's *Ligue Un* (their top division), the very first sign of Wenger's brilliance in both his tactical nous and transfer policy came in 1987; where he was granted the opportunity to manage the luxurious AS Monaco.

Upon arrival on the South Coast, the thoughtful coach set about revitalising his sub-par squad; in a way which recognised the need for balance between explosive youngsters and the more mature head to keep them in check. Following this recipe, in came England international Glenn Hoddle on a free transfer from Tottenham Hotspur, along with compatriot Mark Hateley from A.C. Milan, and legendary French forward Patrick Battiston upon the expiration of his contract with Bordeaux. Together, their experience spearheaded the club to domestic triumph in Wenger's debut season and, but for the sorry state of the club's ownership structure and financial management, perhaps it could've made the next few years by the water far more enjoyable for him.

Alas, the two parted ways in 1994, where Arsène briefly became a technical advisor for FIFA - representing the organisation across the world by delivering key speeches to remind clubs of their regulatory commitments, and to inform them of his own coaching and ethical principles. Around a year later, that itch to return to management became too strong to ignore and, luckily for him, the higher board executives at Grampus Eight in Japan had attended one of Wenger's addresses - signalling out the Frenchman as the front-runner for their vacant managerial position.

Wenger was initially reticent to join the club given their lacking global reputation, but was reportedly enthused following a brief chat with Gary Lineker (who had seen out the twilight of his career at the club), and the assurance that he would be given the financial freedom to enact the changes he so longed to do whilst at Monaco.

Promptly, Wenger's first season awarded him with the J-League Manager of the Year award in 1995 despite not even finishing as the season's winners. He was an immediate fan's favourite to the local support and his naturally respectful and dutiful persona had meshed in well with the Japanese culture. Better still, this admiration is mutual; with Wenger himself personally relishing his time in Japan and since crediting the club's treatment of him as providing the confidence from which his forthcoming legacy had sprouted. And the beginning of said 'legacy' came after a very timely incoming phone call from David Dein.

As it turned out, Dein had also sat in on a number of the Frenchman's mentioned FIFA conferences, and had followed him closely while he briefly implemented some of his bragged-about philosophy in Japan. But still, to task him with replicating such success on as grand a scale as the emerging FA Premier League – a domain which *he* had helped to form, was an almighty risk. Nevertheless, the chairman believed in his new manager and committed to his long-term vision.

To begin with, things looked a little rocky when the new manager's arrival at Highbury was stalled due to a contractual dispute over his committed time to Grampus Eight, and the clubs had to arrange an off-the-table settlement just to pay their way out of his contract.

However, never one to waste his time, Wenger had already singled out two Frenchmen who he'd intended to unveil along with himself before his official announcement ceremony. Dein set about recruiting his wish list behind the scenes and, two months into the 1996 season, Arsenal bid *adieu* to Bruce Rioch, and *Bienvenu* to life under Arsène - side by side with new signings Rémi Garde and Patrick Vieira.

Then, having officially set up shop in North London, he set about critically analysing the rest of his squad to see what other changes needed to be made.

The back five of David Seaman, Nigel Winterburn, Lee Dixon, Steve Bould and Tony Adams needn't be fettled with. Therefore, a lot of the new coach's efforts went into renovating the midfield and attack. More specifically, to help mould the squad's collective efforts around the man who he dreamt of as the nucleus for his new-look Arsenal side. Any guesses as to who it might've been? Well, here's a clue: He's Dutch … *obviously*.

Of course, I'm referring to Dennis Bergkamp; whom Arsène had already highlighted in many of his preliminary meetings with David Dein, as the primary focus for his resulting tactical and recruitment strategy for the team. Like many of the pure football academics from a similar time, Arsène was besotted by the ways of Cruyff and the Netherlands, and the sentiment wasn't lost on Dein where, although Rioch was installed as manager by the time Bergkamp was signed to Arsenal, the evidence seems to suggest that the coach wasn't the man in control of the deal. And today, it's widely believed that Dein had signed Bergkamp in anticipation of luring in a man like Wenger who could get the best out of him. And boy, did he know how to do that!

It's very difficult to put Dennis Bergkamp's professional career into a condensed speech without it detracting from his enormous legacy at the Gunners, but I will say this: if we can safely say that Johan Cruyff is the figurehead for Holland's elegant style across Spain, then history ought to remember Bergkamp as the man who brought it to England. Funnily enough, Dennis' youth career was overseen by the man himself - who gave him his professional debut against Roda JC in the Dutch Eredivisie in 1986 - aged 17. From then on, he went from strength to strength at Ajax before earning an illustrious move to cash-rich Inter Milan six years later. Unfortunately for Bergkamp, but thankfully for the rest of us, his time at the San Siro was spent at the mercy of Italy's inherently 'negative' ways – thus, finding it difficult to gain a yard on the centre back and play with the level of freedom with which he performs best.

Having said that, the odd strong European performance from the false-forward had highlighted his everlasting quality before being brought to Highbury in 1995 and, in hindsight, his high £7.5 million price tag seems more reflective of his supposed natural ability (like what he'd shown at Ajax), over his temporary drop in form in Italy. It's also worth mentioning that he practically tripled the club's record spend upon signing - something that didn't seem to rattle the composed Dutchman, as he sought to repay the faith shown in him by his new chairman and looked set to rejuvenate his career under a new manager who considered him vital to his tactical plans.

"You do not find a player like [Dennis] everywhere you go, it was a **blessing**, a *gift* when I arrived"

– Arsène Wenger

Bearing in mind many of Dennis' stand-out qualities, Arsène saw fit to align his recruitment policy on freeing up the Dutchman to take on that 'False 9' role made famous by its inventor. They started off by pinching the industrious and dependable Emmanuel Petit off of Monaco, along with Gilles Grimandi and Christopher Wreh. Unfortunately for

Wreh, his time at Arsenal was limited due to the competition in his place, though the likes of Grimandi and Petit did very well to establish the foundations of Arsenal's new-look midfield; transitioning the play and selflessly allowing the virtues of Bergkamp to sing.

Then, after finishing 3rd in their first season together - which is a more than strong return to begin with - Wenger sought after more explosive additions to the front line in order to maximise the Dutchman's playmaking attributes. Let's begin with Nicolas Anelka.

From practically every angle, this transaction was nothing short of inspired. When signed, the teenage Frenchman did not have the respective pedigree of some of his compatriots; with his senior appearance tally barely reaching double figures after graduating from the French Clairefontaine academy to Paris Saint-Germain's first team. So, this deal spoke greatly of Wenger's unerring knowledge of his home transfer market, and the benefits which could be reaped from it when he's allowed to experiment.

Once signed, Anelka's youth, explosiveness and composure in front of goal worked perfectly alongside Bergkamp's more deft qualities. And the price for all of this lusciousness? A mere £500,000. You know, I'm not quite sure what the French translation is for 'bargains for dayz', but you catch my drift. And given his frightening pace and effectiveness in stretching the opposition back line, Wenger saw fit to double up on his attributes by buying *another* sprinter. This time, opting for the 'flying Dutchman', Marc Overmars.

Now, if you have never seen him play before, then please allow a short while as I tilt my head in pity and offer you a lollipop to get through the day, for you do not know what an 'effective winger' looks like until you've seen a Marc Overmars performance.

Signing at 24 years old - a near prime-age for a pacey forward like him back then - he was *already* a polished, considered and skilful player by the time he'd darkened the doors at Highbury, where he settled in faster than the time it took me to type his name down for you to read.

Together, both he and Dennis represented two very different ends of the Dutch footballing spectrum, and yet they dovetailed in a way where one's performance would maximise the other's. Dennis could pass, where Marc could run, and Bergkamp could supply where Overmars could finish. A match made in attacking heaven. And throw this all in with that Anelka lad as a garnish, and it makes for a rather tasty-looking front line. Though the latter's stay in the English capital would prove to be a remarkably short-lived one.

Despite my admiration for the forward, I think it's fair to say that Anelka wasn't what you'd call a 'one-club man'. He preferred to experience the different footballing cultures on offer and, considering some of the primary causes behind his various moves, was shameless in seeing out a 'journeyman' career.

This began after establishing himself at Arsenal where, before he could make any serious strides at the club, Real Madrid had their pincers at the ready. Granted, he could've rejected their terms and opted to become a household name for the Gunners, but as the fictional forward Gavin Harris explained to Santiago Muñez in *Goal: 2,* "you can't turn down Real Madrid!" Some Arsenal fans may look back melancholically at his departure; simply wishing Anelka had decided to stay and see out what could have been a glittering career with them in the Premier League. Though, whilst I appreciate the sentiment, it seems to ignore the far more fruitful chain of events which occurred after selling him.

The club received a rough £20million profit from his sale; which was a more than healthy amount with which to replenish their striking stock. Plus, had they opted out of the deal, then they ran the risk of having an unhappy Anelka upsetting the balance of the dressing room, so in the circumstances, this ought be viewed as nothing short of a stellar business decision.

Moreover, when you consider Arsène's expert knowledge of his home transfer market, then the club knew that this amount of money was in good hands when it came to finding a replacement. In fact, it just so happened that Wenger had worked with a like-minded forward before – one who had recently come up as 'available' on the market having fallen out of favour with Juventus in Serie A. What was his name again? Thierry … something? It'll come to me.

***

Much like our earlier 'who's the greatest' conversation, talk surrounding who is the 'best striker to ever play in the Premier League' will probably go on forever; and similarly, without a conclusion.

Football is a battle of opinions, and this one is a war. At the time of writing, the easiest case and title can be made and donated to Alan Shearer; who remains the league's leading goal-scorer (with 260 strikes) since its re-branding. But then you get those who'll make the case for

Wayne Rooney, Sergio Agüero, Ruud van Nistelrooy, Didier Drogba and so on; who were all arguably more talented in *other* areas as a forward. So, allow me to make my *specific* case for Thierry Henry who, in my humble opinion, must be labelled as the most *complete* striker that English football has ever seen.

To begin with, he was an unbelievable physical specimen - very strong, enormously quick and weirdly agile. He himself confesses that a lot of his physique was genetic and, instead of bulking out at the gym, his time was spent actually having a ball at his feet on the training ground. And it shows.

Few players can run at his level of speed, and even fewer can do that while controlling a ball, yet Thierry Henry made it look easy. He rarely needed to break stride, was effortless in his movement and was confident enough to try out some of the things that barely anybody in his position would dare to even think about trying. Moreover, he communicated very well with his teammates and led from the front towards the latter stages of his time in an Arsenal shirt - where he'd even receive the odd captain's armband for his troubles.

Plus, the most beautiful thing is that he is part of a wider French influence which was not only positively impacting Arsenal, but for various clubs across the Premier League. Eric Cantona was one of the first after arriving to catalyse the United attack and guiding them to their first Premier League title. And another person to focus on, is somebody who perhaps doesn't receive the level of attention that he ought to.

It's illegal to anglicise his name so don't even go there. Repeat after me, 'David' (like Silva, not Beckham) 'Gee-no-lah' … yes! … very well done to you, my friend.

Like Cantona before him and Anelka/Henry after him, Ginola embodied that French-style swagger and arrogance which encapsulated the fans. When he arrived, he posed an 'unconventional' figure to what the British fans were used to seeing from a winger; where he often vacated his position on the flanks to link up the play in midfield. Though this had sparked a thought in Wenger's mind, who saw this style as fitting to his new-look Gunners attack.

David himself was bordering on 33 by this point - which is closer to an old peoples' home than a Wenger first team - but his was the model that the manager sought after when on his next shopping trip ... only a younger version. His journey took him beyond the length of the Channel and throughout mainland France before stumbling upon the provincial, yet historic club of Marseille.

Propped up in a rather lacklustre and shadier area of the country, Marseille have had their fair share of stars over their history. Recent years have seen the promising developments of Franck Ribéry, Didier Drogba and Hatem Ben Arfa sprout from these ends, though the time in question points to more senior pros in Marcel Desailly, Christophe Dugarry and Laurent Blanc. And among them, a medium-rare Robert Pires

Cut from the same cloth as the man who inspired Wenger's search, he formed the final piece in a formidable attacking Arsenal jigsaw when he arrived in the year 2000 – one year after his colleague Henry and two years after his opposite wing partner Fredrik Ljungberg.

So, altogether, with the pace of the Swede on the right, the style of Pires on the left and the completeness of Henry and Bergkamp through the middle, Arsène had finally implemented his very own updated version of the 'Total

Football' philosophy; and one which extended throughout the spine of the team to complement each other in a way that even Cruyff would've been proud of. By 2003, his build was complete, and that season's team sheet remained largely unchanged from: Jens Lehmann, Lauren, Sol Campbell, Kolo Touré, Ashley Cole, Frederik Ljungberg, Gilberto Silva, Patrick Vieira, Robert Pires, Dennis Bergkamp and Thierry Henry ... look familiar?

> "You don't win things without having that **mentality** ... that ego, that respect for the team. And yes, battles happen... when you have players around you that demand excellence, that is what you are going to bring."

> – Thierry Henry

And so it came to be, as *that Arsenal team* became the first ever in the history of the Premier League to go the entire season without losing a single game - claiming their second ever newly-branded award in the process. Now, I'm not even an Arsenal fan, but even I have to concede that this squad was bordering on perfect.

Christened *'The Invincibles'*, Arsène Wenger's Arsenal were timeless superstars from the moment the final whistle was blown on the last day of the 2003/04 season. Forgotten are the near-misses and stumbles which jeopardised their immortality, because it simply didn't matter anymore. They were legends, the lot of them; and mainly because Wenger understood the importance of having a *balance* in this star-studded squad. It wasn't about 'buying the best players available', but more so to develop a system that works before seeking out those most suited to adopt that system.

For example, Jens Lehmann may not have been the more talented goalkeeper compared to David Seaman before him, yet it was his steely organisation of the back line which kept his brigade intact. Lauren was arguably inferior to the former Lee Dixon but will go down as one of my all-time favourite right-backs - ferocious in the tackle, beautifully consistent and aggressive even when the ball was out of play – perfect for a role which requires mucking in to help out your teammates. Campbell and Touré complemented each other beautifully in the centre, where one would cover the other's advances, and we need not speak much at all on Ashley Cole's ability – for there are plenty of player testimonies out there that'll do the work for me.

Continuing on, Gilberto Silva was highly disciplined in his defensive midfield role, and dutifully protected the back line in order to give Patrick Vieira the license to hone his box-to-box talents, then Pires and Ljungberg were skilful and inventive enough to forge chances on their own - never mind having the masterful Dennis Bergkamp in charge in behind an imperious Thierry Henry. Eurgh! It was just *beautiful!* Solid in defence. Fluid in transition. And merciless in attack. Footballing poetry at its very finest.

In conclusion, I guess this was *one way* to achieve success - commit to a plan over a few years and slowly piece together the elements for realising it on as grand a stage as you can imagine.

Or ... you could just bypass all of that effort and use your privileged resources to pluck the hard work away from others for the benefit of yourself. But who would have the financial muscle and bare-faced arrogance to pull off something like that? Well, ladies and gentlemen, I introduce to you ... the *'Galacticos'*.

~ 15 ~

'THE GALACTICOS'
¡Ay Dios Mío!

The turn of the millennium saw an estranged era dawn upon the fabled Real Madrid; where I imagine the term 'if it ain't broke, don't fix it' must not translate that well into Spanish. Lorenzo Sanz was the club's esteemed president during their two Champions League (the updated version for the 'European Cup') title wins in 1998 and 2000, and yet his apparently 'conservative approach' to running the club had begun to irritate a significant portion of their proud supporters.

Among those, many were reportedly unenthused by Sanz' lacklustre returns in the transfer market and reduced commitment to expanding the prestige of the club. And before he could even get a word out to defend himself, in stepped rival-cum-successor Florentino Pérez to assume the Madrid presidency with a comparatively daring and 'exciting' proposition of his own. Which in hindsight, looked more like some 'noob' messing around with the *Editor* function of a

Football Manager game, than it did a stable manifesto for running the great Real Madrid.

He pointed towards the mounting debts at the Bernabéu as one of the key reasons for altering the club's business direction - claiming that money saved in other areas around the business can be reinvested into an aggressive transfer policy; thereafter, citing corresponding ticket sales and merchandise revenue as a potential breakeven point. To achieve this, he pledged to buy at least one superstar per transfer window for the length of his presidency, whilst using received revenue to bulk up the club's infrastructure for future generations. He dubbed this the *'Galactico'* project.

Let's get one thing straight ...

It's not even a real word!

Loosely translated, you had to be one of the best performing players in the world to be considered a 'Galactico', as well as having that little 'something different' about you to be attractive to this new Madrid.

In other words, you had to have *mass appeal*, where your signature makes a *statement*. So, when they were deciding on who their first buy should be, it dawned on them: what better way to check off all of these requirements at once than by taking away your closest rival's most prized asset? Exactly.

During Pérez' presidential campaign, he made no secret of his desire to sign Luís Figo from Barcelona; and in fact, this ambition did well to add some much-needed gravitas to an otherwise hopeful policy. The Portuguese star was arguably the most complete winger on the planet, and was able to develop a deadly attacking flow with whoever he was sided with. He was fast, powerful, humble, inventive, entertaining … pretty much everything which embodied the beauty of Catalonia and the passion of FC Barcelona; all in one handsome Portuguese frame.

Now, it was just about getting all of the practicalities in line, which proved to be far more laborious and time consuming than Pérez had hoped for. For you see, Figo seemed to have found himself the ideal scenario at Barcelona. He had already spent five years at the club and was revered among the fans as their most prized possession in midfield; leading to successive top division titles in Spain in the late '90s. Plus, Barcelona had recognised his immense value to the club when negotiating his most recent contract, as evidenced by the release clause that they managed to stuff into it.

Here's how a 'Release Clause' works:

When signing a contract with a new team, the club tend to expect complete loyalty and unmatching endeavour for its duration, though players aren't your everyday commodity and are ruled by other things - like emotion, persuasion, life goals and all that. All of which may lead them to wanting a move away before their allotted time is up.

Therefore, in order to appease their assets, clubs will insert a 'release clause' in their contract, which stipulates how much the club would be content with receiving by any future buyer before the contract expires. And only when a buyer pays a fee which matches it, is the player then legally allowed to consider their offer. Until then, get your head down and focus on where you are now.

With Figo, the Barcelona hierarchy intended to multiply their initial investment almost thirty times over -

setting his release (you can use the word 'bail' if you want) at a record-breaking €62 million. 'Cash or card?', uttered Pérez.

> "I really did not think much about the size of the transfer fee when I left Barcelona … because it was all down to market forces, not me"
>
> – Luís Figo

Now, the average business mind would take a single look at this money-is-no-object policy and immediately question its sustainability, for there usually comes a time where your limitless ambition is reined in by your limited means. But the same does not apply to a football transfer, where it can yield great returns in ways directly connected with the demand and interest that it brings. Especially, from a commercial point of view.

In Figo's case, pick up a piece of merchandise and there he was, check out the latest promo poster and there he was, search for a team sheet for the next game and there … he … was. Ticket sales sky-rocketed (even more than they already were), shirt purchases went through the roof, and the world waited in anticipation to see who his next teammate was going to be after his inaugural season in white. And in keeping with Pérez' drip-feed policy, they didn't have to wait long before a one-way ticket to Madrid was purchased in Zinedine Zidane's name.

Frankly, this wonderful man must go down as one of the most cultured midfielders of his generation. No question about it. He was a leader, depressingly talented, insurmountably marketable and so damn cool; so, it's no wonder as to why Pérez wanted him, and wasn't even fazed by his 75 million Euro price tag.

Having said that, not even Zidane's presence could make up for a lack of 'target man' in Madrid's forward line-up. Thus far, we've marvelled at how the game's most innovative tacticians have broken away from convention to develop an aura of their own, though this Madrid side were antithetical to this type of change. Where the formerly addressed eras speak more about developing *styles* of play with a recruitment strategy to fit, the *Galactico* policy was a stars-only affair. So, once you had Figo on the wing and Zidane in midfield, an elite-level strike was next on Pérez' shopping list; thus, explaining their move for Ronaldo Luís Nazário de Lima – or simply 'Ronaldo' to his mates.

Now, I could sit here for hours and happily type out my endless thoughts about *Il Fenomeno*, though as much as it pains me to admit, doing so would be to focus on something which isn't entirely pivotal to this journey we're on. But I simply refuse to go much further without at least saying this: Ronaldo is the most *gifted* striker I have ever seen, and had his injury record been more scarce and perhaps his lifestyle choices been more favourable, he would be the unequivocal selection for 'the greatest striker to have ever played the game of football'. Bar none.

Anyway ...

With their frontline bulging with talent, Madrid romped to a hoard of domestic honours; including the 2002/03 season's *La Liga*, Intercontinental Cup and Spanish Super Cup - with their latest investment coming good in both finals of the two latter tournaments. And after their successes together, where most people would have rested on their laurels to bask in the success that they'd managed to create, Pérez decided to do the opposite; instead employing his club's analysis department to find any gaps in his squad that was worth plugging.

On assignment, a brief look at some statistics from the *Galactico* trio's first season together revealed that the majority of their return came from open play - with little influence from set-pieces (e.g. free kicks and corners) providing some variety to their goal threat. Therefore, upon hearing of some trouble between manager and star player over at Manchester United, the ambitious Spaniard went after their dead-ball specialist, David Beckham.

A superstar in his own right, Beckham had become something of an icon during his time at Manchester United. Away from being an immensely technical football player, his hard-working personality, relentless work ethic and tendency to pop up on the big occasions had endeared himself to the Old Trafford crowd. Though his partiality for the odd brand deal and tabloid article had left a sour taste in his manager's mouth – forging a rift between the two founded upon this idea that the Englishman wasn't 'focused' enough to continue his career in a United shirt.

And though time has seemed to work its magic on the pair's relationship to date, it hadn't activated quickly enough in order to resist Pérez' advances – thus, soon unveiling Beckham as the fourth addition to a list of largely successful *Galactico* signings.

So, *surely*, this is the part where I monotonously list out all of this side's honours on the domestic and European scene; while poetically reminiscing about every orgasmic element to their successes? Well, no. For while their policy may have made their team *seem* more effective on paper and in mind, there was a monumental oversight which ended up plaguing their *actual* impact on the pitch.

You see, in the same transfer window which saw 'Golden Balls' Becks walk through the doors of the Bernabéu, midfield anchor Claude Makélélé passed him on his way out – and took most of the balance of the team with him!

For any high-level sports outfit to be successful, the concept of striking a harmonious balance between their offensive and defensive quarters is absolutely pivotal, and in this case, simply ploughing the team with 'flashier' attacking players proves worthless without something to pick up the slack behind them - the *yin* to the *yang*, if you will. And Makélélé was the 'yang' to that entire Real Madrid side!

Whenever the team came under pressure with the opposition breaching their midfield line, Makélélé was the ideal protector to have sitting in front of their defensive wall. He was always full of energy, highly combative and very efficient at reading the game to decipher the key point at which to get involved. So, without somebody like him patrolling that position, you leave a gap in front of the defenders which exposes them to the opponent.

Worse still, considering that most of the money brought into the club was recycled into the side's 'more exciting' attacking threat; and not in reinforcing the defence, the impact of Makélélé's sale only became more evident as time went by. And, forever the visionary, the poetic Zidane was on hand to provide a carefully-worded rendition as to how the Makélélé sale would eventually impact Pérez' Madrid:

"Why put another layer of gold paint on the Bentley when you are losing the **entire engine**?"

– Zinedine Zidane

To make matters worse, Zidane's sentiments were shared by his head coach Vicente del Bosque who, though ecstatic with the arrival of such 'galactic' superstars to breathe his attacking philosophy, envisioned a slippery slope without the commanding presence of a Makélélé in midfield to offset it.

The closest person they had in comparison to the dynamic Frenchman was Esteban Cambiasso, and even then, the Argentine was more adept in a deeper-lying playmaker's role - more passing, less tackling. So, when Del Bosque decided to voice his opinion to the president, you'd hope for an equally considered response to the issue. But, instead, his ego took hold.

Pérez had suddenly decided that it was better if he had a manager who more blindly accepted his vision, as opposed to one like Del Bosque who 'questioned its credibility'; a man, apparently, like Manchester United assistant manager, Carlos Queiroz.

A successful understudy to Sir Alex Ferguson by the turn of the millennium, he was naturally calm, considered and very technically sound in his understanding of the game. He also seemed to hit it off with Pérez and, after explicitly committing to the *Galactico* model, Queiroz was installed at the beginning of the 2003/04 season; only to return a year later to Old Trafford with his tail tucked firmly in between his legs. And, well, if that doesn't communicate the torrid state of affairs in Madrid, then I don't know what does.

Things quickly began to fall apart from this point on; with Madrid failing to claim a domestic title for the next three seasons, and Pérez losing his campaign for re-election in 2006. Thus, bringing to an end a once-promising idea by simply failing to implement it in a more careful and considered way. But that's not to suggest that his efforts had gone completely unappreciated.

In fact, it had inspired some unknown Russian gentleman over in London to see if he could one-up the Spaniard through a *'Galactico'*-type project of his own – the very same man who now owned the club that had just purchased Makélélé from Madrid!

~ 16 ~

'WELCOME TO 'CHELSKI''

- Roman Abramovich's latest plaything

Pérez' little pet project, though not as successful as it could've been, had completely revitalised the transfer market, and had briefly shown what *could be* possible if you were to put your finances to work in the right way. And luckily for one London club, this is something which aspirational businessman, Roman Abramovich was all prepared for in advance.

Beginning as a street dealer in his homeland flogging overseas wares to unassuming punters, the Russian had developed an all-consuming empire which spread across over twenty different industries within Eastern Europe by 2003. Atop his vast commercial kingdom, I suppose the young billionaire sought after a new challenge and, when observing the ballooning development of the Premier League, he couldn't help but take a slice for his own; hereby signalling out London as his preferred destination for finding a club in which to invest.

With Arsenal digging their heels in the sand and staying loyal to their batch of owners who drove them from mediocrity to invincibility (bit harsh, I know - but it sounds nice), sights were set slightly lower on their rivals; Chelsea and Tottenham Hotspur. It was also believed that Fulham endeared themselves to the businessman ... though news of their sullen yo-yoing to and from the top division soon put him off the idea.

Beginning with 'Spurs', looks were very deceiving. Despite being the type of club where David Ginola, Les Ferdinand and even Paul Gascoigne couldn't say 'no' to, the place was being run into complete submission.

Shedding a light on their inner turmoil, is the delightfully revealing autobiography of a certain Claude Littner. Of course, a more updated recollection of Littner will present the stern-faced tycoon in a sharp outfit just to the left of Lord Alan Sugar during BBC's *The Apprentice* schedule. Though it may surprise some of the younger readers, to discover that Littner cut his teeth as a businessman specialising in turning around the fortunes of ailing organisations - one of them being his boyhood club in Spurs ... which was chaired by none other than Lord Sugar himself. Funny how things work out, isn't it?

Coincidence aside and ignoring the stellar job Littner did to improve Spurs, Abramovich preferred a more 'open' prospect than that of White Hart Lane – where he could be in position to completely revitalise the club with very few elder states-people getting in the way of his vision. Namely, that prospect was Chelsea FC; whose recent fourth-placed finish (thus, earning a spot in next season's

Champions League draw) proved to be the operating cause for the Russian's debt-clearing £140 million takeover bid.

Once the relevant papers were signed, their new owner appeared to want to emulate a transfer policy whose aggression resembled closely to that *Galactico* thing from Spain. Though critically, he intended to give just as much attention to the incumbent aspects of the club as he did with any exciting new recruits - something I imagine Pérez curses himself for not doing.

He began with an obvious commitment to the club's youth resources; by blueprinting a state-of-the-art development facility for their academic sides in Cobham, Surrey. Having visited myself, I can assure you that it is a rather impressive facility; rife with gymnasiums, spas, analysis studios, presentation halls and a series of real-grass pitches which house the majority of their U-23 and U-18 home fixtures. It was eventually opened in 2007, and only after securing its permission for its build, was it then time to take his wealth into the transfer market.

Deciding to stick with existing manager Claudio Ranieri for the time being, the rest of the club experienced a complete sea change during the course of the 2003 summer transfer window, though most alterations seemed far more tactical and reasoned than the Spanish equivalent.

Here, it wasn't *just* about signing a 'big-name' who could 'hopefully do well for the team', as it was more about bringing in a high-calibre player whose characteristics would blend in well with his teammates; in order to boost the *overall* capabilities of the squad under whatever system the manager employed. And in terms of 'boosting' your team's efficiency, signings don't come much more tailored to this than that of the aforementioned midfield anchor, Claude Makélélé. A truly wonderful purchase.

> "[I] would concentrate only on defence and let the others go and do what they had to up front. They would take the risks; **I would take care of the opposition's attacks.**"
>
> – Claude Makélélé

It is a true testament to his legacy and ability that the eponymous 'Makélélé position' remains at the forefront of transfer policies for any major club today – hence, paving the way for the likes of N'Golo Kanté, Fernandinho and Fabinho in particular, to thrive within the Premier League after him. And much like these later mentions did for their respective clubs, signing Makélélé had re-calibrated Chelsea's recruitment strategy; where his presence allowed a *Galactico*-esque approach to finding his teammates.

But remember, the idea here was to be a lot smarter with their money than Real Madrid had been showing themselves to be at the time; and not to splash the cash on random signings who were doomed to fail from the beginning. Instead, they needed a considered strategy in place, with a select few suitable signings coming in to realise the manager's vision. And on this point, Ranieri's newer purchases simply didn't fit the bill; a trend which began with the hopeful signing of Juan Sebastián Verón.

Evidently blessed with all the attributes of a hallmark 'powerhouse' central midfielder - pace, physique, shot power, vision, skills etc. - the Argentine's impending arrival in London seemed to be foreshadowed by his lacklustre return at his first English club. Where, before Abramovich had even heard of Chelsea, Verón was signing for Manchester United; thereafter, finding difficulty in grasping the English language just as badly as he did to secure a nailed-on place in Sir Alex's trusted 4-4-2 setup.

Throughout his career, he had been able to drift around the midfield and impact the game wherever it suited him, and this didn't translate well into the more formative structure of United's midfield; as Chelsea would soon experience first-hand before making a rough £25million loss on the iconic South American the following year.

The misfortune continued once Chelsea made a bold and controversial move for Romanian forward Adrian Mutu, who would later go on to compensate the Blues for the cost of his transfer after testing positive for cocaine use. And just when things couldn't get much worse, even the more successful acquisition of world-beater Inter Milan forward Hernán Crespo, failed to overshadow the manager's resultantly strained relations with incumbent goal-getters (and personal favourites), Jimmy-Floyd Hasselbaink and Eiður Guðjohnsen.

Sprinkle this in with an imbalanced strategy which didn't revitalise the team's defence anywhere near as he tried to with the attack, and Ranieri ended up relying far too heavily on much of his existing squad to pick up the pieces which his new recruits had dispersed. And though they didn't fare too badly – finishing second only to that 'Invincible' Arsenal squad – it was clear that the Italian had made a mess of efficiently utilising the financial privilege provided by the new owner.

Not to mention the fact that Ranieri had also failed to make any substantial impact on that year's Champions League campaign; an issue compounded even further when you consider who was brought in to succeed him.

***

Located on the north coast of Portugal where the Douro River cuts through the city before marrying the Pacific on its way to the States, the neighbourhood of Porto is a delightfully cultured and beautiful place to visit. Adopting a landscape which mirrors the up-and-down hills of San Francisco, the people are humble, the food is glorious, and the wine is ever-present. Though humility is not exactly the word I would use to label their largest club's manager at this point in their history – José Mourinho.

Unironically, Mourinho's earlier career was given flight by somebody we've already spoken about at length; not Cruyff this time, but Sir Bobby Robson. The esteemed Englishman had himself managed Porto for a brief spell on a series of European getaways before he'd signed for Barcelona, and he'd been introduced by one of his local advisors to Mourinho as a translator / wannabe coach during an even earlier stint at Sporting Lisbon. The pair became inseparable during this time and took their relationship to the next step once Robson went to Barcelona; where he remained the Head Coach of the side, and Mourinho graduated to become his latest First Team Assistant Coach.

Despite their innate connection to one-another, they were almost polar-opposites in terms of their management style. Speak to anybody about their time with Sir Bobby and the words 'man management' will invariably splutter out of their mouths, though his pure *tactical* instincts rarely come to mind. Whereas it's the opposite story for 'Captain Tactics' José Mourinho, who spends endless hours developing systems and styles to directly thwart the opposition on the occasion it is required. Together, they *yin* and *yang*-ed delicately to add depth to their overall management aroma, but away from each other, definable differences have since explained their respective careers.

Arguably, though Robson may court a more blissful reminiscence from his disciples, Mourinho's approach appeared less outwardly affectionate; and more purely geared to winning a football match. And his tactical application to approaching the game had boded particularly well on the European stage, where he took great pride in studying and scheming over how to overcome continental opposition - as evident in the 2003/04 edition of the UEFA Champions League, during his inaugural stand-alone coaching position for FC Porto.

Despite finishing second in their group (which generally decrees a tougher opponent in the next round against a team who topped theirs), the 'Dragons' remained resolute in the face of adversity; overcoming Manchester United, Olympique Lyonnais and Deportivo de la Coruña on their way to the final in Gelsenkirchen where they would square off against Wenger's old stomping ground, AS Monaco.

In a line-up containing future French internationals like Ludovic Giuly, Gaël Givet and Patrice Evra, they had more than enough talent on show to trouble the Portuguese domestic champions. Nevertheless, goals from Carlos Alberto, Deco and Alenichev soon put the game beyond doubt, as Porto ran out deserved European champions which, though expected in the turn of events on the night, was a real outsider's shout at the beginning of the tournament.

Hereafter unofficially lauded as a 'God among men' in Portugal, there wasn't really much else for the Portuguese to achieve at Porto. And a timely meeting with the Europe-obsessed Chelsea owner soon enticed Mourinho through the doors of Stamford Bridge - the ideal 'next test' for him, and the ultimate statement of intent for Abramovich.

> "I don't think I am one from the bottle,
> I think I am the **Special One**"
>
> – José Mourinho

From this point on, there was no such thing as 'subtle' when it came to how Mourinho carried himself in Chelsea blue; and it seems only right and proper to begin with the self-proclaimed 'Special One's' fire sale before the 2004 season, directly before lining up some grander like-for-like replacements.

This began by booting top-signings Hernán Crespo and Juan Sebastian Verón out the door to either side of Milan, and then a rather heartless discard of Hasselbaink to Middlesbrough. And before directly replacing his departing goal-getters, he thoughtfully started his shopping spree off by reinvigorating the part of the side that prevents opposing goals from going in; thus, we arrive at the inspired signing of legendary stopper Petr Čech.

Blessed with a large frame and cat-like reflexes, the man dominated between the sticks for the best part of a decade since arriving; soon becoming a fan's favourite at the Bridge and voted as their 'Greatest Ever Goalkeeper' in 2012. He's even the club's Technical Advisor now, which is a lovely touch; and is serving to make his current boss' job just as easy as Mourinho's from when he was deployed on the pitch. In front of the Czech 'keeper, Mourinho stuck to what he knew by plucking a couple of crucial defenders from FC Porto; Ricardo Carvalho and Paulo Ferreira. Both of whom were key presences in the Portuguese's Champions League-winning side, and seemed more than capable of holding their own in a competition as fast-paced and interrogative as the English Premier League.

Looking further forward, Mourinho sought after the highly coveted Dutch speedster Arjen Robben who, having been courted for the majority of the summer by Manchester United, had been enticed to the Bridge through the coach's promise for first team football and a complementary formation within which to make best use of his agile attributes – a promise which was more than fairly upheld in the seasons to come.

In front of Robben, the arrival of a former PSV teammate in centre forward Mateja Kežman acted as foreplay before the main event. Though an accomplished forward with an enviable scoring record in Holland, Chelsea memories from this time tend to conjure up a more domineering image for its strike force - that of prolific ex-Marseille striker, Didier Drogba.

He was tall, strong, physically imposing and had an unequivocal winners' mentality - fuelled in no small part by his desire to retain his new lifestyle after experiencing what could have been without it. Forever humble and hard-working, he was the ideal outlet for someone like Mourinho; who wanted his players to work as hard and relentlessly as was business as usual for someone like his new striker. It's no wonder then, that the Ivorian native soon became the figurehead of Mourinho's tactical deploys from hereon in.

True to form, Mourinho remained anally consistent in his team selection throughout that first season: Cech would be in goal, organising a defence captained by academy graduate John Terry who was surrounded by Ricardo Carvalho, Paulo

Ferreira and Wayne Bridge (a bit awkward, if you read the tabloids, but all was fine back then).

The midfield was propped up by Claude Makélélé spraying the ball forwards to Frank Lampard and Tiago (also purchased this window), before being hoisted into the path of the marauding Damien Duff and Arjen Robben to feed an insatiable Drogba at its peak - cogs in the machine working in perfect harmony.

'Premier League Champion' status was a mere bi-product of this team's chemistry and consistency throughout the season and, though they appeared strong enough to repeat that feat without much background change, such a free financial situation posed too fruitful of an opportunity to not exploit in the following season. Therefore, explaining his decision to sell Scott Parker and Tiago in central midfield, to make way for the unerring box-to-box presence of Michael Essien

Again, poached from under the noses of Fergie's United, the name 'Michael Essien' became a byword for sturdiness and dependability during his time at Chelsea – thus, proving a worthy investment for a figure north of £30million. Asier Del Horno and Shaun Wright-Phillips came in to varying degrees of success at the Bridge in their respective wide defence and midfield areas, meanwhile the sale of Mateja Kežman to Atletico Madrid outlined Mourinho's utmost faith in Drogba, who would promptly go on to be named the PFA Players' Player of the Year when they doubled their collection of Premier League winners' medals by the summer of 2006

Now, *this* must surely be the point where I start talking about how this Chelsea side went on to continuously dominate their forthcoming years in the Premier League; whilst poetically reminiscing about every orgasmic element of their off-pitch and on-pitch synergy in order to achieve such results? Well … no.

The apple really doesn't fall far from the tree does it? Flick back a few pages if you can be arsed, and you will clearly see me mulling over Pérez' over-influential style of ownership unnecessarily interfering with management and, in turn, the welfare and performance of the Real Madrid squad. Well, it appears as though history has unfortunately repeated here in the case of Abramovich's title-winning Chelsea side.

Sensing a dynasty on his hands, the Russian never quite sat back to appreciate the gravity of his team's accomplishments; instead, he went above his manager's head to ensure that the level of performance didn't drop. 'And how did he do that', I hear you ask? By plunging into the transfer market *himself* in an attempt to bolster the side's attacking options by providing some 'necessary' competition for Drogba's coveted first team spot.

Granted, the Ivorian was picking up the odd injury here and there, and Chelsea looked a far more threatening prospect with him in the squad than without, but this should have been purely Mourinho's issue to deal with. I'm unsure of any behind-closed-doors meetings between manager and owner regarding Chelsea's attacking welfare, but it's clear to me that Mourinho wasn't particularly interested in bringing in another striker. But he didn't sign the cheques now, did he?

In his quest for another frontman, only the best would do for the Premier League doublers, and so the billionaire dipped into his bottomless bag of contacts to see what he could pull out. Many representatives came and went, and the Russian seemed only interested in players who were a) registered to a major club and b) possessed elite European football experience – remind you of anyone? So, I suppose it's therefore no wonder that his search had eventually settled upon Andriy Shevchenko.

Here's a tip …

If you're ever feeling nostalgic and are looking for a little cheat code on *Football Manager 2006*, all you have to do is pick a rich club and purchase Shevchenko from A.C. Milan. Around £20million would do … then stick him up front and let that 20/20-rated finishing do the rest - as was empirically based on his prolific time in Italy, where the Ukrainian racked up more than a goal every other game across seven full seasons in the Serie A (including domestic and European outings). That's Marco van Basten territory! So, *surely,* he'd be a hit in London, right? Well, he may have if not for one critical thing; that José didn't really appear to want him in his football team

His Chelsea side played with one striker up top. So, given his affection towards his current choice, the 'Drogba or Shevchenko' conundrum was solely dependent on the former's availability. After all, he was the first-choice striker, and José was loath to alter his winning formula just for the sake of massaging his owner's ego and including his pet-project … no offence, Andriy … big fan!

This really was a sad turn of events for everybody involved, and even for me in particular, as I *adored* Shevchenko. Though, through a mismatch of systems and a series of false promises, the Ukrainian simply couldn't be anywhere near as effective for Mourinho's Chelsea as he had been in his career up until that point. The poor guy went from being the 'main man' at Milan; heralded by his teammates and loved by the locals, to a frustrated figure that was overlooked or played out of position by a manager who might not have asked for him.

And to make things worse, the entire Shevchenko saga was merely the touchstone for a less than savoury transfer window as a whole for Mourinho and Chelsea.

We've already explored previously how Chelsea loved to stick it to United when it came to signing certain players and, technically, there was nothing wrong with that. Just because you beat your rival to a signature of someone who just so happened to be their target as well, that does not reflect poorly on you at all, especially when you act in accordance with recruitment guidelines and in good faith to all parties involved. But in one such case, Chelsea got this balance completely wrong.

John Obi Mikel was the next purchase to arrive at Stamford Bridge despite having been highly touted for a permanent move to Manchester United, though *this time*, a deal had actually already been *in place* to take the hopeful Nigerian to Old Trafford. Brandished in national newspapers wearing a Manchester United shirt after signing a pre-contract in January, he was contractually obliged to turn up as a United player at the beginning of the 2006/07 season.

Instead, the powers that be in London looked to go one step too far in enticing the defensive midfielder to Chelsea at the eleventh hour. Technically, should Mikel have decided along the way that he did not want to go, he could have compensated United for any losses in the form of punitive damages, and in worser cases (if extenuating circumstances meant that the transfer couldn't happen as scheduled i.e. through injury or personal issues), then the transfer could be considered void unless picked up after the issues dissolved -

as was the case when United held out for Ruud van Nistelrooy when he was injured in a post-negotiations training session with PSV in 2000. But this case didn't fit into either of these categories.

Instead, Mikel was *illegally* approached by Chelsea, offered a better deal to what he'd accepted from United, and had cheekily cited personal circumstances as the reason for his change of heart - a decision which would cost Chelsea around £10 million in compensation to United, and a distinct tarnish upon their club image when the authorities saw through the ruse.

But wait, there's more ...

I can't imagine the debilitating effect transfers like these have on squad morale, but you'd think that after two decidedly media-centric transactions, it's worth adopting a more subtle technique to bring in your next target. The thing is though, that is quite impossible when you're dealing with Ashley Cole.

Instead of discussing Ashley Cole: the media pariah, let's explore Ashley Cole: the left-back - because they may as well be two separate people. As a player, I believe Ashley Cole to be the greatest left-back that England has ever-produced. Described by Thierry Henry as a 'warrior', he was never afraid to put his body on the line, rarely ever shirked his defensive or attacking duties and was painstakingly motivated and consistent when called upon.

Also, a key figure in that 'Invincible' season with Arsenal after having cut his teeth in the club's academy, he established his intention to stay when the rumour mill conjured up a move away from Highbury. But loyalty really is a funny old thing isn't it, *especially* when money plays its part – one thing that Chelsea didn't lack.

It's a *meme* among the footballing community nowadays, that Cole was reportedly offered a £60,000 p/week contract extension - with a sign-on bonus in the early millions – from Arsenal when Chelsea substantiated their interest in 2006. Where he, instead of gleefully accepting the new contract while extending a deep and tender hug toward Arsène Wenger, the England full-back was supposedly taken aback by the sheer cheek of being presented with such a 'low-ball' offer.

Granted, by today's hyperinflated standards, that offer is quite a modest living for a Premier League champion, but back then, they may as well have offered him the gold-plated keys to a sub-Mediterranean island! Evidently, Ashley Cole did not think that, and a taxi soon dropped him off down the road to complete one of the most audacious transfers in English football history.

Having said that, a star left-back was a key move for Chelsea at the time; with Wayne Bridge falling out of favour and Del Horno proving a little too inconsistent for Mourinho's liking. So, make no mistake about it, the intention behind Cole's transfer was rooted very firmly in his exceptional footballing ability, but it just wasn't presented in that pure way. In context, it looked like another distasteful act of power play on behalf of the champions.

As a trio, Shevchenko remained on the periphery of the side, and his signing began to alert the fans as to 'who was really in charge of the club' - causing this feel of disenchantment to cascade over Stamford Bridge which must have been tangible in the dressing room. And once in there, the two purchases which succeeded him couldn't have done much to quell any unrest.

I doubt that anybody would've really known what went down with the whole John Obi Mikel fiasco, though the media didn't relent on Chelsea's inexcusable behaviour in diverting his route to London from Manchester United. And then, when they finally looked to have bought in somebody who was suitable for their squad, he himself took a while to be accepted by the fans; who were disjointed at having to cheer for an ex-rival, leave alone the man directly responsible for seeing favoured centre-back William Gallas leave in part-exchange.

All of which manifested into watching United top the majority of the 2006/07 season before taking the trophy back to Manchester – leaving Chelsea faces as red as the cup's latest adornments. Two seasons of hard work practically undone in the third.

Then, just when it looked like things couldn't get much worse for Chelsea, the love affair with Mourinho was over just as quickly as it began for them; with the enigmatic Portuguese coach sacked before Christmas in 2006, with the club falling 9 points behind United in the run-up to the January transfer window. And where it's easy to lambast the manager for being central to the club's eventual downturn, I personally believe that Abramovich's new-found lack of patience after tasting success, is more to blame than anything else for Chelsea's short-term dominance under José.

Mourinho was the *perfect* Chelsea manager and his recipe was working for them. He achieved what he set out to do and, perhaps if he was left alone in that now-infamous transfer market, Chelsea may have even continued in the trajectory that he had set before.

Of course, there's no saying who he would've brought in, or if he would've reaped the yields that I'm theorising over. But what's for sure, is that his owner's perceived lack of trust and respect for him is what became the club's undoing. And thus, began a series of appointments where Abramovich's clear impatience became an infamous part of the Chelsea job, where a succession of short-term managers serve as little else but to illustrate my point; eventually leading to a fall for the club where they never quite reached that level of imperiousness which Mourinho had created.

It's an easy trap to fall into isn't it? You achieve success, you want to maintain it, so a miniscule sign that it's depleting may lead you to act rashly in the vein of restoring what you feel like you're losing. But one club that didn't fall into this trap for a very long time, was Manchester United.

~ 17 ~

'MR. CONSISTENT'

Fergie's Manchester United Empire

It's probably best now to mention that I'm a proud, lifelong Manchester United fan, so did you honestly think that I'd go through an *entire* book without talking about them at all? Myth! Having said that, our journey into the history of United will begin and end with their Premier League endeavours, and what I ask you to do is to take them as a case study against their rivals.

For where the likes of Real Madrid and Chelsea in particular were hell-bent on completely changing their teams to keep up with the times, United sustained much of their success through faith and consistency - utilising the market to build upon their foundations rather than altering them.

Back when Alex Ferguson joined in 1986, he quickly realised that, much like his legendary predecessor Sir Matt Busby had discovered for himself, a strong youth policy is often the more reliable alternative to regular market purchases - as you can elect either to establish the spine of your squad by using them, or look to turn a profit on them if an overseas competitor looks more alluring. So, it works both from a tactical *and* a business perspective whereas the market option often omits one; a sentiment shared by both employee and employer by the time he was signed.

When Fergie arrived, there was a distinct synergy formed between himself and the chairman, Martin Edwards. Together, they shared the view that, up until the Premier League came into view, the club had failed to expand on any real, tangible aspect in proliferating their identity since the glory days of Busby, and it seemed sensible to go back to basics in focusing on the club's dedication to their academy.

All the while, Edwards would work his magic on the club's commercial enterprise – to provide a solid-enough platform for Ferguson to experiment with any new ideas which sprang to mind. But before Edwards' own prowess could come to the fore, it was down to Fergie to assess his existing crop of youth talent. And 'crops' don't get much better than this …

The 'Class of '92' have to go down as the most talented horde of graduates to ever come out of an English club's academy at the same time. Not least because of each inclusion's own personal talents, but for their chemistry and collective on-field understanding for each other's styles. Better still, they stretched right across the pitch – posing telepathic partnerships from defence right through to attack. Beginning with the former, we have the Neville brothers, and culture dictates that we begin with the eldest, even if this was just by a few minutes.

Often played on the left side of defence despite being right-footed, Phil Neville was your quintessential 'manager's dream' in terms of his can-do attitude, broad versatility and unassuming optimism. Whenever he was on the pitch, you got the feeling that he truly relished and appreciated his position as a football player - and just wanted any and every opportunity to represent his boyhood club. As was the case with his brother Gary; who was presented with even more first team opportunity than his elder.

The fact that Gary Neville has titled the first edition of his autobiography '*Red*', tells you everything you need to know about his dedication and love for the football club. The kit was his uniform, the pitch was his office, and he rarely ever took a day off. At right-back, he was quick, nimble and often well-positioned-enough to scalp out opposition attacks before feeding the ball forward.

Having said that, Gary needn't really be arsed with having to develop an Alexander-Arnold-like crossing efficiency, when you remember who was in front of him. I mean, has there ever been a better crosser of the ball than David Beckham? I'm not so sure.

Forever immortalised by the Anglo-Indian community in the film, *Bend it Like Beckham*, Parminder Nagra (playing the eager and die-hard Becks fan, Jasminder Bhamra) valiantly searches for her own ways to perfect a dead-ball situation, before solemnly concluding that nobody could 'bend a ball like Beckham', and I agree.

As the tattoo-bearing left arm of the Englishman swung intravenously with his incoming right boot to meet the ball at its valve, we all knew what to expect, and I am yet to see somebody as technically consistent as Beckham proved to be throughout his career. Whether it be an unimportant corner in the 36th minute or the late game-altering mid-range free kick, he would approach either situation with the same level of intensity and care as only he knew fit.

Sure, he may not have been the paciest of guys in the line-up, but he more than made up for it with his unequivocal technical qualities which provided another prong to United's attacking options. Now onto the opposing flank, where we have pace personified.

On top of this, Ryan Giggs was also a fairly competent crosser and a strong team player who would give his all for the side at every opportunity, yet most commendably of all, he was very direct. He refused to let up on his opponents and maintained a yogi's level of body conscience and discipline to ensure that he was able to consistently perform at the highest level for as long as was humanly possible. And 672 appearances later (with 100+ goals to match) across a 20-year-plus career are merely circumstantial numbers when you consider his relentless dedication to the United cause.

Though where his creativity and intelligence on the ball was something to be developed and cultured in the lab of United's seasoned professionals, a slight, ginger-haired pupil of the same Class needed nothing other than a stage upon which to showcase his God-given ability.

"You rarely come across the complete footballer, but Scholes is as close to it as you can get. One of my regrets is that the opportunity to play alongside him never presented itself during my career."

— Zinedine Zidane

Beginning as a forward and slowly reverting to a more creative and space-making central midfielder, this later evolution would establish Paul Scholes' legacy as one of the most naturally gifted servants ever presented to the United roster. He played there his entire career, was a favourite under Sir Alex Ferguson, retired and rose from the ashes in Fergie's final season, and through his reserved personality, a tender love for the club shines.

In behind 'Scholesy', you had someone who doesn't get *anywhere near* the credit he deserves - Nicky Butt. Nicky-'won't leave you alone'-Butt. Let's be completely honest with ourselves, if you were to make an XI with those who you thought were the best players of United's Premier League era, would you even consider including Nicky in your team?

Personally, he would be extremely close to the first-team squad - with Roy Keane's captain status being the sole reason for why Nicky would be omitted. But this is not a fair representation at all of the player he became and the role he adhered to with such success. His passing ability was criminally underrated, he was delightfully humble, unnaturally consistent and very satisfying to watch do those 'simple' yet vital roles for the squad. Respect his name, please. Because not enough people do.

And there we have the nucleus of the squad; full-backs in Phil and Gary Neville, Ryan Giggs and David Beckham in front of them, with Nicky Butt and Paul Scholes linking together in the middle of the park. They were talented - extremely talented actually - but very young, immature and inexperienced; not exactly the foundation for a title-challenging side on their own.

The Students needed their Teachers …

The 'teachers' in this case are qualified as 'leaders' in the dressing room, and in his first few years at the club, a handful of Fergie's initial signings had been brought in with this role in mind. You had Denis Irwin brought in from Oldham, then in came Steve Bruce from Norwich, Gary Pallister from Middlesbrough, Paul Ince of Inter Milan, Mark Hughes for a second stint at the club, and that mentioned Cantona fellow from Leeds; altogether forming a spine of experience throughout the squad from which the sponge-like 'kids' of '92 could absorb some valuable know-how on how to realise their potential.

And while Ferguson ensured that their marriage was an amicable one, Martin Edwards was working his magic on the club's commercial side; not just to finance some of the mentioned transfer moves for his manager, but to also secure the long-term proliferation of the Manchester United brand as a whole. And this began by floating the club as a public entity on the New York Stock Exchange in 1991 – directly before that 'FA Premier League' thing was set to be released.

This became the basis from which the club's current status has grown, and it had stabilised them to a point where it could accommodate for the next few years' worth of technical game changes and player price fluctuations. So, while they may have been 'lucky' to be gifted with the Class of '92 for free, the essential improvements made to the team, its facilities and global visibility were as strategic and intentional as it gets.

Six league conquests out of a possible eight come the turn of the millennium, and Manchester United became a force on the pitch which suited their growing commercial portfolio. And as a bi-product of all this business-y stuff, Fergie had the freedom to sign practically whoever he'd wanted, could employ a very well-experienced backroom team to help him out and use his own innate managerial prowess to bring it all together. All in all, this would culminate in that prime 1999 treble-winning side which has preserved its mystique to this day.

By the early 2000's, they had officially become the Premier League's most successful club, though a change-up proved necessary to cope with their innovative rivals. Usually, it would be a two-horse race between United and Arsenal to see who would ultimately be crowned champions at the end of the season – with United's closer-to-prime squad preventing Arsenal from distorting their dominance.

But as everybody got used to writing the year with a 'two' in front of it, it's clear to see that the tide was beginning to turn – with Arsenal reaching their peak state and United descending from theirs. Due to this, it was back to the drawing board for the Red Devils, where, even a club as powerful and profound like Ferguson's Manchester United, weren't immune to making some key mistakes when this task presented itself to them; hereafter known as their 'transitional period'.

Fergie kicked this period off with the record-breaking transfers of Juan Sebastian Verón and Ruud van Nistelrooy; and things swiftly began to fall apart from here.

As mentioned, Verón did not make much of an effort to learn the English language let alone to identify himself with the laymen of the Manchester area, whereas van Nistelrooy; United's most prolific ever goal-scorer (in terms of a goal:game ratio), possessed an unwavering obsession with scoring goals and the personal accolades that followed. No doubt, he was an undeniably clinical striker, but, *respectfully*, didn't seem all too eager to drop from his designated spot if it meant that he wasn't in a position to score goals; and United's game-plan became rather one-dimensional with him upfront as a result.

Even considering this, there's no doubting the fact that United had an enormously solid striker in van Nistelrooy and, having also whipped out the cheque book to bring elite defender Rio Ferdinand to Old Trafford, they were a couple of thoughtful signings away from being on par with *La Arsenal* and *Chelski*. But unfortunately for them, the mentioned duo would prove to be the pinnacle of Fergie's recruitment structure from this time, for it appeared that ulterior agendas had thwarted any further positive development for Manchester United.

Bring in the blunders!

To avoid any libellous allegations for anything I'm about to say, allow me to remind you that these are just *my opinions* ... about what *I* think ... regardless if the data backs me ... which it does ... as do most United fans ... as will you ... but still. Let's start with Cameroonian midfielder Eric Djemba-Djemba who arrived in Manchester after a positive showing in the FIFA 2002 World Cup. So good they named him twice? Not so much.

The 'next coming of Roy Keane' was one on a long list of hail-Mary plunges into the transfer market; made by the United hierarchy in a bid to directly recapture the success that the fans had longed for ... and that was the problem in a nutshell.

As we all know, it is nigh-on impossible to search for something which is directly as compatible and effective as something you've once lost. The only way to do this is by getting back that thing or searching for an alternative and going down a different path entirely. And in football, it's not like you can bring your old club legend out of retirement and expect them to put in prime-time performances, so you have to go out and re-develop your team. In accordance with this, signing somebody in an ex-player's mould is only going to breed a disappointing outcome. As was the case with Djemba-Djemba; who was never able to truly establish himself under the weight of expectation that comes with being compared to someone like Roy Keane.

The club's administration team then had to deal with David Bellion and Kléberson winding up on their books. I mean Kléberson wasn't a total loss and was a decent midfielder during much of his career, but the Premier League proved far too fast-paced and physical for the Brazilian to truly enjoy himself. As for Bellion, his transfer was certainly not worth the hassle of stealing him from another club. I mean, Sunderland fans must be absolutely over the moon with that one. They got compensation and everything!

Now here's where I might sound a little controversial ...

I've looked at many of these so-called 'new stars' careers before winding up at United and some things simply don't add up. Barring perhaps Kléberson whose stock had risen significantly having teamed up with *Il Fenomeno* at the World Cup, I fail to understand why United would feel as though it was wise to go after relatively unknown quantities in their search for re-capturing their pre-Y2K aura.

For me, considering some of these players' evident qualities (or lack thereof), it seemed as though signing some of them was more of a commercial stunt than a genuine on-pitch decision – in an attempt to court wider domestic markets by signing one of their territory's own. Like I said, it's a bit of a controversial statement, but hear me out ...

Djemba-Djemba would be the next African player to follow Quinton Fortune into Old Trafford and, after the former's involvement in the famous Nantes setup in France, it seemed somewhat worthwhile to take a punt on him. However, to splash out over £4million on an unproven central midfielder, make forced comparisons of his combativeness and hard-man style to that of Roy Keane ... all the while you've presumably made back your investment on the deal via shirt sales and added televisual rights in mainland Africa, only to sell him two years later after an average of ten appearances per season, is that really a footballing decision? I'm not convinced.

Then, moving onto another continent, Kléberson vague World Cup-inclusion doesn't seek to hide much of what I believe to be a larger desire to make some commercial strides into the South American market; especially when paired along with the other stumbling signing of Uruguayan hit-man Diego Forlán.

Neither of them had necessarily set the world alight in Manchester, yet by signing them, the club had gained access to an area of the world that was besotted by the game of football, and whom would have been overjoyed at the idea of having one of their own playing for them.

Correspondingly, as habitually dedicated as they are, local Latinx fans were now driven to tune into United matches in support of their compatriots. And from the club's own standpoint, more eyes on their games leads to a greater fan-base, which in turn drives another revenue funnel from a previously untapped part of the world. So, as you can see, there are lot of background positives to be gained from operating in this fashion, but it yielded a very inconsistent return on the pitch; because none of these players were actually *suitable* to play for Ferguson's Manchester United – both in style and in ability.

However, before they were made to bask in the shadow of their mistakes and gear themselves towards rectifying them, there was one major territory which was inexplicably left unexplored. Africa was checked off, South America sorted, so how could they leave out Asia! Well, spotting another commercial breakthrough, their recruitment journey brought them to China, and what must go down as the most obvious representation of the ulterior motives behind United's transitional business.

Scoring a supposed two goals across just under thirty appearances in China, doesn't quite give off the air that you're about to purchase a world-beater, now does it? I suppose one could argue that *potential* could have been a driving factor behind sanctioning a move for this kind of player, but that often relies on them arising from a more competitive league, or at least a nation which shows an outward dedication to the sport.

So, I'm going to go ahead and preface this case study here as a massively callous and near-sighted commercial endeavour – one which was made in a desperate attempt to soak up some Asian interest in United, without really considering any substantial future detriment to the subject of the deal; a young, aspirational front-man by the name of Dong Fangzhuo.

£500,000 was all it took to transform Dong from a humble kid working at becoming a footballer in China, to becoming the powerhouse's first ever East Asian player. Though such an unprecedented circumstance arose legal issues in relation to his registration, meaning that he would have to play elsewhere to gain enough first team experience, before being granted a work permit to run out in red.

A two-year loan spell followed where Dong donned the white and red of Royal Antwerp in Belgium - the result of which was another innovative commercial angle for United. Between 1998 and 2013, Antwerp and United had established a long-term, no-questions-needed, loan partnership. This would mean that, should United have a crop of youngsters developing in their academic ranks who were at the stage for first team involvement, Royal Antwerp would then be obliged to bring these players in on a short-term basis at United's request.

When in Belgium, the English side would often set expectations as to the player's involvement i.e. whether they would be there to make up the numbers, appease the agreement or play week in and week out. Well, Dong had a certain number of appearances to rack up before being granted a work permit, so I suppose the latter was in effect.

Unfortunately for him, his swansong in Belgium would be as prolific as it got for the striker - not registering a single competitive appearance at United before his search for a worthwhile career took him back home. And it came to be that Dong would be on the receiving end of persistent mockery in China for his failed stint in England. Such was the abuse that he decided to undergo plastic surgery – in the hope that his new appearance wouldn't attract the level of hostility that his previous one did.

Now, it is grossly unfair to place the blame of Dong's later suffering solely at the foot of Old Trafford, and I will not do so. Though it is a dire indictment of United's lost recruitment policy at the time – one which wreaked greater havoc on the subject of their near-sightedness than it ever did on them. It was time for a rethink on their part.

As we've seen, United were beginning to stray away from the identity which had brought their success in the first place. Forever, their glory was founded upon the guile, dedication and talent of young, hungry and gifted players - who would be moulded and shaped under the stewardship of senior pros to breed a title-winning squad.

So, it was high time that they had enough with these little bits and pieces which strayed away from this concept, and onto a spot of old-fashioned scouting in line with their revised outlook. First stop, Lisbon.

Question time:

Who do you believe was the mastermind behind Cristiano Ronaldo's transfer to Manchester United?

A very simple question that seems to have a very simple answer, isn't it? It must be the manager, or possibly even Ronaldo's agent? Not so much. The answer is located right beside Sir Alex Ferguson; and upon the shoulders of his tanned, silver-haired assistant, Carlos Queiroz.

Over in Portugal, word soon spread from his little black book of contacts of a young, flamboyantly haired, wonky-toothed winger who was beginning to make a name for himself in the setup of Sporting Lisbon. Wasting little time, Queiroz sought to organise the soonest flight he could in order to arrive at his own conclusion, though this proposed trip was postponed by around a year to sew his managerial oats with Pérez' Madrid. Back on *terra firma* at the United training complex, Queiroz picked up where he left off, and happened upon a radical suggestion for how he and Sir Alex could get a better look at this talked-about Portuguese teenager. And this was to organise a pre-season match-up between United and Sporting as the latter unveiled their new stadium – not only testing the youngster's quality against their own defence, but also earning them some pocket money for their involvement in the tie. 'Two birds', and all that!

As the players of Sporting Lisbon and Manchester United arrived to a ticker-tape welcome in front of a freshly-painted, sold-out arena, the players shook hands at the centre-circle and readied themselves for a supposed 'friendly' fixture to simply usher in Lisbon's time at their new home, though this introduction was about as pleasant as it got between the opponents.

As soon as you watch any video of this match (which I greatly suggest that you do), you'll think about sending poor John O'Shea a condolence card. Word on the street is that Cristiano Ronaldo had been courting for a move out of the club from the season before; and knew of Queiroz' initial interest prior to his manic Madrid moment. So, to have him return to United, *and* for them to come onto his home turf, was a once in a lifetime opportunity to prove how good he was to them.

So, what O'Shea expected to be a gentle affair, turned into a relentless massacre at the hands of Ronaldo. His trademark step-overs, tricks and break-neck speed were all on display for the boss to see. And whatever the Irishman did to combat him, whether it be to post up to him, lay off, show him onto his 'weaker' foot, expose him into midfield … nothing seemed to work … and ninety minutes wasn't long enough to be able to figure out what would. He was snapped up by

United quicker than O'Shea could compose his thoughts about what just happened to him, with many of Ronaldo's future teammates proving instrumental to Fergie's ultimate decision; the same lads who broke onto the scene at a similar time in their developments as he did.

The Evolution of the 'Class of '92'

The very boys who were once posed as those budding graduates looking to take their claim for first team regularity earlier on in the Premier League era, had now become seasoned professionals in the camp; whose opinions held great weight to their manager.

Plus, not only were they extremely vocal in their support of signing Ronaldo after this performance, but the Portuguese himself would be in a position to flourish under their very guidance whenever the formalities were ticked off.

Considering this, the role of the Class of '92 (minus Beckham who'd just moved onto his *Galactico* chapter) would come full circle - from fledglings who needed to be tutored themselves, to being responsible for passing their knowledge onto new boys like Cristiano.

The 'students' becoming the 'teachers', if you will, and just to add a little flavour to the marinade, it is now common knowledge that Arsène Wenger, had reached Ferguson's conclusion before he did; seeking after the pace-merchant to add to his bulging ranks of would-be 'Invincibles'. So, but for this timely intervention by Queiroz and United, the Red Devils' fortunes could have been oh-so different.

***

Signing Ronaldo had ignited the touch paper on United's new, more positive transfer strategy, and Ferguson now had a whole new set of criteria for his scouting department. New signings needn't have a certain global appeal or commercial viability, instead, a humble attitude, raw talent and untapped potential would be the order of the day.

So, where to next? You'd think after finding Cristiano in Lisbon, that the Scot would've taken fancy to the sun, so maybe Majorca? Madrid? Barcelona? Porto? Greece? Erm ... no. Fulham was the next stop ... in Autumn. Though it just so happened that United had to travel there for the fourth game of the 2003/04 season anyway, so no need to delve into the travel expenses purse for this one.

Typically, you would expect an average United side to overcome most Fulham sides. But things didn't go quite to plan on this particular afternoon, as United fell to a 3-1 defeat at the hands of the Cottagers. There were just shy of 70,000 to witness the butchery that took place at Old Trafford, and although much of the media attention went on the Frenchman Steed Malbranque for officially sinking the United ship, it was his elusive teammate which drew greater attention from Manchester.

Deciding to make lemonade out of lemons, Fergie and his merry men took particular fancy to Malbranque's strike partner, Louis Saha. And please forgive my lack of impartiality here but, I *loved* Louis Saha, and from a fan's perspective, was *ecstatic* when he joined United. It showed that Fergie was clearly on the warpath to develop his squad in this new, hungry direction, and you'd be pressed to find somebody who embodied this better than Saha.

He was a rather unconventional striker for his time and almost the polar opposite of the single-minded Ruud van

Nistelrooy. The Dutchman was the type of goal-scorer for whom the final score runs second fiddle to his own personal tally, whereas Saha was wired in the opposite way - prioritising the team's welfare over any personal accolades.

He was selfless, full of energy, a real handful to deal with and never seemed to mind sacrificing a goal-scoring position for the benefit of bringing his teammates into play. So, when they brought him in and practically ousted van Nistelrooy as a result, it was a clear indication of United's outlook at the time, especially so when the Dutchman's vocal disdain at this arrangement was met with yet another striking addition in the mould of Saha.

A surprising story given his affinity to Leeds at the time, Yorkshire-born striker Alan Smith swapped Elland Road for Old Trafford in the summer of 2004. A raw centre-forward in his own right, you need only glance up at my description of Saha if you're wondering what signing Smith was geared to bring to the club.

Unfortunately for him, a mixture of injuries (karma, probably) and an inability to stick to his position hindered his progress at United, before sustaining an awful leg-break at the hands of Liverpool left-back John Arne Riise. The Gods of irony really were on top form here, weren't they?

Get this, the supposed *Leeds* fan makes a fateful switch to represent *Manchester United,* only to be critically injured by a *Liverpool* player ... and not by a clash of studs or anything of that sort ... but by the *ball* itself, you cannae write this stuff! Satire aside, Smith had undoubtedly lost a yard of pace after recovering from his injury, and found solace in a shallower central midfield position which was too stacked to flourish in with United. A trip to the North East with Newcastle beckoned, thus beginning a journeyman career at the heart of midfields in Milton Keynes and Nottingham. But, maybe this 'other striker' United signed shortly after his leg-break would have better luck? One can only hope.

"Ladies and gentlemen, introducing sixteen-year-old
... **Wayne Rooney**!"

– Clive Tyldesley

Everton v Arsenal
[Rooney's First Team Debut]

Be honest, what were you doing at sixteen / what do you plan to do when you reach sixteen? For me, I was whittling my life away without a care in the world - a PlayStation controller in one hand and my crotch in the other. Occasionally, I'd go out and watch a movie, court a young lass and all the rest of it, but overall, I was a lazy, moody and broody teenager ready to let the sands of time dictate my life's tale. And here Rooney was, banging them in at the highest level for a Premier League club - cue the 'you could have been a doctor' comments now.

Looking back on Rooney's first outings in the league, there is a distinct whiff of 'Gazza' about the teenager; as both played best when they were left unrestricted and able to express themselves under a supportive manager. Luckily for Gascoigne, he found this situation with Sir Bobby Robson and England, and likewise for Wayne, who got on well with club manager David Moyes.

Under him, the figure of a young, stocky lad donning a *Keitan*-sponsored deep navy-blue kit with 'Rooney - 18' across its shoulders, became a common sight at Goodison Park. I imagine the plan was to manage his development very carefully so as to not over-expose him into a competition he wasn't ready for, though almost seventy appearances across two seasons in Merseyside, points to his unavoidable talent and crowd appeal - both of which didn't require a prolonged grace period.

Given his rapid inclusion within the first team setup, a couple of seasons was all it took for Rooney to get itchy feet. As cruelly evident in a press conference at the beginning of the 2004/05 season, where a despondent-looking David Moyes seemed resigned to losing his prized starlet after he had handed in a transfer request; in a supposed ploy to forward his career on the national stage amidst interest from comparative 'big boys' Chelsea, Newcastle and Manchester United.

As strange as it may sound to Newcastle fans born into the emotionally draining Mike Ashley era, they were a very intriguing proposition for Rooney when their reported £20million bid was rejected by Everton. And in theory, a more stable environment with a prolonged Sir Bobby Robson tenure (yes, him again) may have shifted the tide in favour of Tyneside. Then again, the concept of stability, unity and professionalism lay firmly with the club who made the £30million bid that was eventually accepted.

At only eighteen years-old, the fee agreed between Everton and Manchester United would assert Rooney as the most expensive player in history under the age of twenty; a tagline which could've proved far too weighty to ever exceed under for your average prodigy. However, an eventual career which led to the Evertonian topping both United's and England's scoring charts, suggests that Wayne Rooney was anything but 'average'.

For the next half-decade, A typical 4-4-2 formation headed by Giggs, Ronaldo, Rooney and Saha would terrorise defences up and down the country. Very few were able to oppose the directness of Saha, the all-rounded ability of Rooney, the trickery of Ronaldo nor the composure of Giggs.

And with some astute acquisitions at the back line like Edwin van der Sar, Nemanja Vidić and Patrice Evra, Fergie's millennial side grew into an all-conquering force which saw them become the most successful club in the land once again - winning *another* hat-trick of Premier League titles from 2005 to 2008. How fitting. The new era began with Rooney scoring a hat-trick on his debut (which again, is another match that you need to see) and culminated in a hat-trick of Premier League accolades to fit. I tell you; football can be pure poetry at times.

The Ultimate Rebirth was complete

Personally, I believe that *this* is the period where Sir Alex Ferguson truly stands out as one of the all-time greats in football management. Not to throw mud on his '90s efforts, but the initial success he experienced during the previous decade was unparalleled - limited only by their imaginations and not weighed down by expectation. Moving into the 2000s, the club were experiencing a slump that they had never before encountered in the Premier League era, and were facing an uphill battle to change their immediate fortunes around.

Even in this book, we've seen so many clubs over the years have their time in the sun and bow out when the times move past them, so to restructure the club itself around these changing times in order to preserve your place at the top is a mightily impressive feat to accomplish. Not to mention the fact that, he went against the grain of what many desperately big clubs were doing to return to the heights from whence they dropped and was able to pinpoint his misgivings before acting upon them in the most efficient way possible.

In conclusion, Ferguson's United had gone full circle throughout his first two decades in management, and the Scot proved himself to be an absolute master at learning from his mistakes.

He'd had his blunders, splashed the cash, tried different methods and ultimately stuck with the winning formula he ended on. And if ever there was a team which needed to learn from their mistakes, it was that pesky *Galactico* version of Real Madrid.

For them, the vision was there but the execution was very poor. And if ever they were going to bounce back, their next venture needed that Ferguson-esque 'long-term vision', that Wenger-style level of innovation, and even a somewhat Mourinho-like level of arrogance to not let any opponent get in their way. Especially so given how tough their task had become since falling from their perch.

~ 18 ~

'UNA CORTO SERIE DE EVENTOS DESAFORTUNADOS'
A Short-Term Madridian Nightmare

The story of Florentino Pérez' relationship with Real Madrid is reminiscent to that of a man who wronged the love of his life and begged for a second chance to do the right thing. So, let's first look into what separated the two lovebirds in the first place.

The club was progressively being hindered by the obligation of signing a world-beater every summer, where the numbers of available superstars were dwindling as the windows drifted by. Therefore, with the calibre of *Galactico* declining, the imperiousness of their brand was slowly beginning to diminish with each newcomer being more underwhelming than the last, a task which, in itself, was made even harder by the impending retirements and departures of treasured stars Zinedine Zidane and Ronaldo. Therefore, unable to steer the ship away from its impending collision, Pérez had lost a lot of support from the fans and any hint of another presidential term was extinguished by January of the 2005/06 season; thus, leaving incoming president Ramón Calderón the unenviable task of picking up the pieces.

Cursing his luck, he began by appointing ex-A.C. Milan war-captain, Fabio Capello as the team's new head coach; which was a decent tell as to Calderón's intent for *his* version of Real Madrid.

By bringing in somebody as technical, ruthless and independent as Capello, it seemed as though it was an active attempt to rid the club of the egotism which followed the *Galactico* name, as well as any of the harboured dead wood which arose from that mentality. All in favour of bringing in (or developing in-house) players which were suited to an *actual* system invented by the Italian. Which, though very reasonable in concept, largely failed to materialise given how unstable Calderón's canvas became. Especially so given that David Beckham had *also* recently announced his own intentions to leave before the new president had even had time to sit down!

Now, it's fairly accepted amongst the hard-to-please Spanish media, that Calderón couldn't do much about the first two stars leaving, as their intentions were made pretty clear from the time Pérez was at the helm – with the Frenchman opting to retire after that Summer's World Cup, and Ronaldo's lifestyle choices signalling a preference away to a less pace-centric league. But Beckham was a different story, and though this was never his direct intention at time, it's easy to see why his reasoning ended up undermining Calderón's presidency before it had even had a chance to breathe.

"What do you mean he's going to **America**?!"

- Ramón Calderón … probably

Footballers are faced with this decision whenever they're put up on the market. They assess their current ability; consider what type of challenge/culture they want to play in and seek a move within those parameters. In this particular case, we have a just-after-peak David Beckham, whose powers would surely have a wealth of top-level clubs coming in for him. And should he go to a club of that kind of stature, then perhaps fewer questions would have been aimed at Madrid to explain why he left.

However, in a situation where the buying club are nowhere near the same league as the sellers, then it has the opposite effect. And this is exactly what happened when the Rapunzel-styled ball-bender somehow wound up on the shores of California with an LA Galaxy shirt in his hand – a club registered with the newly founded Major League Soccer ['MLS'] franchise in the United States of America.

The story of the rise, fall and re-emergence of soccer in America is a fascinating tale; and one that we will revisit later on in this edition. For now, all you need to concern your pretty little self with is the fact that it was nowhere near where it is now.

Back then, the 'MLS' was little more than a collection of ideas based on what they *aimed* to achieve following the failure of their first attempt with the 'NASL', and they were looking for a rather large name to attract some positive attention to their new venture. So, by all accounts, Beckham was the perfect candidate for their requirements.

And from Beckham's own point of view, he was the centre of attention, the star of the new league and was able to personally benefit from the myriad of commercial opportunities afforded to sports icons in America. What's more is that he had a better quality of life ahead of him in

California – a less visceral crowd, more welcoming environment, a bigger house (apparently) and a playing schedule which suited his family lifestyle as well. But nobody really recognised any of this at the time; especially if you held an affinity to his previous employers.

Back in Spain, the story was never really about analysing why Beckham chose to make the move for *himself*, and instead a lot of negative attention was fobbed off onto the 'ex-*Galacticos*' to explain why he would reject *them* to go to the Galaxy.

Inevitably, the blame was pointed at poor ol' Calderón, who was ostracized for reportedly 'playing a part' in Beckham's departure. When in hindsight, he was the easy target in an aimless search for a reason to the madness, and *even then*, something like that is the manager's decision - with Calderón taking on a much less intrusive standpoint to what somebody like Pérez was comfortable doing.

Plus, Beckham was a mature-minded, seasoned professional before Capello was even appointed; and no longer the petulant kid who fell out with Sir Alex Ferguson before arriving at the club in the first place. So, as far as he was concerned, he was making a long-term career decision which benefited him in ways that many were too ignorant to conceive.

He wasn't making any decisions in spite of any tense relationship between him and Capello, nor any other torn ties against the new president. He simply made a careful, considered choice which required more aforethought than much of the media seemed to possess at the time. Nevertheless, the vultures circled in the way that they did, and Calderón became the unfortunate casualty out of all this uncertainty and speculation. Quite frankly, it didn't matter what the *real* reasons were, it only mattered what went along with the narrative that the media were happy to portray.

And as far as they (and their readers) saw it, Pérez was out, and now we had 'boring' Calderón come in to replace him who, despite his idealistic interpretation of how the club could grow under his guidance, had: not managed to talk Zidane out of retiring, nor keep the fridge door locked before Ronaldo stuffed himself en route out the door to A.C. Milan (for less than half of what they shelled out for him), and now couldn't help but lose Beckham to a league that hadn't even started yet! Doesn't look great when you think about it like this, and it was a mindset which proved difficult to shift.

Galactico-less and under constant scrutiny, two exceedingly underwhelming seasons on home soil only heaped further pressure on Calderón. It also didn't help that his delightfully warm and calm persona was taken as being 'uninterested' or 'placid' in the face of adversity; especially when it was directly compared with his fiery predecessor.

What's worse is that the poor treatment of Calderón is especially harsh when you consider that he'd actually spent well in the transfer market, with the elder Fabio Cannavaro and Ruud van Nistelrooy joining in and around the same time as players like Marcelo and Gonzalo Higuaín – thereby following those policies which had earned him his original presidential spot.

He'd also purchased Chelsea's Arjen Robben and Ajax's Wesley Sneijder before the 2007/08 campaign, but even that wasn't enough to calm the storm - with many of the younger stars not being in a position to achieve the short-term yield that Calderón really needed in order to get the pincers off his back.

And as things quickly trekked on to their inevitable end, the nail in Calderón's coffin came courtesy of Catalunya, and the insurmountable task posed to the Whites if they ever dreamed of toppling the new form of FC Barcelona that had taken the European continent by storm. And whose dominance looked eerily similar to that brought by the man who'd given reason for much of this book to be written in the first place.

~ 19 ~

'THE SECOND COMING'
Rijkaard's Revival / the Tiki Taka Time Capsule

Throughout this book, I've made it my mission to shine a light upon some of football's most significant moments in ways that we perhaps haven't considered them before. To the point where I am loathed to simply include an incredible team / moment purely on the basis of how great they / it was. This is all about linking things together, taking a different viewpoint and viewing it all in this 'how did it help us develop' context.

And though I will briefly happen upon this team's ungodly number of honours, I'm much more interested in how it got to where it did and, more importantly, the knock-on effects for those who looked on in envy of their accomplishments. With that settled, let's go ahead and talk about that *glorious* Barcelona side from 2007 (whose efforts have underpinned much of their current success), and discuss the chain of events it resulted from and what has since transpired from them.

Before the time when the glistening bald scalp of a revolutionary, cardigan-wearing Adonis would grace the Camp Nou dugout, the club juxtaposed this image by employing the crazy-haired Frank Rijkaard to precede him, who, after a fantastic playing career in *that* famous combining-the-styles Sacchi Milan side, enjoyed a rather unconventional journey into coaching before being given a 'leap of faith' opportunity with FC Barcelona in later 2003. And boy, did he have it all to do!

To give you an idea of the scale of the job at hand, one must remember that he'd signed just in time to watch Ronaldo and David Beckham parade around in a Real Madrid shirt; with many expecting the *Galacticos* to blow away the competition, including their previously close rivals from Catalunya. And make no bones about it, Barcelona were indeed deeply affected by those big-spending Whites, *especially* so by the Beckham and Ronaldo transfers, though not in the way that anybody would have expected at the time.

Let me explain …

Beginning with Beckham, it is believed that a deal was agreed in principle to bring the set-piece specialist to the Camp Nou, with everything but a flick of the wrist in place for the deal to be completed. But as we know, the riches of Real Madrid proved too alluring to turn down for both Becks and United, and the midfielder was soon brandished at the Bernabéu.

So, this left Barcelona with a problem to solve and an equally big statement to make; to bring in somebody who could ideally attract a similar level of anticipation and excitement around their transfer, like Becks would have done with his. Thus, the club searched far and wide before their travels brought them to the fashionable city of Paris, where a Samba-style Brazilian superstar was marinating nicely under the Parisian lights. Some lad called Ronaldinho.

Strangely enough, there was a very strong chance that Ronaldinho could have donned the red of Manchester and not the multiple colours of Barcelona. But, luckily for Barca, they had their own ambitious newly elected president in Joan Laporta; who'd set his sights firmly on the Brazilian and aggressively outbid United when their attempts for Beckham fell on deaf ears.

Days later, €30 million brought Ronaldinho to the Camp Nou and everybody in Catalunya had pretty much forgotten about the Beckham ordeal. As for United, they were pretty peeved, but I'm sure Queiroz' bottom-of-the-ninth reconnaissance mission with Sporting Lisbon mended any bruised egos.

How crazy is that?!

Beckham is wanted by Barcelona, then Madrid sign him. All the while, United are courting Ronaldinho as Becks' replacement, and Barca rebound onto him when they lose out on the Englishman. Then, having lost out on Ronaldinho, United signed Cristiano Ronaldo.

It's so funny how things work out sometimes.

And as we see how the Ronaldinho transfer arose from the knock-on effects of the 'Greedy *Galacticos*' signing Beckham, there's also a case to suggest that the Brazilian's strike partner's stint at the Camp Nou may not have happened but for the policy which attracted Ronaldo to Madrid. With lightning winding up to strike twice, here's how the purchase of Ronaldo had correlated with the sale of Cameroonian star-in-the-making, Samuel Eto'o ... though this is far more convoluted than the earlier example, so please bear with me here.

Initially plucked from the local Kadji Sports Academy from a wandering acquaintance who held ties with Real Madrid, Eto'o uprooted his homeland and moved to the outskirts of the Santiago Bernabéu in 1997. Then, while maturing delicately in the club's *Castilla* developmental setup, Pérez' introduction a couple of years later had forced the African fledgling out on a number of short-term loan arrangements as a presumed opportunity to impress his employer's from afar upon his eventual return.

Whilst out, his most successful stint came at RCD Mallorca in the Second Division of Spanish football; amounting six goals in thirteen appearances in a single half-season, thus, prompting his latest employers to express a strong desire to make this agreement a long-term one for the future.

So, slowly creeping up to his nineteenth birthday, the young forward had a decision to make: wait it out to see if his efforts went noticed back in Madrid, or to work permanently for Mallorca to hopefully continue his strong run of form. It's a point where you ask yourself as a footballer: is it better to stay at the *bigger* club with *less* open opportunities to impress, or to attempt to prevail at the *smaller* club where greater opportunities have already presented themselves? As we all know, it takes a brave man to turn down Real Madrid, but I suppose being pushed out the door would do that to someone.

Here's where things get complicated ...

Eto'o's ultimate decision was very much dictated by the concept of player percentage ownership - a pervasive influence in much of European football despite its taboo-like representation.

The concept is that anybody who has made a monetary consideration for the development and well-being of a player, should be entitled to a percentage stake in that player which amounts to however much they've invested in them.

So here, if you hold the majority 'stake' in a player's career, then you can have the deciding vote on where the player is transferred to and/or you're able to veto any unwelcome interest. All the while, the minority is owed compensation in value of the percentage they have vested in the player. These parties can be clubs, representatives or even the player themselves.

Eto'o found himself in this exact position when Real Madrid had inserted a clause in his original contract, where they would maintain a 50% stake in the Cameroonian once he'd returned from his loan spell - giving them right of first refusal if his development at Mallorca attracted offers from further afield. It was a tidy insurance policy to protect their asset in case he became good, but Madrid had completely misused it by undervaluing Eto'o, showing no intention of giving him a first team role at the Bernabéu (as a perceived 'non-*Galactico*') and forcing him into the arms of Mallorca.

Whilst there, the pace, guile and sharpness of Eto'o shone on the Spanish isles where, despite his slight and nimble frame, he proved a formidable fixture up front; as his game-reading intelligence matched his outright desire to get on the scoresheet. In doing so, he quickly endeared himself to the fans, and more than paid back the record fee required to secure his services permanently from *Los Blancos*.

By the time 2004 came around, it was clear to see that Eto'o's exploits in Mallorca would be short-lived. He lovingly recalls his development at the club and still holds a place in his heart for the fans who helped him throughout this period. But sometimes, when bigger clubs come calling, you can't help but answer - especially when that club is FC Barcelona – a direct rival in stature, ability and history to the one he wanted to stick it to.

If only Real Madrid weren't so caught up in their narrow-minded policy, then maybe recognising the depth in quality they *already possessed* could have gone some way to achieving what they were trying to do. Ah, well ...

There we have it, a series of seemingly innocuous events had brought two of Barcelona's greatest ever players to the Camp Nou. After this, no amount of *Galactico* aforethought could make up for their insufficiencies in the same policy. And with their two 'gifts' in Ronaldinho and Eto'o, Rijkaard's Barcelona were beginning to reach the form of old - forging a crow-like path towards two Spanish La Liga titles - with Samuel Eto'o obtaining the Golden Boot in both seasons, whilst his ever-smiling fellow front man Ronaldinho captured the imagination of fans worldwide.

But *even then*, even after dismantling Madrid's stranglehold over the league and making a mockery of their all-conquering outlook, the mere fact that Barcelona didn't win a treble had attracted an inquest by the media to find out why that was. And with a Pérez-less Madrid no longer attracting the same level of attention as it once did, the vultures set to the Camp Nou in search of a story to tell. Vicious, aren't they?

Failing to win the 2006/07 campaign (directly after Pérez' departure) led many to believe that Barcelona's side was getting too egotistical for its own good. Yep. That same band of lads who'd worked tirelessly to retrieve the mantle from a club who was *actually* run with egotism as its core value, was now being disregarded for the same thing simply because they were winning. I may be jumping the gun by insinuating that this was the primary cause, but that's exactly how it looked.

Add this onto another win-less season the following year with a spattering of ageing signings to boot, and the Barcelona hierarchy decided to change tact - thus amicably relieving Rijkaard of his duties in their quest for somebody that would detract from any of the unfair negativity which tarnished his tenure.

In his place, they wanted someone younger, more innovative, hungrier and naturally more devoted and relatable to the club in a way an overseas star like Rijkaard couldn't ever be.

Preferably, they needed someone from Catalunya; with a connection to the fans, a knowledge of the setup, a vision for the club's academy and a set of tactics geared towards putting Barcelona back on the top of the world stage for good.

Enter: ex-midfield maestro-cum-academy-manager Josep Guardiola ... or 'Pep' to his mates.

Right, where do I begin with Guardiola? And how do I manage to accurately quantify his overall influence on FC Barcelona? Well … it's impossible for me to do here. However, if you want to go into greater depths as to the specific stories behind his success at Barcelona, then there are copious amounts of texts to provide your fix. Or just watch a few videos with Guillem Balagué in them – as he would certainly know more than I could research and re-communicate to you in a chapter or so.

But having said that, we're looking to focus here on linking up some of the older data to identify a trend or two which pertains to learning about the past's influence on the present - and there's little more in the world of football which illustrates this better than Pep Guardiola and his Barcelona story. As we alluded to briefly a little earlier on, Guardiola began as a decorated defensive midfielder at Barca - both under Cruyff and even briefly under Sir Bobby Robson.

Blessed with extraordinary eyesight and with the audacity to realise some of his vision, he was an almighty strong passer of the ball and was the beating heart for his side's on-the-ball efforts. He really was a fantastic player and it's a shame that a lot of his younger talents have since been largely put to one side, though perhaps that just speaks even greater volume of his post-playing managerial prowess.

As with a lot of managers we've spoken about, it's often a case of getting a number of anonymous qualifications before teaming it with your playing prestige to elbow your way into any ol' job. But Pep didn't want to go down this route. He was as much a talented footballer as he was a natural academic, and chose to take a two-year reprieve from the game whilst he soaked up all the textbook knowledge he could into how a team operates, so he could therefore form a vision of how he wanted his eventual side to work. And it turned out to be very blessed moment of aforethought from the Spaniard. *Typical, really!*

By the time he had officially declared himself 'ready for employment', he only really ever looked destined to remain in Catalunya. His desire to be a part of Barcelona was palpable and, after helping out here and there in their *La Masia* academies upon retirement, he was officially offered the head coaching position for the club's *B* team in 2007. Coincidentally, Rijkaard's faltering stint in the first team dugout contrasted with Guardiola's coming-of-age story in the background. Then, once the Barca hierarchy had altered their job requirements, very few fit the bill better than Pep. Particularly so when he came to his interview armed with a proposal to completely change the way the team was playing under the Dutchman.

His ideas had completely juxtaposed Rijkaard. The former was rather 'flashy' and direct in how his team attacked, where separate plays and formations were the ballasts behind why they were able to win a football match. But Pep opted for a format which was intrinsically ingrained within the squad; where his team would adopt a more 'complete' mentality which encouraged them to: look after one another, make up for each other's defaults, work towards making each other better and ultimately to control the outcome of the game by possessing the majority of the ball - and indeed hounding the opposition whenever they dared take it from them.

It's **Total Football**. Repeat after me: Guardiola went to Barca and implemented yet *another* version of *Total ... Football.*

First Michels, then Cruyff, a splash of Sacchi, a dollop of Wenger and now the crowning jewel in Pep Guardiola. Though unlike the aforementioned Italian and French versions which rose before his time, the Spaniard's buffering adaptation was set to be the *only* homage developed by somebody who had played under the main man himself! Well, this should be good ...

Almost *inevitably*, his plans worked better than anybody could have ever dreamed of when Guardiola walked in, and even more so considering how haphazardly he'd approached Rijkaard's squad. What am I talking about? Well, Guardiola's entire policy had centred upon proliferating the talents emerging from *La Masia*, and basically ousting many of the larger profiles who'd claimed a space under a Rijkaard as a consequence.

To prove the point, here's a brief list of some of the big names he sold over the next two-three years:

- o   Deco;
- o   Gianluca Zambrotta;
- o   Giovani dos Santos;
- o   Edmílson;
- o   Oleguer Presas ...
- o   *Samuel Eto'o* and;
- o   *Ronal-* ... *-dinho*!

And in their place, came a whole host of fresh-faced graduates, namely: Sergio Busquets, Xavi Hernández, Andrés Iniesta and some Argentine 'wonderkid' called Lionel Messi.

Beginning with Busquets, the gangly-looking deep-lying midfielder is stationed the furthest away from the attacking export of the quartet. His game, much like the manager during his time, was to calm things down at the back and get the ball rolling in the right direction; which usually meant fobbing the ball off to Xavi or Iniesta ahead of him.

When the ball was with Xavi, he too preferred to keep things simple. In my opinion, he was an equally as talented passer as Busquets, though his low centre of gravity made him look more elusive and cuter than his teammate. On the other hand, Iniesta slightly beats these two as far as pure dribbling ability is concerned.

The ball was *his* to control, and whatever he commanded, the object understood and set off in order to please its master. He even popped up with the odd key goal here and there as well, which is nice. But then again, he didn't really have to worry about scoring goals, did he?

Right, so what have we considered so far?

We've looked at the most *influential* player ever in Johan Cruyff, the most *naturally gifted* goal-scorer of all time in Ronaldo, and the most *complete* striker in Thierry Henry. So, using this same form of questioning, I suppose we have to say that Lionel Messi, just *is* the most naturally gifted *overall* footballer to have ever played the game.

And I know you want me to do that almighty Cristiano Ronaldo vs Lionel Messi comparison, but quite frankly it's redundant. Their approaches are very different, Ronaldo played in different leagues, Messi isn't as physical, Ronaldo isn't as agile etc, and comparing them tends to detract from their own personal achievements. Instead, let's just admit that Lionel Messi is a God among footballing laymen, and move on …

When adopting Pep's new Total Football alteration (hereafter referred to as *tiki taka* – supposedly a phonetic description for how quick his team's inter-play was), the mentioned players were the operating causes behind the esteem adorned by this Barcelona side. Of course, there were highly talented players all over the park, such as Carles Puyol, Víctor Valdés and even Thierry Henry who wormed his way out of a struggling Arsenal team. But the Busquets, Xavi, Iniesta and Messi four-way were in a league of their own.

As a microcosm, the play begins with Busquets, onto Xavi, a little foreplay teamwork with Iniesta before Messi arrives at the point of climax. As a macrocosm, you get a treble-winning season in 2008/09, a dominating string of 6-2 and 5-0 triumphs over Real Madrid, and even an unprecedented domination at the 2010 Ballon D'Or awards - where the bronze, silver and gold awards were all earned by *La Masia* products.

Oh yeah, and there was even a World Cup in 2010 (located in Johannesburg, South Africa), where Iniesta himself scored the winning goal in the final for Spain against the Netherlands. And yes, the coincidence isn't lost on me – a player moulded under his manager's adoption of the Total Football style, had gone on to defeat the very nation from which the creation was born. Brilliant stuff, this 'linking things up' malarkey, isn't it?

In a mere *two seasons*, let me say that again, *two … seasons*, Pep Guardiola had completely changed the trajectory, vision and image of FC Barcelona.

It was a Ferguson-like 'relying on youth' empire which brought Cruyff and Michels' philosophies into the twenty-*second* century - never mind the twenty-first. It was simply breath-taking. And with that settled, I wonder how Real Madrid were faring in their shadow …

~ 20 ~

'PLEASE … I CAN CHANGE!'
Florentino's Second Chance

Whether they wanted to or not, Madrid had to admit that they'd fallen well behind their domestic rivals. Not only were Real lacking in a man-to-man comparison with them, but their enemies had *also* established a longer-term vision predicated on an innovative style and a policy which lessened their reliance on the transfer market; an absolute mountain to climb for the already-under-fire Calderón.

Then, in the wake of Barca's brilliance, Calderón was derided in the press for: a perceived lack of ambition, his side's lacklustre form in the league, and the diminishing returns for his own transfer market activity, not to mention the mis-appointment of Bernd Schuster whose tenure failed to yield the rewards expected of his heralded playing reputation. All things considered, it's no wonder that the man resigned from his post in January 2009; almost three years to the date of succeeding Pérez, and roughly a year before the next scheduled election.

Naturally, Madrid called another emergency election to fill the gap left by the departing Calderón. And in stepped none other than Florentino Pérez in a bid to restore his dwindled reputation, this time, armed with an amended version of his original world-beater doctrine.

To the delight of those in white, where the previous era failed is where he sought to directly improve. In his various electoral addresses, he seemed to finally understand that buying the likes of Figo, Ronaldo, Zidane and Beckham, had marginalised his unconscious efforts to boost the *Castilla* academy.

Whereas now, he proposed the signing of players with a long-term future who would all work harmoniously within a tailored tactical system and, critically, he vowed to prioritise the squad's incumbent qualities rather than going on a shopping spree to immediately replace them before consulting the manager.

Having said that, it looked like a 'my mother was right about you!' situation when, upon his official return to presidency, his inaugural (is it inaugural when he's been there twice? I don't really know) mission statement was riddled with the prospect of signing Brazilian superstar Kaká.

Ricardo Izecson dos Santos Leite, mercifully nicknamed as 'Kaká', was a central attacking midfielder of … 'galactic' proportions. Signing initially with A.C. Milan after making a name for himself back home with São Paolo, the graceful playmaker had stormed his way to the 2007 Ballon D'Or award with a rough one-in-two goal contributions to games ratio in Italy. So, on the face of it, he's about as typical an 'original' Pérez signing as it gets, though there seems to be a deeper reasoning this time if you're willing to look for one.

No doubt, signing the game's most recent 'World Player of the Year' was a monumental statement of intent, as is breaking the world transfer record to make the deal happen. But more poignantly, Kaká's own line-breaking approach to his position enabled him to fit into a multitude of styles; without altogether seeking to distort the balance of the midfield. Also, he still had a few prime years ahead of him by joining at the age of 26, and his naturally non-egotistical personality permeated much of his globe-topping aura. So, when we look at things in this way, his signing represented: versatility, longevity and non-egotism – some of the things which played into the detriment of those before him.

Unfortunately for Kaká, a culmination of injuries and a resulting lack of confidence led to a relatively underwhelming return for the ex-Ballon-D'or winner Granted, an average of a goal in every four games is not bad at all from a central attacking midfielder, but it wasn't the yield expected from a transaction as committed as this. Though fortunately for Real Madrid, the man they signed ten days after Kaká didn't know the meaning of 'under-delivering'.

***

As a die-hard Manchester United fan, I unconditionally *adore* Cristiano Ronaldo, and I personally hold an even greater respect for how he approaches his profession. And by the time Real Madrid had sorted themselves out under a 'changed' president, Ronaldo had become the perfect person to drive home *Los Blancos*' new journey under him. Again, Madrid committed a rather princely sum for his services, though it did very little to weigh negatively upon Ronaldo's impact at the Bernabéu.

On top of being an outstanding football player, he was a hard-worker, dedicated to the club, versatile across the front-line and a relentless goal-scorer. And better still, he had a very good crop of players to work with at Madrid already, who were all geared to a system in which he could thrive; where Barcelona's motive was to pass around you and exhaust your confidence, Real Madrid would simply run through you and bruise your ego on their way out. Perfect for someone as direct as Cristiano.

Before we look deeper into the squad, I suppose we ought to reference the more notable omissions from the team's books; those which made way for Ronaldo's eventual long-term colleagues. Firstly, it wouldn't make much sense if the bright and bubbly Cristiano was immediately disgruntled upon waltzing into the Bernabéu dressing room, and a sure-fire way of preventing this is to move on anybody with whom he had already developed a tense relationship. Off you go, Ruud.

Considering their past quarrels, it's heart-warming to see that the wonders of time appear to have worked their magic here, and that they're both able to concede the undoubtable qualities in the other. Though back when the flames still roared, van Nistelrooy's criticism of the fuddy-duddy style of Ronaldo at Manchester United, was as pungent as ever when they were reacquainted in Spain.

However, fortunately for the both of them, the Dutchman understood that his career was maturing beyond Pérez' new vision, and couldn't find a reason to stir up any unnecessary drama with Cristiano at centre-stage; before swiftly seeking a 'Bosman' move to Hamburger SV in

Germany to officially end the beef - all's well that ends well, I guess.

After Ruud, Real purged themselves clean of a lacklustre Klaas-Jan Huntelaar to A.C. Milan and an injury-prone Arjen Robben to FC Bayern Munich – thus, freeing up Robben's right-wing position for Cristiano himself, and Huntelaar's centre-forward role for somebody who best complemented Ronaldo's style. And in search for his ideal partner, Pérez would've been stupid if he hadn't taken a leaf of inspiration from the winger's time in Manchester.

> "The power of Wayne Rooney is his **mentality** and **strength** … and he **never stops**"
>
> – Cristiano Ronaldo

Whenever Rooney was powering forward with the ball at his feet, the broad strides of Ronaldo were following him to his left, and whenever Cristiano himself burst down the throw-in line, Wayne would set-to in earnest to support him. Together, they were frankly unstoppable, and had spear-headed much of United's domestic 'three-peat' and UEFA Champions League success during this period.

Realising the importance of this partnership to bringing the best out of 'Ronnie', the logical choice would be to launch an approach for Rooney himself to pick up where they left off. Though, I doubt even the Real Madrid president was brave enough to risk Ferguson's wrath by wiring across an official bid.

Instead, word soon spread of a broad, stocky, young forward by the name of Karim Benzema out of French club, Lyon, and the deal arranged to bring him across had boosted

Madrid's summer spend over that €200 million mark. But, ignoring the financial implications behind 'just another *Galactico* spending spree', these deals were far more considered and tailored than his first era ever dreamed of being.

And, rightly sensing that he was going in the right direction, he pushed on with his wish list which now centred upon somebody with the ability to control his midfield. Enter, Liverpool's Xabi Alonso

Don't get me wrong, my love of Manchester United is of a religious disposition, therefore Liverpool should represent the antithesis of everything that I believe in. But above all else, I'm a football purist, and have to resign my personal biases in favour of noticing true quality on the pitch. So yes, I have to say, even before Alonso proved to be a true Adonis among disciples in Madrid, he was astonishingly good at Anfield, and managed to stand out in what was an already-commendable Reds selection.

His vision was impeccable, he possessed a wonderfully powerful strike and this all-consuming aura of 'don't worry, we got this' which assured many of his teammates. And as Real searched far and wide for that midfield general to organise their inner trio, whilst picking out the perfect pass to the wings to assert their game plan, there really was nobody better available to them than Xabi Alonso. A truly great buy, and the ideal interlude before blueprinting some much-needed renovations for the back line.

With the departing Fabio Cannavaro on a one-way ticket back home to Juventus, his unwavering professionalism and experience seemed to wear off well on the developing Sergio Ramos and Pepe, who were able to display signals of the Italian's intelligence and game-reading ability when affixing themselves at the heart of Madrid's defence over the coming decades.

The right-back position would prove to be the biggest headache for a while, but it was a situation solved by the re-signing of Dani Carvajal from Bayer Leverkusen over a year later, and his opposite number on the left-flank was equally as sorted by some promising Brazilian from Campeonato Brasileiro outfit, Fluminense.

An immensely hard worker, very talented on the ball, and atypically mature in his decision-making in the final third; Marcelo soon flourished into an all-round wonderful left-back throughout his term in Madrid (which is still ongoing). Moreover, given that he was often deployed on the same side as Ronaldo, the pair soon struck up an instinctive partnership once they understood each other's game; where they knew exactly what to expect from one-another to ensure that the team wasn't overawed on their side, and proved an essential pairing whenever *Los Blancos* launched forward.

Typically playing in a 4-3-3 formation, Real Madrid's midfield were also beginning to move into an era of balance previously overlooked by the initial *Galactico* period.

Fernando Gago and Lassana Diarra did their best to assume that fabled 'Makélélé' role, but were outshone by a more consistent Mahamadou Diarra (no relation to Lass, I'm told). Though perhaps not as agile as the man who gave his role its name, he was equally as intelligent at reading the game and if not more forceful in winning possession back. Sure, he might have got a few more cautions in the process than what would have otherwise been advisable, but it's nice for the fans to see one of their own fighting the good fight for them.

In front of him, passage of play often moved to newcomer Alonso, and his senior partner in a more advanced midfield position whenever Kaká was ruled out - like Guti or Raúl. Options on top of options. And having *all of this* as the foundation for an attack including Ronaldo and a fresh-faced Gonzalo Higuaín, then you have the makings of a squad that can more than hold their own against Pep's boys.

A successful first season ended with Real Madrid scooping up the *La Liga* and *Copa Del Rey* titles away from Catalunya, and the 2010 FIFA World Cup gave cause for Pérez to pinpoint a few more promising young talents to reaffirm his changed ways.

For a club like them, the World Cup has historically presented itself as the ideal opportunity to scout and acquire the competition's biggest stars - like a Ronaldo or Zidane. But this was a new Real Madrid, a *sensible* Real Madrid. So, by all means, sign the competition's best performing player if that's what the situation dictates that you should do, but first make sure that they fit the new brief set out by the club.

Remember: talented, hungry and determined.

Forever remembered for its ghastly 'vuvuzela' soundtrack and wayward Jabulani football, the football on offer here was rather *unpredictable*. To illustrate the point, it was a year when a certain Diego Forlán rose to South American stardom as he guided his Uruguayan squad to a semi-final place, Ghana became everyone's second-favourite nation as the most successful African club of all time when they reached the quarters, and Luis Suárez became Public Enemy #1 for deplorably thwarting Ghana from an unprecedented semi-final spot.

Adding to this, and in spite of Spain remaining consistent enough to win the whole competition as expected before it kicked off, a youthful Germany side were attracting more than the odd favourable glance in their direction. In fact, all eyes were on them in the lead up to a tumultuous 4-1 win against England in the quarter final. The Lions' heaviest ever defeat at a World Cup competition.

> "Of all the things I have done, the goal I didn't score is what I get asked about most!"
>
> – Frank Lampard

Undoubtedly one of the ignition points for the introduction of technology in football, the game was on a knife-edge when Frank Lampard's off-the-bar looping volley was ludicrously ignored for 'not crossing the line'.

Right up until this innovative invention called a 'replay' managed to reveal that the ball had quite obviously voyaged beyond the goal line by roughly four feet - much to the disgust of *BBC* commentator Mark Lawrenson; whose tirade towards disgraced *FIFA* president Sepp Blatter has proved a welcome distraction for those England fans who had to watch their side get dismantled by a simply sprightlier and hungrier Germany team.

At the heart of it all, the Germans were blessed with a myriad of starlets from back to front, which England's ageing squad were ill-equipped to compete with. Explicitly, Manuel Neuer in goal, Sami Khedira and Mesut Özil in midfield, and a pimple-faced Thomas Müller at the tip. And though they were presented as this centre of German excellence who were the pride of their own homegrown clubs, they soon attracted unignorable attention from further afield. Not least from Real Madrid.

Out of the four, neither Neuer or Müller proved realistic and/or necessary acquisitions for *Los Blancos*, but the same couldn't be said for their midfield teammates. Beginning with Khedira, he was an ideal mix between the two roles which take on that defensive midfield position - combative yet a visionary, and he proved to be an easy-enough acquisition from Werder Bremen whose standing in the Bundesliga proved a pivotal aspect to Khedira's decision to leave.

Özil was a 'flashier' signing by comparison whom adopted a similar role to Kaká in the advanced playmaker role. By contrast to the Brazilian, he wasn't anywhere near as established, nor as goal-oriented, but he presented a cute, nimble alternative whenever the game needed a bit of 'pizazz'. He was also far more assist-based than anybody else on Real's books which is even more important considering the mindset of their front line. Without hesitation, a €15 million bid was accepted by FC Schalke 04 for their product, and Mesut soon became a prime creative outlet for his new side in the years to come.

Together, they were two very good deals for two very special young men, and had helped to set the scene for the next half-decade's worth of unprecedented feats achieved by Real Madrid, both on the pitch and in their recruitment. They managed another *Copa Del Rey* win the season after the World Cup (against Barcelona, no less!), a chart-topping 32nd ever *La Liga* triumph and the heralded *La Decima* win - a term coined for their tenth ever UEFA Champions League success; the most of any European side to date.

During this time, they changed managers from Manuel Pellegrini, to José Mourinho, to Carlo Ancelotti who between them, had managed to attract Ángel Di María, Toni Kroos and Gareth Bale to the team - all over boosting the squad's quality which allowed Cristiano to surpass Ferenc Puskás as Madrid's all-time leading goal-scorer, as well as breaking the record for the most goals scored by an individual with *sixty* in the 2011-12 season.

You have to give credit where it's due …

During the president's second attempt, Real Madrid had unequivocally developed one of the greatest and most well-rounded outfits ever assembled in the history of the game; especially commendable when you consider that a lot of their squad was derived from the market and not a fortuitous influx of academy grads.

So, much like how Ferguson had re-developed a title-winning squad having lost his way in the eye of that 'big signing' storm at Manchester United, Pérez had done something similar with Real Madrid; where the greater spend accounted for both how good Barcelona were and the fact that he couldn't benefit from having someone like Sir Alex Ferguson to rely on.

In fact, they were *so* successful, that some of the high-profile sales and omissions from this era were largely forgotten. For example, to sell Raúl would have been unthinkable at one point, and yet he was let go on a Bosman. Fabio Cannavaro - the talismanic leader of the dressing room - met a similar fate after being boomeranged back to Italy and, even more notably given his relative potential, a promising young Brazilian was sold onto England for another project that was unravelling over there.

I wonder how this one would go …

~ 21 ~

'A GUIDE FOR WHAT *NOT* TO DO'

The Cautionary Tales of Blackburn Rovers, Newcastle United and Queens Park Rangers

The concept of a financial takeover is nothing new. Sometimes, it's the wholesome case of a local businessperson taking the plunge to bring their homegrown club into a brighter horizon. Other times, it's a group of investors looking to add a football club to their growing commercial portfolio. Either way, you'd better get your ideas straight before you consider it.

One of the first of these stories from the Premier League era is that of Jack Walker; a bubbly senior who fobbed off his metalworks empire proceeds into the ailing financial deck for Blackburn Rovers Football Club. Where, even prior to assuming full operational leadership in 1991, his intentions were clear: balance the books, get them out of the Second Division, challenge the new 'Premier League' elite and rise to the top. He began by selling his dream to prospective manager Kenny Dalglish, who took to Walker's vision with aplomb. And as a legendary striker in his heyday, he started things off by seeking a younger version of himself to lead his brigade; eventually settling upon a young Geordie lad in Southampton who had caught his eye. Alan … *something*?

The story goes that, while playing in a number of county and district sides in Newcastle, a scout at Southampton picked up on the talents of Alan Shearer. And after persuading the young kid and his family to have him travel down and live on the south coast, he matured quickly enough to earn a first team place within a year of joining the Saints. Thereafter, a mixture of first team appearances, links with the England squad and his untapped potential contributed to Shearer's inflated £3.5million price tag.

Considering his pedigree, this does seem like an outlandish figure for the time, though Blackburn weren't the only ones who weren't totally put off by it. So, it's a good thing that Walker was rich, and possessed a far more liquid portfolio than that of his nearest competitors.

In case you haven't been privy to an Alan Shearer punditry clip for more than five minutes, then you may not have lasted long enough to hear about his two failed moves to Manchester United. Focusing on the first, United's float on the Stock Exchange had ironically frozen much of their immediate funding for the transfer; leading them to having to borrow the money in order to finance the deal.

All the while, Walker (armed with an immediate payment) arranged a meeting between Shearer and Dalglish to pass the owner's vision onto the forward. It worked a treat, United couldn't keep up, and Shearer embarked on his hopeful journey with Blackburn Rovers. Then, after having looked on in envy as United stomped toward the first set of

Premier League titles, Walker reacted by purchasing a strike partner for Shearer in a bid to double-up on their attacking output. Chris Sutton was his man off the back of a strong season with Norwich City (these really were different times), and the 'SAS' partnership flourished in a very simple, yet highly efficient Rovers side.

With seasoned professionals like Tim Flowers, Colin Hendry and Tim Sherwood forming the spine of the team, wingers Stuart Ripley and Jason Wilcox were best suited towards the styles favoured by the two big lumps up front; whose 'I can't be arsed to run, so put in a good cross' instruction made way for a nail-biting title win at the end of the 1995/96 season.

"I'd grown up in the Highlands kicking a scrunched-up Coke can around the back yard. Now, I was a *Premier League winner*. Where I was from, **it was unheard of**."

– Colin Hendry

Away from the detail that a single United goal stood between failure and success, the fact of the matter is that this plucky, unassuming Northerner had managed to plunge his millions into a football project which *actually* worked. Blackburn Rovers were Premier … League … Champions.

Look where they are in the EFL setup right now, and imagine them winning the top division in three seasons. Bit unreasonable, right? But it happened … IRL. 'Though if you're wondering what else they achieved after this, then you're wasting your time. Because for all the ambition Walker had shown to get to this point, his lack of long-term vision hindered any further progression for Rovers once he'd reached here.

By re-familiarising yourselves on the reasons for why Walker purchased them, you begin to understand why Blackburn's joys were short-lived. In the simplest of terms, he wanted to 'stick it' to the big wigs of the league, and have his beloved club become the best team in the land by the end of the season. But football doesn't end there. We repeat this whole 'my team's better than your team' routine year after year. It's a demanding and cruel mistress which will run you over if you're unable to keep up in the race. And lo and behind, Blackburn Rovers were never to replicate the success of the 1994/95 season, and Walker was sadly unable to donate as much time and effort to stabilise the club as his health deteriorated - ultimately leading to the good man's death from cancer in the year 2000, aged 71.

Looking back, Walker's short tale is still a very uplifting one. A young man who worked very hard, made a fortune and invested his earnings into making his city happy. Though I fear that his short-sighted outlook of becoming a football owner has shrouded his legacy in a way that it never deserved to be.

Moving on from Blackburn, we travel up to Newcastle United and the summer of 2007, where a new reign was set to take shape at St. James' Park. Succeeding a much beloved representative in Freddy Shepherd (Bobby Robson sacking aside ... yes ... *him again*!), Magpies from around the world were made to chirp to the tune of retail giant Mike Ashley.

Now, in the context of the Premier League as a whole, Newcastle were and remain to be a fine institution in English Football. They are responsible for a number of key moments throughout the competition's existence and, but for an allergy to defending, may have even been etched into the trophy itself early on in the '90s; something I'm sure their manager Kevin Keegan would've 'loved' to have achieved.

And speak of the devil, 'King Kev' just so happened to be the front-runner to return to the manager's job when Mike Ashley took over – practically a decade on from when he left the first time. So, would lightning strike twice for the honorary Geordie? Would Keegan finally be able to go one further than he had managed to go before? No. He would not.

From what I can gather from Keegan's refreshingly honest autobiography, Ashley was a very stand-offish owner from the get-go. Not dissimilar from your average conglomerate owner, his money would be used to fuel the companies within his portfolio while simultaneously employing people to whom he can delegate responsibility. Of course, there isn't much *wrong* with this approach, but this only works well provided that you employ the right people in the right positions. And did he employ the right people? No. He did not.

As mentioned, he started quite well by persuading Keegan to come back, but if only he'd managed to install a suitably experienced background team which befitted his reputation, then things might have *actually* turned out 'alreet' for his Newcastle reign. But instead, Ashley proved to be naive in his recruitment, unaware of the requirements needed to take up a hands-on role behind Keegan, and he seemingly opted to employ whoever won him over; as opposed to who was best suited for the job at hand. And if we're being completely honest here, even *considering* a man like Derek Llambias as the club's new 'Managing Director' is testament to that, let alone hiring the fella. The first of many poor decisions from the new owner.

According to Keegan, it is believed that the velvet-tongued Llambias wormed his way into St. James' Park by focusing on his South American heritage - presenting himself as the key middleperson between the Magpies and the most sought-after talent from over the Pacific. But, as the manager suspected, there was very little evidence beyond his mother tongue to back this up, and at the very most, it was a mere cloak of charm and false promises to obtain a role he wasn't suitable for; a feature which was cruelly evidenced by an inexplicable 2008 summer window for the Magpies fans.

Acting as 'Managing Director', Llambias had reportedly assumed much of Newcastle's transfer responsibilities from this time, and used this window as the ideal opportunity to showcase to his employer (Ashley) the fruits of his employment … even if it wasn't authorised by the manager (Keegan)- you know, the guy who's in charge of *working with whoever he brings in*. Looking from afar, it seems as though Llambias was more concerned with proving his non-existent worth to the United hierarchy than he was for working directly for the benefit of Newcastle United, and I presume that Mr. Keegan shares this opinion.

Tensions soon grew into vocal disdain once Keegan called into question Llambias' intentions behind being linked with a number of sub-par Latinx players in 2008.

And as it turned out, the gaffer had every right to be sceptical, with it later being divulged that Llambias had attempted to broker a 'you scratch my back, I'll scratch yours' relationship with some of the region's most successful and well-connected agents / middle-men.

In theory, it presents an opportunity to succumb to a short-term loss under the promise of a long-term gain. In reality, it's insanely risky, highly unethical and almost equally as immoral as the crime which convicted George Graham over a decade earlier at Arsenal. So, needless to say, Keegan's patience was wearing almightily thin watching all this unfold.

This summer saw the arrival of four players into St. James' Park, each bringing a starkly comparable reception from their new manager - with very few of them being positive. But, before we get onto the more problematic ones, let's start with a couple of the brighter signings. And frankly, they don't get much brighter than the very tidy £5 million deal for winger, Jonás Gutiérrez.

Regardless of football orientation, you simply have to respect this Argentinian pony-tailed beauty. On matchday, he was a tireless workhorse who gave his all for the crowd in attendance, and the man wasn't too bad to watch on the ball either. He could dribble, had a decent shot on him, probably wouldn't set the world alight but a cheeky little signing, nonetheless. What's more, he became somewhat of a cult hero during his six-year stint on Tyneside, before a testicular cancer diagnosis in 2014 halted his career in its tracks.

Upon realising that his condition was malignant, a thankfully successful procedure was performed before Gutiérrez was discharged in early 2015. And instead of listening to his doctor's orders to pack everything in and gear up for an early retirement, he instead chose to pay an emotional show of respect to the Newcastle crowd in a short, yet beautiful, substitute appearance at Anfield in April later that year.

An altogether wholesome ending to a great story for Jonás Gutiérrez and, whatever he's doing now, I hope he's doing it with that same smile on his face for which his professional career has been guided by. Ah! That was a nice story, wasn't it? Yeah … now it's time for the not-so nice. Remaining on the sunnier shores of Western Europe, the remainder of Newcastle's purchases were a mixed bag, beginning with an ambitious, though largely unwelcome move to bring defensive midfielder Fabricio Coloccini to the club; for twice as much money as was required to secure Gutiérrez.

Of course, if you're a *Football Manager* fan from this time, then this is a great signing for any topflight club at the time - he was supposedly quick, intelligent, experienced and would presumably provide some steel and flair to Newcastle's shallower midfield line.

However, his talent was misused greatly while in the Premier League. He played the majority of the time in defensive midfield while contracted to Deportivo in Spain, and his transition into a no-nonsense centre-back didn't pan out so well in the Toon. Only further highlighted by the fact that his elevated fee could've been better placed in Newcastle's other problem areas. Particularly in attack. But … don't worry … because … erm … Llambias had … erm … *thought of that?*

Every player has their level, and unless they can call upon their dedication to bettering their craft, the majority of ballers will assume the station to which their ability is assigned. This isn't an issue provided that they align with a club who matches their quality, but a serious problem arises when they are clearly inept for the club they're employed by. And unfortunately, we have a sizeable problem here when assessing Ignacio González' and Xisco's time in black and white.

Neither signing (despite some significant financial commitment) managed to make a single start in their maiden season under Keegan — which could have been as much reflective of either's innate lack of quality, as for the manager's personal antipathy for the man who authorised their deals. Nevertheless, and more significantly, arrangements like these had unequivocally undermined Keegan's status as Newcastle United manager.

> "It's my opinion that a manager must have the right to manage and that **clubs should not impose upon any manager any player that he *does not want*.**"
>
> – Kevin Keegan

To this day, he remains their most vocal, outwardly passionate and daring manager since the Premier League began, and I'd be surprised to see somebody waltz in and do a better job than he did. Yet, Ashley didn't appreciate this and was made to pay the price, particularly once a botched James Milner contract negotiation (with new Sporting Director, Dennis Wise) had forced the winger out the door … with Keegan following closely behind. All in all, the new owner had a very strong manager at his disposal, and his leadership (or lack thereof), had made his position completely untenable; and this had rather set the tone for Ashley's entire reign in the North East.

But at least he's the last case study we have of an impulsive owner who doesn't know anything about running a football club tarnishing a club's name, right? … oh wait, there's *another one*? I don't think I have time for this …

I'm aware that this is a football-based book, however one of my other favourite sports within which to indulge is Formula One. It's an industry filled with adrenaline, risk, controversy, an enormous amount of wealth and a fancy to be fanciful. I understand that it's not everyone's cup of tea, but personally, I deem it to be one of the most demanding, specific and impressive sporting products ever created. And whether it be for better or worse, two of their most famous patrons in recent years have been Bernie Ecclestone and Flavio Briatore.

While Ecclestone was nearer to the head of the organisation as a whole, Briatore cut his teeth working his way up to be the team principal of Benetton racing. As such, he would be the person who ultimately: decides the racing strategy, employs the team beneath him, has final say on the selected drivers and is at the forefront of the media's attention when things go wrong … which typically happens on any given race weekend unless you're a Mercedes or Ferrari.

He then went on to manage Renault in 2000; where a certain Jenson Button has since had a fair few things to say about his principal's troublesome management technique. Apparently, the Italian was never one to mince his words when dishing out his frequent criticism of his brigade, and it's no wonder that he ruffled a few feathers in their aftermaths. Nevertheless, both he and Ecclestone were major forces within the industry and were never afraid to innovate and dare to go where very others would.

Yet, even by their exhausting standards, combining forces outside of their F1 comfort zones to take over a struggling English Second Division side was an almightily diverse undertaking.

On the other hand, if you were a Queen's Park Rangers ('Q.P.R.') fan in 2007, then this was a more than welcome announcement. Not too dissimilar from the cloud surrounding Newcastle when Mike Ashley took over, the

West London club were craving some loving attention in order to stay afloat, and the doors were left ajar for anybody with enough wealth to save the club from the abyss - regardless of their background or ulterior interests.

Then, like a stormy cloud to a parched tree, a Monaco consortium alongside Briatore and Ecclestone came billowing by; promising to bring the club into brighter pastures with their now-infamous 'Four-Year Plan' – search these very words into *Amazon Prime Video*, and you're in for some light evening entertainment, I assure you.

The strategically arranged fly-on-the-wall documentary features Briatore's controversial banishment from Formula One, which led to the longing for another project. Therefore, he centred upon turning around the fortunes of Queen's Park Rangers under the advice of agent-cum-sporting director, Gianni Paladini, and the hands-on impact from the club's amiable chairman, Amit Bhatia. Together, their intentions were as daring as they were clear - to take Q.P.R. from their mid-table EFL Championship standing, into the Premier League within four years from taking over.

> "It is completely wrong to compare Q.P.R. with Chelsea. We want to do it **our way**"
>
> – Flavio Briatore

However, unfortunately for Briatore, the hangover of his dismissal from F1 had rattled a few nerves over at the FA; who were concerned as to whether or not his indiscretions in motorsport would carry over in his new role at Rangers. Not to mention some of the applicable imprudence which may call his entire new venture into question. So, while they did their homework before inevitably readying their case for his exile, Briatore still had a decent chunk of his proposed four-year programme to leave an indelible mark upon his club. Now that I've said it aloud, I don't think 'mark' is the correct word to use here … let's go for 'smudge' instead. More appropriate.

In typically brash fashion, the new owner did away with many of the club's managers in any of their early signs of discontent. He dismissed incumbent Iain Dowie before their first season kicked off, mutually terminated the deal with Paolo Sousa after a media-related bust-up concerning top goal-scorer Dexter Blackstock, said 'hello' as quickly as 'goodbye' to both Jim Magilton and Paul Hart once results started to flip, until finally making good of that dastardly 'plan' with Neil Warnock at the helm by the end of the 2010/11 season.

By which point, Briatore was largely out of the picture and Bhatia more front-and-centre than before. And with synergy achieved between ownership and management, the 'R's were crowned Premier League newcomers on the final year of the consortium's forecast. But, much like with Jack Walker's tenure at Blackburn, they didn't look like they knew what was supposed to happen next.

To make matters worse, much of the sustainability that went into their promotion push was largely forgotten atop the perch they wanted to climb. Soon, they became far too caught up with focusing their new-found wealth onto bringing in new players, that little attention was paid to establishing a steadier foundation to prop up the club's long-term run. They also developed the sort of 'slap-dash' bunch of squad members which emphasised their unclear recruitment directive. The Championship-winning season saw the arrivals of the likes of Jamie Mackie and Ishmael

Miller (on loan) - young, hungry recruits who were eager to prove themselves and be a part of the project which earned their way into the Premier League. But once they got there, the club looked to have lost that focus on youth – instead agreeing to the odd overpayment here or there to bring in experienced Premier League players who weren't up for the expected relegation scrap which ensued at the end of their first season in the topflight.

Shaun Wright-Phillips was well past his best when he stepped up to the plate, and Djibril Cissé was as effective as he was injury prone. And as far as Kieron Dyer and Joey Barton were concerned, please refer back to my previous assessments … in that order. Deals like these were a microcosm of what came to be in Rangers' time in the English Premier League, which didn't last nearly as long as it could have done, had they acted more sensibly.

They just about escaped relegation the first time round before the appointment of Mark Hughes set their fate in line. Though they managed to bring in Loïc Rémy who enjoyed a brilliant spell in London from Marseille, the acquisitions of Ji-Sung Park (fantastic, though passed his prime), Rio Ferdinand (ditto) and Christopher Samba (kind of) did nothing but expand their financial obligation, and relieve their squad of the rigour required to stay in the league.

They'd risen high, fallen harder and nowadays, they'd be lucky to spend in excess of £2million on any player, while their training ground and academic facilities are even more worse for wear – neither of which should ever have been the case given how much of a privileged position they were in to prevent it.

***

So overall, in Blackburn, Newcastle and Queen's Park Rangers, we have three major league examples of what not to do when taking over a football club.

Therefore, anybody with a modicum of common sense would approach their own venture a lot more sensibly in light of cautionary tales like these. Especially where a lot of ambition and money is at play. Manchester City; over to you!

~ 22 ~

'WATCH AND LEARN'
Sheikh Mansour's Premier League Project

In an ideal world; where the skies are always blue, our oceans are beautifully preserved and Rihanna *actually* follows up on that 'new album' promise, the best way for a new owner to enter the fray would be to amalgamate the approaches of Martin Edwards' United and Abramovich's Chelsea. Essentially, to combine the financial power of the latter with the commercial acuity of the former.

And to start things off, I assume very few were concerned with the monetary aspect once a certain Sheikh Mansour showed interest in purchasing Manchester City.

After years of laying comfortably under the red shadow of United, the City faithful were bestowed with the modesty that befalls any set of fans that were simply happy to be where they were. And when word began to spread that an Abu Dhabi conglomerate was looking to add City to their collection in 2008, nobody really knew what to think ... except that it *might* be better than what they were experiencing under Thaksin Shinawatra, whose financial mismanagement of the club left them pretty much 'owner-less' but for the Middle Eastern interest.

So, in one fell swoop, the club went from nearly dissolving altogether to potentially having access to one of the most enviable financial portfolios ever presented to a sporting franchise, though after the Sheikh's representatives had provided proof of funds to substantiate their superior's interest, the Abu Dhabi Group required a requited level of commitment from City themselves, before officially signing off on the ownership papers. Even by doing this, it proved that the club had a rather conscientious bidder at the table, and the East Manchester club were willing to do everything in their power to appease their saviour. And they'd better get cracking, because the task at hand wasn't an easy one.

As he didn't want his money to be underappreciated during his reign, he asked the club to self-finance a big-name signing before he officially took over; which would (in theory) prove to him that their incumbent staff were 'worthy' enough of putting his money to good use once things fell into line. A sort of 'dance for me, and I shall reward thee' demand.

The responsibility of sourcing and attracting this 'big' signing fell upon the restless shoulders of Manchester City chief executive, Garry Cook, who fully appreciated the conditions within which his little club had found themselves in. The search was as expansive as was humanly possible to find a Mansour-appropriate signature, with the Sky Blues limited by nothing more than their imagination to secure their archetypal headline-grabber.

Atop their wish list was Kaká, though as we know, the Brazilian rebuffed any interest from Manchester to experience life in Madrid. In fact, there was even suggestion that the playmaker's representatives had flirted with City in order to use their interest in a negotiation battle with the Spanish giants to achieve their asking price. Either way, a lot of time was wasted, and it was back to the drawing board for Cook and his crew.

A mooted discussion reportedly took place with Chelsea captain, John Terry, though the centre-back's allegiance to the Blues didn't allow their interest to extend beyond the post office of Stamford Bridge. By contrast, a much more advanced situation concerned Tottenham Hotspur and their lackadaisical marksman, Dimitar Berbatov; whose two-year stint in North London drew plenty of plaudits from all over the Premier League.

No sooner had he joined Spurs as a relative little-known quantity from Bayer Leverkusen, had he established himself as a thoughtful and elegant target man worthy of his market value, and he proved vital to the Lilywhites' unlikely six-placed finish and FA Cup final showing in 2008. Plus, with his game being more unconventionally balanced in favour of assists over goals, he proved to have a more favourable arsenal of skills for the rest of the squad than your average selfish goal-getter.

So overall, he looked like a steady and long-*ish*-term proposition for Manchester City, especially when Spurs announced their willingness to part with him for £30 million - 'chump change' in the eyes of somebody like the Sheikh. And from the player's perspective, he was outwardly seeking a move to challenge for domestic and European honours, and was therefore all too happy to fly to Manchester to strike up a deal on Deadline Day. Though he must've gotten into the wrong taxi when leaving the airport; because it looked like he was on his way to Old Traff- ... oh, well this is awkward.

Admiring Berbatov's technical qualities from afar, his avantgarde methods hadn't gone unnoticed by those in red, and vocal interest from their 'noisy neighbours' only prompted Fergie to take action even quicker than he would've done without it. A bid was tabled, promises were made, and pictures of him being ushered around Old Trafford came as news to the public as it did to City. And with the deadline fast approaching, they couldn't afford another slip-up with their backup choice.

By this point, the rumour mill was in overdrive, and various names were mentioned, before an ounce validity was given to somebody who very few could imagine in a Sky-Blue shirt – and it just so happened to be a man whose arrival would directly correlate with that second galactic tenure going on in Spain.

As it happened, the president's return had reportedly disgruntled Brazilian trickster Robinho who (having established his place in the line-up under previous ownership) had assumed that his role would be marginalised against the incoming Cristiano Ronaldo. Therefore, sensing a future rotting away on the Bernabéu bench, he began to entertain a number of offers which came his way; of which there a were number of keen, serious candidates.

Whilst at work, Robinho was *very* exciting to watch. He was direct, skilful and had that extra bit of creativity to qualify as the 'marquee signing' that City craved. But much like with Berbatov, City were going to have to compete for his signature under a time constraint, this time from Abramovich's Chelsea. Both had put in £30 million + offers for the Brazilian and had met with his representatives to hash out personal terms before the transfer deadline passed. It would then be a case of the most alluring offer leading to his ultimate decision.

But for whatever reason, Robinho had decided that his representatives were best placed to decide upon his future without him, and he wasn't as aware of City's interest as he had been about Chelsea as the Blues had been linked with him long before an official bid was lodged. So, I suspect it came as a big surprise to him to learn that City had presented the most favourable terms, and that he wouldn't be travelling down to London after all.

Regardless, he was indeed presented as a Manchester City player on Deadline Day of the 2008 window and, but for an awkward slip of the tongue at his unveiling where the winger mistakenly confessed his gratitude at joining Chelsea, his signing for the Citizens was enough to convince their future owners that they were worthy of the investment - and the takeover documents were signed not too long afterwards.

Even to this day, I'm not sure if Robinho himself quite understands how pivotal his actions were into creating the Manchester City that we all appreciate today, because if we're being honest, his unveiling on the east half of Manchester was one of many dominos to fall.

However, with the winger's transfer coming in at the eleventh hour, much of City's new financial muscle would have to be flexed in next year's window, plus whatever was able to be concluded in the preceding winter period. And in a time which has become somewhat infamous for its difficulty for concluding permanent deals, City must be commended for attracting a number of notable names to set them up for a largely *glamorous* summer affair.

Starting between the sticks, they managed to sign a personal favourite of mine in Irish 'keeper Shay Given. By modern standards, he isn't the most graceful on the ball nor is he as physically imposing as you would expect for an elite stopper, but I challenge you to find me many others who match Given for his raw reflexive talents.

After him came the combative Nigel de Jong to marshal that equilibrium point in the midfield, and then Wayne Bridge to sure up their left-back berth. They even brought in Craig Bellamy to support Robinho in the attacking third, though they both really did need some additional support in and around them if they were ever going to have the impact that their talents warranted. Fast forward to the summer of 2009, and things were on the come-up for the sky-blue brigade.

Gareth Barry, Roque Santa Cruz and even Patrick Vieira were lured in by the City vision. But there was one particular signing of this window which signalled City's intent better than any other. A deal for which the audacity and brashness to make happen would become synonymous with their Premier League mission statement. And a player whose talent and prior allegiances would help to alleviate the new Manchester City up alongside the league's elite outfits. A player by the name of Carlos Tevez. The *ultimate* statement signing.

Enigmatic in his own right, the Argentine had become a fan's favourite during a two-year loan spell at Old Trafford. And having prolifically elbowed his way into Louis Saha's role as a 'pressing forward' in Fergie's setup, it was widely expected that United would be chomping at the bit to tie him down to a permanent deal before anybody could beat them to it.

He was a selfless team-player, a good goal-scorer and perhaps United's greatest South American import to date. Not to mention, that the supporters clearly wanted it to happen, and many of us were waiting in anticipation of the deal going through. Yet despite all of this, negotiations stalled, and the hard-working frontman became a stranger to all of us in red once again.

But perhaps it was down to a cultural fit?

According to his teammates, namely Louis Saha (as mentioned in a podcast with *MUTV*), Carlos kept himself to himself when outside of usual working hours. From the moment training was over, he was rarely ever seen socialising with the rest of the squad, and perhaps this arose a slight concern for the manager when it came to approving the purchase of a potential pariah within his close-knit ranks.

I am theorising here, but as a loanee, he could most likely 'get away' with coming in and 'doing a job' as that is the purpose of a loan signing, but permanently, getting on with your squad and being a part of the team's more all-encompassing lifestyle seems pivotal to success; and here's where his out-of-the-way tendencies may have played against him in the eyes of management.

But whatever the true reason, it's clear that the Devils' had acted hesitantly when procuring a long-term Tevez deal, and this had presented an opportunity for their neighbours to weigh in on the saga – with their own motives seeking to align with a man who was ready to renounce his United bond.

Finding a Common Enemy ...

With United being the top dogs in the Premier League at this time, and the Berbatov signing probably still stinging a little bit, what better way to pipe them down a peg, then by poaching one of their closest prospects? Football is a jealous game. A petulant game. And any opportunity to disgruntle a rival is often a popular one.

So here, Tevez was contractually obliged to see out his loan deal with Manchester United, though there was nothing tying him down to the red half once the loan expired. Thereafter, it became a simple case of whichever bidder could satisfy his 'parent' club's (West Ham United's) valuation to release him from his permanent contract. And once that was done, the power laid firmly at Tevez' feet to decide which of the presented offers looked most attractive to him

Eventually, when it came down to making that choice, it was a toss-up between an eager City bid and a responsive United one. And to him, the Devils' hesitance must've felt akin to being rejected by them. So, what do you do when someone rejects you? Well, if you're weak or desperate, you long for their touch and wait for the phone to ring. If you're Tevez, you realise your self-worth, watch *Bridget Jones*, re-assess your options and make an empowered decision.

Altogether, I can rest easy at night with the belief that Tevez went where he felt more *wanted*, and perhaps wouldn't have wound up on the East Side of Manchester but for United's stuttering negotiation technique. Either way, that wasn't going to stop City from milking the situation for all its worth.

The Carlos Tevez saga as a whole, had represented a lot more than simply *another* 'big-money signing'. Indeed, the required £40 million figure was a princely sum and worthy of recognition in its own right, but it was more the fact that this was concluded right on United's door-step - that a world-beater like Tevez had *directly* rejected a permanent transfer to Old Trafford in favour of being a part of the Abu Dhabi project on the opposite end of the city.

In making this move, City had beaten United at one of their own games, and were staking a claim for their project to attract far more acclaim than it had done up until this point. Not to mention their succeeding marketing campaign which only sought to drive the knife further into the spleens of those in red. If you're not sure what I'm referring to, then another cheeky *Google* search will cause a chuckle or two.

"Welcome to Manchester"

– Manchester City's Carlos Tevez

Whether you were a neutral football fan or the most cynical critic of City's revolution, you hadn't much choice but to stand and applaud the vulgarity of their new venture. And, considering their bottomless financial stash and proposed continuing transfer activity, it seemed as though the Tevez deal was to ignite a cataclysmic shift in favour of the Citizens; provided that their recruitment choices would be the correct ones to accompany their latest attraction.

And though they had acquired some much-needed Premier League experience over recent years, it wasn't enough for the club to challenge for domestic honours given the remaining strength of their rivals. Hence, City went for broke in the 2010/11 pre-season window, by attracting a number of foreign talents who were geared to directly catalyse their efforts to disturb the order of title challengers in front of them.

***

When tracing back through the modern chronicles of Manchester City, many will highlight Sergio Agüero's acquisition as the most pivotal of the Mansour era thus far. And frankly, acclaiming the club's all-time goal-scoring record is a pretty fair indicator for this honour. However, I personally have reason to assign that tagline to his diminutive partner in crime, David Silva. Not least because the timing of his £25 million deal was absolutely spot-on from both a tactical *and* business perspective for the club.

Originally contracted to Valencia in Spain, the club was being picked apart after a number of poor performances on home soil. Gone seemed to be the glory days of Santiago Cañizares, Roberto Ayala and Pablo Aimar, and their nouveau-youth-centric policy proved inescapably alluring to clubs looking to get their hands on a fledgling Spaniard for their own; particularly given their promoted notoriety under Pep at Barcelona and with the resulting Spanish national side.

City were no different and joined a long list of bidders looking to get their hands on somebody like David Silva, but had to bide their time after initially being quoted a £125million+ settlement for him and his strike partner David Villa, when an initial enquiry was launched for the pair of them in the summer of 2010.

Now, strictly speaking, Manchester City were in a position to cough up a price like this for the two of them if they felt inclined to do so. Sure, it may have pulsated a number of shockwaves through the sport, but it was technically possible for them to commit to that obscene level of expenditure. Though instead of bowing down to Valencia's demands and reaching an arrangement with them, they waited patiently in the wings to see what the next season would bring – with both of them creeping a year closer to the end of their current deals.

Then, by a stroke of good fortune, Valencia were unable to keep hold of David Villa who was soon on his way to the Camp Nou, and with a year's reflection guiding City's eyes away from Villa as their number one striking option (and onto Sergio Agüero), they could focus solely on obtaining a now-lonely and unsettled David Silva; which they managed to do for almost half the price required for Carlos Tevez. I suppose patience *can* be a virtue after all!

Upon arriving at the newly branded 'Etihad Stadium', David Silva quickly proved to be one of the most intelligent and elegant footballers ever attracted to the English Premier League. Never one to flirt with the media or overtly scream at his teammates for underperforming, he had adopted that advanced playmaker role made legend by a number of notable names in this book. And I'm sure City fans are dreading his impending date of retirement, as he's not somebody who is very easily replaceable.

Refreshingly, City also acknowledged the need to stabilise the likes of Silva via somebody in behind him in the midfield with a more robust skillset. Hence why the subsequent deal to bring Yaya Touré in from Barcelona stands on par with him as one of the most important deals made in the history of the football club; especially insofar as bringing future stars to play alongside him.

"Yaya was different. After we signed him, every top player began to see the possibilities at City. He was like a **Pied Piper**"

– Gary Cook

Linking up with his brother Kolo (who had incidentally moved across from Arsenal the season before), Yaya instantly settled into his new role at the Etihad. While at Barcelona, he fell out of favour for his style simply not adhering to that beautiful *tiki taka* mantra glorified by Pep, and he was subsequently put up for sale to any buyer who could make better use of his supposedly more abrasive and less aesthetic methods.

One man's trash became City's treasure, as they matched up Yaya Touré's box-to-box style nicely to the dynamism, physicality and speed of the Premier League. And, together with David Silva, the pair of them helped to completely transform the team's attacking threat and defensive stability.

Moreover, the rest of the team was soon bolstered with a number of dependable and versatile recruits to supplement the catalysts I'd just mentioned e.g. James Milner and Aleksandar Kolarov; thus, improving the overall dependability, robustness and stature of the squad. So, by the time they were ready to attack the 2011/12 season, many hopes were raised on the blue half of Manchester, that *at least* they'd go some way to proving just how far they'd come under the Mansour reign. Though I doubt that even the most optimistic of fans would have dared to dream about what would come of that season's early outing away at United – the first genuine indication of how well their new-look side would perform in the season to come.

Some call it 'the Old Trafford massacre', others call it 'the ultimate revenge'. But I call it 'the day where everything changed'. Sunday, 23rd October 2011. Oh boy, here we go ...

Looking at the two sets of line-ups from that day, it is clear that Manchester City trumped United in most departments on the pitch; both in terms of world experience and directly comparable attributes in their position. For example, David de Gea wasn't anywhere near as confident or experienced as Joe Hart at the time, and Darren Fletcher was incomparable in terms of his presence or passing quality to that of Yaya Touré. And it proves to be a similar summary across the board which largely explains how the events transpired on the day.

City's forward play was slicker, more direct and far more confident than their rivals; with United struggling to cope with their attacking width, defensive press and relentless bite. Altogether, this resulted in a complete humiliation for the Devils, as City recorded an unprecedented 1-6 thrashing of their supposedly 'better' rivals.

As we know, Manchester United have long been lauded as perennial record-breakers in the Premier League era - the first club to record a domestic and European major league treble, the first to win back-to-back-to-back domestic titles, all the while a hoard of transfer records and off-the-pitch commercial antics had founded international partnerships with some of the most recognisable brands across the world e.g. Nike, Chevrolet, Hublot and Audi. But on this day, this critical day, they were breaking records for all of the wrong reasons.

Expectedly, this was the first time that the comparative younger brother in City had ever scored six goals in a single Manchester derby, and is their greatest ever margin of victory for this specific tie. More tellingly, they were able to inflict Manchester United's worst ever defeat in the Premier League era, have them succumb to their worst home loss at Old Trafford for over half a century, *and* force them to concede six goals on home soil for the first time since before the Second World War. It was *biblical* stuff!

In a single match, the margin between the two clubs which was once a chasm in favour of United was quickly eroding under the Emirati ownership of City. And it formed the benchmark for the most exciting end to a title race in English Football History. Again, United fans: look away ... if you haven't already. But for everybody else, I encourage you to escape into the beauty of the story for it is pivotal to understanding the lion's share of City's resulting aura.

The entire 2011/12 season was a tug-of-war between the two Manchester clubs - with the experienced United striving for their twentieth overall topflight triumph, while City were eyeing up their first of (hopefully) many. Momentum shifted to and fro throughout the season between them and, coming into the final game of the campaign, a botched 4-4 draw between Everton and United at Old Trafford handed control over to City. All they had to do was overcome a struggling Q.P.R. side in their final tie and they would be crowned Premier League champions - four years on from Mansour's sugar daddy drop ... a rather different 'Four-Year Plan' to what we've discussed previously, as I'm sure you'd agree. Meanwhile, United would have to do the business away at lowly Sunderland and hope for their neighbours to slip up.

Rooney had put United in front with a trademark placement finish early in the first half, and Fergie's men proved solid enough to withstand any of the Black Cats' advances to record a deserved win. Most remarkably, 'Lady Luck' seemed to be smiling over the men in red as the Etihad

Stadium became a painting of embarrassment and anguish throughout the majority of their fixture with Rangers.

Initially, things went as expected when, on the 39th minute, Pablo Zabaleta quelled a spirited Q.P.R. side to send City 1-0 up into the break - a vital pre-half-time goal to settle the nerves. Djibril Cissé however, ironically an ex-Liverpool employee, didn't get the memo regarding how this day was supposed to go; swiftly firing his side back into contention with a close-range blast beyond a hapless Joe Hart in goal. 1-1. Then, despite having their captain Joey Barton sent off for a second yellow card offence, the unassuming figure of Jamie Mackie burst beyond City's defensive line to send the away side 2-1 up ... with 20 minutes of normal time left on the jumbotron's timer.

'Tick, tock' went the clock, until we arrived at the 90th minute; at which point, a growing sense of dread began to wash over the Etihad stadium - that they were about to throw away the most glorious of opportunities to prove themselves on the domestic stage.

You have to remember; their ranks did not possess much Premier League-winning pedigree by this point, and there wasn't much reason to believe (if any) that they possessed the resolve and knowhow to fight their way back into the match; especially given the amount of time remaining for them to complete an unlikely turnaround ... which only makes the report of what transpired over the next few minutes even more sensational.

A blast from the past ...

There is a very intriguing note in an interview between *Sky Sports* and ex-United and City 'keeper Peter Schmeichel who described, in detail, the chain of events leading up to the Red Devils' miraculous European U-turn against FC Bayern Munich in the late summer of 1999. Even to this day, many of the plaudits lie at the feet of Ole Gunnar Solskjær - the 'baby-faced assassin' who poked in a Sheringham header to send the Nou Camp into raptures and bring the treble home. However, Schmeichel himself prefers to highlight the equaliser that was swept home two minutes earlier in injury time by Teddy Sheringham himself - the reason? Because it "gave us a shot" - it gave them *hope*.

In football, a game so fraught with emotion, *hope* is a powerful thing. It's the driving force behind success and underpins the majority of key moments which become synonymous with it. So, when Edin Džeko popped up from the depths to equalise for Manchester City in injury time, his teammates started to believe in themselves again. To the untrained eye, there were only two minutes left, United had already beaten Sunderland, so the game (and Premier League crown) looked beyond City's reach. But this is football. It doesn't follow the rules. In reality, it gave them ... *'a shot'*!

Anybody who was emotionally involved in this occasion will remember where they were when it all unravelled. Personally, I was at home with my dad and, before a ball was even kicked, we took the mature stance of believing that the season was already over. In our minds, City were the champions (and rightly so over the course of the season), and we would simply be the team than ran them to the end of the wire - *anything* other than that would be a lovely little bonus though it would feel undeserved - particularly after they spanked us 1-6 back in October.

But Q.P.R. gave us some faith that things could turn around ... and I still hate them for that.

When Džeko equalised, I retreated to the solace of my room as I couldn't bear to experience what could potentially occur. Though unfortunately for me, the walls in my family home were gut-wrenchingly thin, particularly that of which guarded my microscopic single-bedded room where I could clearly hear Martin Tyler on the commentary downstairs - with my father opting to deploy his new Bose-powered surround-sound speakers for the occasion … cheers, Dad (!)

My naivety and boyish optimism allowed a faint grin to appear in the corners of my mouth as the game drew to its climax. 'We've done it!', I thought. 'I don't know how, and I don't care how, but we've done it!' and … well … I almost don't want to write this next bit.

City launched their final attack which, according to Mr. Tyler, was their last chance to divert the title's journey away from Old Trafford. And after a series of hoofs and ricochets, the ball fell to Mario Balotelli, who poked it to the right-side of the penalty area into the path of that Sergio Agüero fella.

The Argentine seems to forget the stress of the occasion, takes the ball in his stride, arrives near Rangers' goalmouth before mercilessly lashing the ball home at the goalkeeper's near post. Thus, marking the end of the most enthralling, heart-breaking and *beautiful* Premier League season since its inception.

I - like all United fans on the day - was completely crest-fallen when that goal went in. And as weird as it may sound to your average philistine, I liken the emotion of this occasion to one of mourning. I mean, we had our hopes raised above the mountains only to be crashed to the depths of the ocean; all within a matter of seconds, and televised for the world to see in an era where it will never be forgotten and constantly brought up.

Then, once the dust had settled, the club as a whole had to concede that the most sensational moment in Premier League history (an era that they'd dominated since its birth) now belonged to their inner-city enemies. And to make things *even worse*, the Hollywood-type ending of this campaign did more for City than they could realise at the time of Agüero's winner, for they now had an empirical example which directly paired up with their takeover ambitions.

Until that point, bringing in a new player was a question of whether or not they could buy into the new idea for the club, but now, their pitch was a hell of a lot easier to start off. It went from being: 'imagine the scenes if you could help us do this', to: 'we're Premier League champions … roll the VT'

What's more, is that they announced themselves on the title-challenging scene in the most emphatic way possible; thus, directly playing into this 'audacious' narrative idealised during the league's rebranding, whilst directly rubbing their new-found success in the noses of the supposedly imperious force in the league.

As I'm sure you'd agree, it was a truly miraculous end to an equally miraculous story, and this would prove to be only just the beginning for them in their rise to prominence on home soil. Whereas for their embarrassed adversaries, it looked like the beginning of the end.

'THE FALL OF A GIANT'
A Manchester United Story

With the sound of goading Sunderland supporters echoing deafeningly in the away dressing room, Ferguson remained uncharacteristically calm and considered in that dreaded game's immediate aftermath. In fact, his debrief was short and to the point: 'we're going to make sure that what happened today doesn't happen again'. Translated from Scottish: 'we're going to get our title back'.

Not wanting to waste any time, Fergie set about securing the club's twentieth Premier League title the following season; in a bid to re-assert United above those storytellers over the road.

And having technically forfeited the title via goal difference, the team's technical department had set their sights on bolstering the manager's front-line - with an A-list playmaker and an out-and-out goal-scorer – to ensure that history wouldn't repeat itself. Subtlety wasn't an option this time round, so when looking to satisfy that ever-elusive striker position, he simply went for the previous year's top marksman Robin van Persie ... then contracted to Wenger's Arsenal!

Throughout 'the year that must not be named', the Dutchman had shone brightly in a sub-par Gunners side - tallying thirty goals for the season as they secured another UEFA Champions League spot. Now, more often than not, deals for one competitive rival's star player to another is a rare one. But here, Wenger's antipathy for the number thirty (his age, not his goal return) had made Robin a little easier to let go - something which accelerated Ferguson's interest; who only envisaged needing him for a single season ...

Oh boy, here come the waterworks ...

Time has since revealed Sir Alex's intentions at the beginning of the 2013/14 season, where, both he and David Gill (later installed after Martin Edwards in 2003) had already decided to step down from their perch as Manchester United manager and Chief Executive respectively come the end of the year; regardless of its outcome.

Over the years, the pair had cultivated a wonderful squad who worked in harmony over successive years in the world's most prestigious domestic league competition, and in fact, it's commonly believed that they would have hung up their suits a year earlier than they eventually did but for City's Cinderella story. But as you could imagine, Ferguson preferred to go out on a high – and few ways come higher than by winning United's twentieth English top league title in dominant fashion; both as a bid to restore their local pride in Manchester, while building a morsel of breathing space between them and Liverpool as England's most successful ever football team. Therefore, signing van Persie was a clear marker of this intent - a short-term solution for concluding a long-term task.

Thereafter, he was ominously provided with the number '20' shirt; serving as a constant reminder of his purpose in the team. After him, it looks as though Fergie shifted his attention onto making life a little easier for whoever would eventually come in to replace him.

Days later, Shinji Kagawa became the first ever Japanese player to represent United after he transferred from Borussia Dortmund as the Bundesliga's top assist-maker. Adopting that advanced midfield berth, Shinji possessed a delicate touch with a cute arsenal of passing skills - constantly tiptoeing in behind the striker to peer through gaps between the defence before enacting a pass to suit the moment. On paper, a very good signing all round - clearly a talented player who gives unprecedented access to the Japanese commercial scene … old habits really do 'die hard' at times, huh?

Following up closely behind Kagawa, came Dutch full-back Alexander Büttner who, despite a promising start, simply found the gap between the Eredivisie and Premier League too big to bridge. Then, United became future-obsessed with the purchases of promising Crewe Alexandra and Universidad de Chile forwards, Nick Powell and Ángelo Henríquez - players who may have benefited from Fergie's own long-term vision but would be left fluttering in the breeze unless the Scot's successor shared his vision for them. And the following signing of Crystal Palace's Wilfried Zaha only seeks to compound this ideology.

Therefore, looking back on his double-ended transfer policy for the summer, Ferguson's intentions seemed to be to make sure that a) his final season was settled beyond any doubt, and b) to leave behind some groundwork for the new manager to build upon. And Fergie even had a hand here to help locate the club's most ideal new captain; ideally one who'd had a track record of rearing their own youthful squad in the Premier League era, and therefore aptly suited to pick up where he'd left off.

During the search, ex-Everton manager David Moyes' pedigree had suggested that he was capable of achieving greater results with a bigger club after he was freed from his hand-to-mouth existence in charge of the Toffees. But when you *really* think about it, the search itself was flawed from the outset.

Sir Alex Ferguson wasn't a mere 'manager' of Manchester United; who was capable of being replaced by another 'manager'. He *was* Manchester United, and his departure had presented an impossible task for any respected coach to approach successfully.

Allow me to explain …

Fergie's legend, which has since been immortalised with a named stand and bronze statue erected in his honour at his workplace, was unrivalled and his departure was still raw among the United fans. Not to mention the fact that the pain of his exit was doubled by the adjoining David Gill.

Therefore, by leaving, they weren't just taking their immediate qualities with them, but they were also removing much of the infrastructure in place for anybody to come in and build upon what they'd left. Because, in all but name, the club was almost completely unrecognisable behind the scenes. And worst of all, that fact doesn't stop those glory-hungry United fans from maintaining the same levels of expectation that the Fergie team had set during their time at the club; ergo, imposing a standard that very few managers would have been able to live up to given the changes that your average fan couldn't see.

So, considering all of this, Moyes was not welcomed into a stable environment, and his various, ill-informed reaction to such unexpected conditions have since brought his cut-short tenure at Old Trafford into unbridled infamy.

To begin with, in an attempt to bring *some* sort of familiarity into an otherwise alien surrounding, Moyes went about hoarding in a select few of his Everton cohort to help him out with his new job; both on and off the pitch. And though it seems a fair approach to taking on such a difficult position, it had unsettled many of United's incumbent playing team, whilst simultaneously relieving the club of a title-winning backroom brigade. A retrospective recipe for disappointment.

Moreover, his usual 'hoof the ball upstream and see what lands nicely' style of play didn't suit the demanding fans of Manchester United; who'd grown accustomed to an all-guns-blazing mantra with skill and endeavour being the order of the day.

As such, the team looked largely directionless under his leadership, he failed to incorporate many of Fergie's impromptu youth signings in an appropriate manner, and altogether put his trusted line-up out of touch with the identity which formed the bedrock for the club's all-conquering eras. And as you probably would've derived from this summary, the pulse-slowing nature of watching a Moyes version of Manchester United was never going to last long, and indeed in this world of tactile owners and emotional fans, the initial five-year safety blanket offered to Moyes proved to be nothing more than a false sense of security for the out-of-depth Scotsman. In reality, he lasted a whopping seven months before receiving his marching orders, and United changed tact completely by going for a 'proven European winner' in Louis van Gaal.

Arriving off the back of a solid 2014 World Cup campaign with Holland, van Gaal was as hard-nosed as they come. When you play under him, you are instructed to adhere to his strict formula and no-nonsense lifestyle; at times leaving little room for innovation in place of pure, un-wilting efficiency. And let's just say that watching *his* United side wasn't the most enthralling way to spend a chunk of your weekend, which is a real shame given some of his exciting transfer business from this time.

Thanking his profile, United were suddenly linked with a plethora of high-level talent; of whom, with the greatest of respect, I have doubts as to whether they would've been as equally enticed by the thought of playing under David Moyes.

Van Gaal started by being able to recruit two of the World Cup's stand-out performers - Argentine Marcos Rojo and fellow Dutchman Daley Blind - neither of whom set the stadium alight in the years to come but were promising given their versatility and national pedigree.

But after them, United made Luke Shaw the most expensive teenager for his time when he arrived from Southampton, and then came arguably van Gaal's most successful United signing in midfield dynamo, Ander Herrera who, after an attack-based showing in Spain's *La Liga* with Athletic Bilbao, soon transformed into an industrious deep-lying midfielder who had the engine and patience to add some formidability to the team's midfield.

Once he was brought in and given his orders, I suppose it was time to reinstate United's attacking prowess. And in doing so, they couldn't have set their sights much higher than with South American superstar Ángel Di María; whose stay in Manchester must rank as one of the most frustrating and misunderstood tenures in the history of the football club.

Having come to the fore in a Real Madrid team brimming with quality and spear-headed by Cristiano Ronaldo, Di María established himself a hard-working, dynamic and impossible-to-catch winger who was tearing things up on the European stage. In fact, the Champions League final the season before his move to United, was one of his finest hours - rightly being crowned 'man of the match' for his stellar outing against Atlético Madrid as Real brought home '*La Decima*'.

And just when things couldn't seem to get any better for Manchester United, Deadline Day brought us the news of the elite Colombian marksman Radamel Falcao touching base at Manchester Airport. Got me all giddy, this one did!

Admittedly, stock had fallen in the prolific goal-scorer following a tumultuous start to life with his newest club, AS Monaco, but a year of strife didn't diminish his wealth of achievements prior to arriving in France.

Nicknamed 'El Tigre' for his feisty and dedicated outings at the Wanda Metropolitana for Atlético Madrid, the slick-haired Latinx superstar proved an indomitable force in front of goal for *Los Rojas* and, having suffered a long-term injury at the Stade de Louis, many in Manchester red were hoping that it was a minor blip across a career where his initial loan spell at Old Trafford would help to reignite his standing in the game.

But as we all know, he found it impossible to settle in the Premier League, and his exorbitant loan fees looked a wholly unworthy investment for his return. He was reportedly brought in on a season-long loan agreement with United bearing the brunt of his astronomical €300,000 p/week wage, not to mention being saddled with a potential invoice for €55 million should they wish to fix the Colombian permanently at the club come the end of the season.

Top that all off with a €6 million loan fee required to secure him in the first instance, and you have a rough expenditure of over €12 million per goal that he ended up scoring. It really is a catastrophic group of numbers to get your head around. And even more crucially, Di María didn't fare much better … though his issues were more personal; something I sincerely hope that more United fans have come to realise in the time gone by.

It's very easy for us laypeople to sit back in our armchair and marvel at how easy it is to succeed as a football player. To us, it's a routine of: train, play, get paid, repeat. But this really fails to take into account the mental strength required to sustain a consistent level of performance when things go against you, notwithstanding some of the more relatable issues of how difficult it can be for foreign stars to relocate from one culture to another.

Lest we forget, the weather in Manchester is relatively intolerable when compared to the coastal benefits of Spain, the food is completely different, the dietary requirements at the club were unusual, there were very few other relatable Latinx squad members present to aid in the embedding process, there's a significant language barrier between them and the majority of their new team, and in this particular case with Ángel, the manager failed to develop a formation which brought the best out of him.

Worse still, he had to make this transition under the visceral United press who were becoming progressively irritated by any performance which was sub-par to the standards imposed by Sir Alex Ferguson - with many holding Di María personally accountable for this as the club's most expensive player; a title which had *nothing to do with him*!

Then, the final straw came when a number of United 'fans' brought the club and the game as a whole into disrepute; reportedly breaking into the Argentine's new home and ransacking the place before leaving the fearful playmaker to unravel whatever mess they'd left for him. So, all in all, I'm sure you'll agree with me when I say that's a lot to deal with when changing jobs, and perhaps it's helped to alter your perspective on the lad when casting your mind back to his United days.

All things considered, I personally hold no grievance against Di María for his decision to leave England, and his future successes at Paris Saint-Germain is a welcome addition to one of the most glittering CV's ever assembled in the game of football. And in fairness to both himself and Radamel Falcao, their short-term blips at Old Trafford only seeks to put a faint veil over the true problems pervading at the club.

***

Gone seemed to be the days of breeding a young, fighting and spirited squad to be developed into first-team regulars, and instead the club fell into the very same trap experienced by Ferguson in that aforementioned 'transition period'; the process of panic-buying big-name players as desperate attempts to restore the club's prestige, without having a clear direction for where they were looking to go in the long-term.

Where, even a well-integrated Di María and an on-form Falcao would have done little to quell the bigger problems at hand; much like the experiences of Juan Sebastian Verón and Ruud van Nistelrooy before them.

In fact, this very lack of foresight affected many other players that arrived during van Gaal's tenure. Morgan Schneiderlin was one of the stand-out players in an over performing Southampton side before he found himself out of his depth in the centre of United's midfield, Memphis Depay showed all the potential in the world but struggled to nail down a first team spot when the defensive frailties of the squad reduced his attacking capacity, and then you have the tragic mistreatment of German legend Bastian Schweinsteiger, who was declared too slow and lethargic to be allowed to wear United red.

However, when properly managed and integrated in an appropriate system, I have reason to believe that most (if not all) of the mentioned players may have achieved something worth writing home about, but instead, the fans and United hierarchy soon grew tired of van Gaal's transition, to the point where even the 'Special One' had a shot at it. Allow me to preface my description of Mourinho's United outing by expressing my utmost respect for what the Portuguese has achieved across his illustrious career. But there's no escaping the fact that his styles weren't well suited to this particular job.

Unfortunately, José Mourinho didn't seem to see much wrong with the van Gaal 'let's get some big names in and hope for the best' approach, and aimlessly recruited three high-profile names to see what could come of them; each of whom had made diverging statements as to what the manager's intentions were for bringing them in.

Beginning with Henrikh Mkhitaryan - the first Armenian to ever score in the Premier League - who arrived following a Kagawa-esque stint while in Germany with Borussia Dortmund. Not unlike with Di María, his was a case of not nailing down a single position at United, before a lack of confidence crippled his career at Old Trafford. By signing him, you'd think that the team were aiming to play more freely and fluidly, while instead, he fell victim to Mourinho's negative, counter-attacking tactical choices.

Then came the enigma that is Paul Pogba, whose U-turn transfer saga to, from and back to United is one that's been drawn out and analysed many times, so here's an overview of his troubled entrance into the first team at Old Trafford.

He broke onto the scene as a teenager under Ferguson, was overlooked as a prospect, sought after more playing time, broke away to Juventus via a 'Bosman move', established himself as a dynamic midfielder under the guidance of Andrea Pirlo and co. in Turin, United realised their mistake, ate the most humble of pies, and whipped out their leather-bound chequebook to shell out a whopping £85 million sum to bring him back.

Now, despite the monumental oversight concerning his talent in the Devils' ranks to begin with, the re-signing of a post-pubescent Paul Pogba really should've been the beginning of a revival for this dwindling United team. During his time in Italy, the Frenchman asserted himself as one of the world's most outstanding midfielders - in that he possessed perhaps the broadest skillset out there owned by a fellow chance-maker. Sure, you had the Kevin de Bruynes and Toni Krooses of the world who could certainly match Pogba's vision and passing ability, but do they have his physicality, pace, box-to-box ability and confidence to improvise? Well, it's a tougher debate, that's for sure.

Either way, United now possessed one of world football's most prized possessions, and it was up to them to build a team around him in order to guide them into whatever direction his transfer had indicated. But they didn't do anything of the sort.

His best role is either on the left of a midfield three or as an advanced playmaker in the heart of the midfield duo; backed by more defensive-minded teammates to muck in and do the dirty work while he can be inspired to do the flashy stuff. So, best thing to do would be to sort out all that defensive malarkey to supplement his attacking intent, right? … *Right?*

Well, instead, the remainder of that summer's business was concluded with the confusing acquisition of Zlatan Ibrahimović on a free transfer from Paris Saint-Germain. Don't twist my words here, Zlatan is undoubtedly one of the most talented players of his generation, but the man was 37 years-old by the time he signed a one-year-deal at Old Trafford – and was the mere definition of short-term thinking.

In fairness to Mourinho, the pair did link up well and Zlatan's outstanding goal tally propelled United to a hard-fought 2nd placed finish before injury cut short his fairy-tale swan song in Manchester, but his signing just *didn't make any sense*! Firstly, you can't go about bringing Paul Pogba to your club - somebody within whom you presumably rest the team's creative flair, and then fail to accompany his attacking qualities with the defensive resolution required for him to enjoy himself. And secondly, you can't highlight the club's long-term vision with the signing of someone like Pogba, and immediately pair him up with a striker who had a short-term shelf life. If you ask me, this very contrast of viewpoints encapsulates just how disjointed United had become in their post-Fergie era, and their rivals were resting in the side-lines, basking in their incompetence as they fell even further from grace; and further still from domestic and European contention

***

In conclusion, Manchester United have been and still are a mighty fine institution. The commercial appetite of its company-form converted a historic club into a global organisation; where its continual financial flows have stabilised its ground-breaking developments for: the club's facilities, proliferating their overall brand and revitalising the cyclic terms of their playing squad.

All of which were overseen by money-rich owners, reliable boardroom figures and a strict, consistent figure in the dressing room - the ideal recipe for *sustained* and relentless success. However, all three of these components act in tandem with each other and operate in a tripod-like level of dependency; where without one of these 'legs' of the 'tripod' being there, the others will be unable to stand on their own.

So, the inevitable happened when *two* of them had fallen away in Sir Ferguson and Mr. Gill. Thus, arose years of aimless 'progress' which was put into action for all of the wrong reasons, leading to the fall of the Manchester United empire which is only now (at the time of writing) beginning to show *some* signs of a rebirth. Boardroom disarray aside.

Though, where United seemed to be getting everything wrong, their rivals were enjoying an opposite turn of fortunes, not least those pesky neighbours to whom history ought to attribute the honour of exposing the Devils' eventual frailties back in 2012.

~ 24 ~

'MANCHESTER IS BLUE'
It's Our Turn Now ...

All this zigzagging from one half of Manchester to the other is making me feel nauseous, though as we focus away from the disintegrating legacy on the red side, the blue side was only growing in stature ... and at a menacingly fast rate.

Reading between the lines of what was causing United's downturn, City understood the importance of getting things right behind the scenes before being able to change the scene itself. After all, there's no point employing a top-level actor to star in your movie without paying equal attention to the director in charge of them, nor the script they're reading from.

So, adopting that same analogy here, it was pivotal for City to home in on a central model for how they wanted their team to look/play, and employ a suitable background team who were capable of breeding a title-challenging team grounded upon their chosen philosophies. The idea they went for was FC Barcelona's *tiki taka* style, which required an anal attention to commanding space on the pitch, as well as attracting top-level stars capable of putting such tactics into practise for the Premier League. So, when searching for their 'own version' of the Spanish innovation, City had decided to instead put their financial muscle to good use in order to attract the masterminds directly responsible for Barca's *own* success.

In the wake of incumbent chief executive Garry Cook's resignation (supposedly following a loose accusation of 'trolling' one of the player's relatives), Khaldoon Al-Mubarak, one of Mansour's personal advisers and acting chairman at the club, replaced him directly with ex-Barca boardroom leader, Ferran Soriano, and went one better to sweeten the deal by installing his buddy Aitor "Txiki" Begiristain as the team's official (and inaugural) Sporting Director. Take notes, Mike Ashley!

Begiristain was one of the primary people in charge of recruiting supplementary talents to Barca's *La Masia* spine during Pep's era of dominance in the Camp Nou dugout, namely the likes of Dani Alves, Alexis Sánchez and Javier Mascherano. All the while, Soriano had prioritised the state of the team's academy to ensure that their own positive trajectories would continue.

So, between the pair of them, they had masterminded the foundations for which Guardiola was able to create this 'ultimate *Total Football*-based' ideology - with a beautiful blend of youthful locals and expensive recruits tailored to bringing this *tiki taka* format to life.

Now, we've already spoken about what the Catalonian trio had achieved during that period, but by this point in 2012, Guardiola was ready to move on to a new challenge with FC Bayern Munich in Germany - leaving Soriano and Begiristain to go on without him in Catalunya. Remember what I said about the tripod theory? Well, here we have another one. Only this time, when the managerial leg had fallen away, it had left the remaining members vulnerable to Manchester City's charm offensive. And the timing of everything had just meshed in perfectly as far as the East Manchester club's proposal was concerned.

At the same time when Pep's cold feet marched him out of Spain, Manchester City had bestowed upon us all the most astonishing 'fairy tale' moment in Premier League history. In fact, it's arguable that had the 'Agueroooo' moment not occurred, and worse still, if City hadn't won the title that season, then it would've been a much less stable pitch to the success-hungry, Pep-less hierarchy at Barcelona.

But that's all hypothetical dribble, and in reality, City had an empirical example of the sorts of stories they were capable of writing resulting from their financial transformation; provided that it was guided by the right people. So, altogether, this was something that their latest targets could get behind and run with. And boy, did they ever!

In their new roles, Begiristain was their transfer sage, whilst Soriano would concern himself with all of the other behind-the-scenes business matters - balancing the finance books, keeping the club compliant with authority regulations and launching / maintaining commercial initiatives as a means of expanding the brand of Manchester City. Where the most significant impact he would have directly on the playing squad would simply be employing their new manager; a task which proved quite difficult whilst Pep was settled elsewhere.

To begin with, he was relatively fair in his initial assessment of the current title-winning team and had the presence of mind to provide them with another full season in charge before making any required changes. Yet, despite being the first ever coach to bring them Premier League honours, incumbent head coach Roberto Mancini wasn't best loved at Manchester City.

Players like Richard Dunne, Shay Given and Shaun Wright-Phillips noted the manager's generally despondent personality as being difficult to connect with, and cliques soon formed within the club before the new season kicked off. Then, once the uninspired signings of Jack Rodwell, Javi García and Maicon had all but handed the trophy back to the opposing end of the city, a search-party was launched for his successor almost from the very minute United had re-affixed their topflight crown.

City's subsequent appointment of Manuel Pellegrini was a given – as he was somebody whom the honchos knew well from their time in Spain, and was presented as an ideal short-term fix to keep the ship chugging along whilst holding out for its long-term captain – again, not too dissimilar to what Arsenal's Mr. Dein did with that whole Rioch-Wenger swap in the mid-'90s.

Undoubtedly, Pellegrini was a strong, stable-enough manager to continue this shorter transitional period, and was capable of bringing some trophies in the meantime to appease their newer, glory-hungry set of supporters. But City only really ever had a single target in mind once their new Chief Executive and Sporting Director were installed; and it would be that remaining leg of the Barca tripod ... Pep Guardiola ... *duh*!

After completing another four-year stint, this time being equally as domestically dominant in Germany as he was in Spain, Pep's feet grew cold once more. He had achieved everything he'd wanted to achieve as per his initial contract at FC Bayern, and was now looking for another project to be a part of; one with perhaps a tougher set of requirements and more satisfying yield level. And Manchester City was the absolutely perfect place for him to do something even greater, and in an even more visible league.

But *this time*, not only did he have his pals on his side once again, but now he possessed the financial capability to *literally* do whatever he wanted to do and, perhaps more importantly, there was a lot *more* to do than what he'd been used to.

Both Barcelona and Bayern had a ceiling which was relatively easier to reach than most elite-level outfits. Both of their academies had already produced some of the greatest players ever seen. They were both global powerhouses in terms of their brand and the respect that their badges commanded, and had altogether *already* grown accustomed to being successful; where Pep's triumphs, though worthy of more than this, would simply join a long list of managers who were able to achieve things that looked inevitable to the untrained eye. By contrast, Manchester City didn't have these benefits yet. In fact, they couldn't even carry the momentum from the famous story-ending campaign into the very next season, leave alone being consistent competitors in the league title run.

So, this time, if Pep was to be a success, he would be tasked with developing a legacy *in his own right;* and this is precisely the prospect which attracted him the most about moving to England, especially when he came to realise just how ideal his new workplace would be for him.

***

Finally, after years of courting and silently stalking their prey, Guardiola was officially tied down to a five-year deal at Manchester City in the summer of 2016. And just to sweeten the deal a little bit more, his ol' mate Begiristain arranged for one hell of a welcoming gift, actually, he'd arranged two!

Again, much like the Wenger arrangement two decades prior to this, the pre-Pep City organisation had brought in a couple of players who were ready to embody the philosophy that their new manager sought to bring. And where the Frenchman was treated to Dennis Bergkamp to impose his culture on Arsenal's attacking movement, the first of Pep's presents came in the form of one of the most promising inside-forwards in world football; Raheem Sterling.

Peculiar running style aside, Sterling appeared to be a quick, tricky and exciting winger when breaking through into the Liverpool first team as a teenager. Then, as his development continued, he was linked with a number of big-money moves that often garner the careers of young talents in modern football. Both City and Real Madrid were reportedly able to match the post-£50 million valuation of the Englishman, so it came down to where the player himself could visualise his long-term future. And the potential of signing for Pep had apparently proven far too exciting for him to ignore.

Then, shortly after the major move for Sterling, the City cohort's eyes were drawn to some bright-haired Belgian cooking up a storm in Germany.

Now before I go on, I'm going to just put this out there, and say that Chelsea have made some truly *awful* transfer blunders in the Premier League. Many of whom have come to highlight the frailties behind their inherent short-term policies and floundering loan affiliate setup.

On the 'lower' end of the spectrum, they gave up on the development of Nathan Aké who has since carved out a commendable Premier League career in Bournemouth (before being sold onto Pep's City in 2020), and on the higher end they'd discarded Romelu Lukaku to Everton where he tripled in value before signing for Manchester United. But among their most embarrassing blunders to date, giving up on Kevin de Bruyne before fobbing him off to VfL Wolfsburg is a candidate for top spot.

Initially purchased by Chelsea as a slight, European prospect who showed some potential for growth back home in Genk, there seemed to be no real plan to sustain his development once he'd arrived at the Blues.

Over the seasons leading up to De Bruyne's capture from Belgium, Chelsea had this God-awful habit of having a loan list longer than their league registration list; meaning that they often had more players out on loan at other clubs than they had available to select for their own club. Now, as a concept, this isn't a *terrible* idea as it allows for certain prospects to develop their first-team acumen elsewhere before (ideally) rivalling any incumbent selections in the Chelsea squad.

But that only works when you can successfully assess the qualities of the loaners you have; which isn't likely if the sheer volume of players doesn't allow you the time to efficiently figure out if they are worth the continued investment thereafter.

So, by adopting this one-for-all option, they were inevitably going to allow a number of notable names to slip through the net, as was the case with Kevin de Bruyne who, having been loaned out to Werder Bremen one season, felt inclined to move away from the Bridge permanently in the next.

During that post-loan single year with Wolfsburg, he amassed an outstanding half-tonne of appearances with a prolific one-in-two goal inclusion ratio to boot; before quickly courting interest from City and (surprise, surprise) Real Madrid. Though, much like with Sterling, a more enticing route was carved out for the Belgian in Manchester, and the Sky Blues wasted little time in re-smashing their personal club transfer record to bring him to the Etihad. Not a bad way to usher in the new manager's arrival is it? I would've gone for an ice cream cake and some flowers but … each to their own, am I right!

Anyway, with things practically set in terms of their player and backstage recruitment in the lead up to Pep's eventual union with the Sky Blues in the 2016/17 season, City could attach some focus onto a number of off-the-pitch motives in an attempt to secure their business future and build their growing brand identity. And, when looking for a blueprint to adopt, they need only look back over the road to find a play-by-play rulebook on how this should be done.

***

I know I'm a fan, but hear me out. Away from the titles and team honours, there is another very important reason for why Manchester United is one of, if not *the* biggest club in the world. They became masters in the worlds of business partnerships and marketing.

To illustrate my point, one of the very first things United did in order to make their brand more all-encompassing and recognisable, was to finely alter the club crest. As we can all understand, to change a club's crest is to risk changing their identity as a whole, and so you have to tread carefully so as to not ruffle too many feathers through making your alterations. Though thankfully, for both the wishes of all United fans and probably for Martin Edwards' own safety, he made a very subtle, yet brilliantly effective change to it.

The general appearance of the badge remained largely untouched - it was still an image of two footballs on either side of a devil, who's pictured beneath a sailboat and in between two text sections above its head and beneath its feet. Even the red and yellow colouring remained the same for both the text fill and outer-stroke sections; yellow for the wording and red for the filler.

But instead of sprawling the full 'Manchester United Football Club' in a squashed geometric *WordArt*-type font within its borders, the words 'Football' and 'Club' were removed, and simply 'Manchester' and 'United' remained - signifying that football wasn't the *only* thing that 'Manchester United' should be associated with. And in making this adjustment, United were now able to acclaim a number of ulterior commercial initiatives by virtue of being presented as something more than a mere footballing entity. Subtle, yet brilliant.

Manchester City took notice of this and decided that a club icon redesign was necessary for them to continue on their own commercial journey, though their alterations were far more striking and … erm … *obvious* than that of United.

Before, there was this this eagle-headed dragon-type creature as the main feature of the badge, with a sky-blue banner at its feet and the letters 'M.C.F.C' draped across it. But this was done away with for a simpler shape which mirrored Manchester United's crest. And when I say 'mirrored', just search up a comparison image between the two and you can determine for yourself whether this is an understatement or not.

... Need I say more?

Their recruitment policy also took inspiration from United's tendency to undercut their rivals; either by beating them to the punch for a particular target, or setting sights on a rival's star for their own; most of which led to a dramatic upturn in fortune for the lads in red over the very organisation that they'd asserted their transactional dominance.

You have the signing of Eric Cantona from Leeds United catalysing their earlier Premier League title efforts in the '90s, the purchase of Wayne Rooney from under the noses of Chelsea to steer them away from an early 2000's transition, stealing Cristiano Ronaldo away from North London for the same reason and then, even more audacious than the rest, going straight for the jugular to sign Robin van Persie (reportedly under a substantial City interest) to claim back their twentieth topflight title in Fergie's final outing. And that's just the tip of the iceberg!

United were absolutely relentless. Both on the pitch and in the boardroom, they acted with a type of arrogance and confidence which portrayed a sort of: 'we are the best club in the world, it is a privilege to play here, and you know it' mentality. Now, it was City's turn to see if they could emulate their way of thinking. Both in who they targeted and how they went after them. Needless to say, they haven't fared too badly in this regard.

Their first attempt at this was the proud presentation of Carlos Tevez to their inner-city rivals, then came the signing of German midfielder İlkay Gündoğan, who had been persistently linked with a move to United two years prior to being unveiled at the Etihad and finally, you have Raheem Sterling; poached directly from another competitive rival, *and* out of the clutches of another significant bidder in Real Madrid.

And away from purely 'signing' players, they had introduced an even more sophisticated affiliate club system in a bid to maximise the development of their fringe talents. Though here, unlike your typical loan-based arrangement as previously considered with United and Chelsea, City went one further by establishing what we refer to as a club 'feeder' system.

What is a Club 'Feeder' System?

In essence, this modernised the traditional affiliate club system via more deeply ingrained partnerships; where whatever club they teamed up with would be viewed as an *extension* of Manchester City themselves, as opposed to a stand-alone partner from further afield.

So, where the likes of United and Chelsea simply wanted to develop their own talents abroad and consider integrating whatever players rose from the crop, City would partner with a club, offer up a substantial financial package to rebrand their new partners in line with their own restyling, advise them on how best to establish their academies and first-team setups, and all the while making their brand more recognisable in whichever footballing economy their new partner belonged to.

It was a truly sensational piece of business thinking from the Citizens. Constantly looking to grow, and always ensuring that they maintained multiple funnels for developing their player base.

Soriano himself had initiated this by teaming up with A-League side Melbourne City and later with MLS outfit, New York City FC - both of whom became official members of the Abu Dhabi owners' expansive 'City Football Group' empire. And once inducted into the Group, they almost became parodies of their new Manchester brethren.

Even 'til this day, their badges are similar, their kits are practically identical, and both provided City with a direct link to a fan base which had been largely left alone up until this point. There was even a conscious effort to bring in some big-name twilight players in order to proliferate either of their newly linked Australian or American franchises.

In fact, quite soon after forming their allegiance with the Manchester City team, the likes of David Villa, Frank Lampard and Andrea Pirlo - all of whom had once been linked with a move to Manchester - were now employed as commercial figures to help improve the overall image and identity of the Group.

Moreover, bringing in these superstars not only helped to boost each respective team's overall interest and resulting fan base, but also the abilities for those around them who could benefit from being under their pupillage. As is evident when you consider players such as Aaron Mooy, who grew in City's Australian ranks, and then drew a tidy £10 million profit for the Group's ownership when he moved into the Premier League with Huddersfield Town in 2017.

I'm sure that the Group are hoping that his doesn't turn out to be an isolated example, and perhaps one day, one of those foreign lads might even be good enough to sneak into City's own books. But until this happens, the club can rest easy knowing that they've set up things to a point where something like that is even remotely possible.

Overall, Manchester City must've been a dream for *Green Peace* because all they did was *recycle*. Whatever finance was pumped into the club was constantly revolving around this burgeoning portfolio of affiliate stations which only sought to benefit the focal point of their efforts.

And most importantly, they were very mature in their decision-making - in centring upon clubs in competitions like the A-League and MLS during a time of intense growth which, for the latter at least, looked like it might never happen … but for a Manc changing their fortunes around!

~ 25 ~

'THE RISE OF THE PHOENIX'
The Rebirth of American Soccer

This long-held appetite for football / 'soccer' in the United States can be traced back to the World Cup in 1966, where a reported 1,000,000+ TV-owners tuned in to watch the works of Messrs Banks, Charlton and Hirst. And ever the opportunist when it comes to taking on a sport for their own, the US soon propelled itself off the back of its burgeoning popularity, by trying their hand at establishing their very own soccer league setup.

A series of commercial partnerships between the US' major corporations and many semi-professional soccer organisations which existed at the time, had forged the number of 'franchises' required to produce the country's inaugural North American Soccer League ('NASL') by 1968.

On its registrar, came the inclusion of the aptly named 'New York *Cosmos*'; who intended to turn the entire league on its head by using their industry-backed fortune to attract some of the most well-known players in the world who, though they may have seen better days, would hopefully use much of their crowd-pulling aura to reclaim the Cosmos' investment in them.

But before they were able to do this, changes were made to the league setup itself to increase interest in the sport from the home crowd; by incorporating a number of common aspects of different sports to presumably expand its mass appeal throughout the country. All of which were met with varying degrees of scepticism and, in some cases, outright defiance.

The first of which was the use of a descending stopwatch-like clock (as adopted by the NBA and NFL) - where the time presented to the fans on the large jumbotron screen winded *down* to show how long was left in the game, as opposed to ascending up to represent how long had already passed.

In theory, it wasn't a radical switch nor a left-field idea, considering that it would encourage more excitement towards the latter end of the match and make it easier to get used to the new timeline for anybody interested in exploring the sport on their first viewing.

But, in a game where the time doesn't halt for stoppages and instead adds time on at the end to make up for however long was lost during the original game period, the idea fell flat on its face and proved the naivety with which the US approached the game of football.

And this was only the **beginning** ...

They also went about changing the offside rule which is already confusing as it is! In layman's terms, this rule indicates that: during a team's attacking phase, from the very moment at which the ball is played forward to another attacking player in the opposing half, the receiving player's body (any part of which can score a goal i.e. their torso, head, legs or feet) cannot be closer to the opposition's goalkeeper than their final defender.

It is then the job of the linesman (who patrols the outer-edges of the longer side of the pitch) to dictate whether or not the attacking player had advanced too far ahead at the moment the ball was played to them, or if they had actually remained on the trailing side of the defender for it to be a legal move. Complicated enough? Apparently not.

The US opted to further confuse matters by having a drawn line on the pitch to represent where a player can be offside. The actual rule of being in line with the last defender still remained, but only after the point at which this line was drawn - roughly 35 yards from the penalty area. Again, it's a system which is familiar to a stop-start game like American football; where set-plays are determined by their relativity to the touchdown line, but not in a game meant to be played fluidly like world football, and the change has since been ridiculed by today's knowledge and appreciation of the nuances of the game. But I'm even more surprised at the American take on how a penalty should be taken.

A penalty is perhaps the easiest thing to understand about set-piece football, and something which undoubtedly provides tension and excitement whenever one is taken; irrespective of when it is awarded and what rests upon it.

The concept is that there is an area surrounding each goal where, should an opposing player be fouled by a defending player within it, the opposing team are presented with the opportunity to place the ball unopposed on a spot in the middle of the area, with nothing but the 'keeper standing in the way of the taker slotting the ball home.

And this whole format of: place the ball on the spot, wait for the referee to allow the spot-kick to be taken, do whatever run-up you deem necessary before striking at goal, was as universal around the world then as it is now. But that's not how the Americans take a 'penalty'.

Instead, their version comes from the sport of ice hockey where, over on the slippery surfaces of the rink, the preamble to awarding a penalty is identical to football - for an opposing player to be travelling to the goalmouth before being illegally impeded within the 'keeper's area.

But after this, mainly due to the size of the rink, harshness of the puck and relative striking power of the taker, penalties are begun by skating with the puck from the rink's halfway point, and using whatever tactics deemed necessary to slide it into the net *while the puck is moving.*

For those unaccustomed to this style of 'taking a penalty', it proves to be quite an exciting and stress-inducing spectacle on the rink, but it somewhat loses its *panache* once you bring it onto a wider surface, in an outdoor stadium and without any real consideration for where the goalkeeper should be stationed. Frankly, its result was farcical, and looks far more suited to a *meme* compilation of stupid ideas that should never have been considered, as opposed to 'innovations' trialled as an attempt to include the US fan base.

Thankfully, these ideas didn't stick around by the time of the 1974 World Cup, which would turn out to signal the States' inaugural foray into the world of 'marquee signings'. Where, despite the overall competition being staged in and won by West Germany, Brazil's free-flowing antics had glowed in comparison with tactics of the winners and other finalists. There was something about the samba-style stars which was more *attractive* and *fun* to watch for your 'average' spectator than any of the callous, antiseptic deployments of most other nations.

So, wouldn't it be great if they could attract somebody of a Brazilian persuasion to ignite the new league in America? Why yes, yes it would. They just needed to find the right man and go about attracting them in a way which proves sustainable for them for a good amount of time.

I mean … one out of two ain't bad, right?

The Beginning of the First End …

A big competition needed a big introduction and Pelé fit the bill on that front. Undoubtedly a legendary striker for club and country, names in the footballing world don't come much bigger than his, though he simply wasn't any longer the indomitable force that he once was. In fact, he was due to retire by the end of the 1974 club season, and his protracted move to the New York Cosmos was a clear, see-through marketing ploy. Nevertheless, winning three World Cups and scoring 'one thousand goals' in your career, was never going to come cheap for the new NASL franchise. And herein lies the problem, not just with the Cosmos' ethos, but for the precedent it set.

The Cosmos were unveiled at a similar time to the New York Mets baseball team and were overseen by the same group of chief executives responsible for running Warner Comms - the soon-to-be media conglomerate known as Warner Media LLC to you and me. Therefore, their enviable financial muscle was largely unattainable for the vast majority of their competitors. However, sensing that the Cosmos might pull away from the pack by virtue of their spending power, many competing sides felt the need to inconceivably match their garish output in search for a crowd-puller of their own.

The signing of Pelé, on a reported $1.5 mil p/year settlement, lit alight a touch paper which would engulf the entire league in a mission to out-do one-another; without realising the personal torment it would later cause. So, in its own cruel form of irony, these teams were inadvertently plunging themselves into debt, in an attempt to lure in the star that would presumably lead them to commercial prosperity.

So, when the likes of Eusébio, George Best and the mentioned Johan Cruyff wound up in the 'land of the free' (bet they wish it was 'free'), I'm sure many were overjoyed with the promise and expectation that their names had brought. But their respective investments were overtly disproportionate to their on-pitch yields, and overall business return.

Altogether, this over-expansion (mixed with a smidgen of economic recession) took its toll on the fledgling league, and the NASL was over before it really had a chance to begin. And almost two decades had come and gone after its initial passing before any hopes of a rebirth came to fruition.

Then, with America being America, their re-emergence onto the world soccer scene couldn't be a quiet one, especially with the 1994 World Cup coinciding with a welcome boom to their national economy.

***

FIFA, among many other things, are in charge of sifting through various bidding proposals from prospective nations;

to ultimately decide on who is best placed to host each World Cup whenever they come around. Usually, their most successful bids arrive from 'football crazy' nations, or those whose presentations showcase the level of ambition and financial investment necessary to be a good host. And in this case, America had tasted soccer and liked the way it lingered on the tongue, plus it was a great way to re-introduce themselves on the scene; now that they were in an improved economic position to do a better job of it all, compared to their faltered start in the sport.

Plus, with only Brazil and Mexico appearing as their strongest competitors here, the United States represented the most steady and exciting proposal to showcase the 1994 World Cup. Remember, football aside, the World Cup is meant to be a *spectacle* for the whole world to ingest and enjoy… and if ever there were a country suited to putting on a fitting spectacle for most occasions (once they understand the rules), it was America.

By today's standards, the opening ceremony of their World Cup was a pantomime, but for its time, it was jolly good fun to watch. They had helicopters whirring around the stadium, cheerleaders aplenty, deafening marching band music and even a lip-syncing Diana Ross spooning a penalty wide of an enlarged inflatable goal. What's not to love? And on top of being able to put on a show and commit financially to being a solid host, *FIFA* had also committed the US to establishing a professional soccer league which would stand well beyond the competition's finale. Thus, we arrive at the new, re-branded and *highly more sustainable* Major League Soccer ['MLS'] model.

At first instance, it looked like the old American dog was struggling to learn new tricks, as they focused on luring in some of the bigger names from that year's World Cup into the newly formed league – presumably in order to generate some form of buzz and excitement for their regenerated era. However, the steadier foundations of the MLS (grounded by the requirements necessary to host the World Cup e.g. established franchises, sustainable team management and up-to-code stadium builds), allowed for any short-term buzz-creation; which signings like Carlos Valderrama helped to engage, without desperately hindering its growth going forward.

More critically, this focus on the league's underbelly had helped to funnel some financial muscle into building each franchise's academy; which culminated in a largely MLS-based US national team for the next two World Cups after they'd hosted theirs. Better still, one of their own in goalkeeper Tim Howard managed to attract some *international* acclaim, before moving from the MLS Metrostars to none other than *Manchester United* in 2004 for a $4 million suit.

Thereafter, things slowly trotted along, and the league looked set to continue a steady and modest evolution in a similar vein to stories like Tim Howard - whereby they'd develop their own talents to attract some form of positive attention before being taken seriously. And by doing this, the hope was that any larger names brought to the MLS would've been done sensibly - particularly given the fact that the league's new organisers had placed a limit of three foreign stars to be added to a franchise's roster. So now, not only were teams encouraged to look after their long-term goals, but they were also actively disengaged from ignoring the values on which the MLS was built.

Therefore, being more selective in this way meant that foreign acquisitions were few and far between; with each franchise now operating in a much more considered fashion whenever they wanted to bring in a big name. But there was one club in particular who'd sought after a particular name for a very long time - supposedly not long after the turn of the millennium.

We've spoken about said 'name' before, and though he may not have known it at the time, this player and his to-be employers were about to change the game of 'soccer' beyond recognition. The franchise was the Los Angeles (LA) Galaxy, and the target was David Beckham. A 'catalyst' of an entirely different persuasion to what we've considered so far.

As we know, Golden Balls' time in Madrid had run its course, and among the many propositions made to him upon leaving, none quite turned his head more than the prospect of being MLS' new poster boy. Or 'ambassador'; as I'm sure he'd much prefer.

Throughout his illustrious playing career, Becks had proven to be just as impactful on the commercial stage as he had been on the pitch, and neither of these areas should take anything substantial away from each other. His Jekyll was football and Hyde was his brand; both comparative by appearance but identical in substance. And above all else, he was a different kettle of superstar than had ever before washed up on the shores of the United States. A 'marquee signing' he was, but a 'short-term cash cow', he was not.

Not only was he insanely fit and had many of the Galaxy's formations tailored around an even longer-lasting career for him, but he was almost considered a business partner to his new franchise; and would have his forthcoming stint in Los Angeles morphed specifically to ensure that: he played *only* when required, was in a position which best suited him, and worked a commercial schedule to maximise his celebrity association. Pretty decent gig!

> He helped elevate the quality of the league, obviously he helped elevate the focus on the league, and **the league's growth during that period of time was unprecedented**."
>
> – Bruce Arena (LA Galaxy Coach)

Now it would just be a case of whether or not he could fulfil much of the promise that his transfer had created. And the fact that a bronzed, slightly misshapen figure of Beckham still protects the Galaxy stadium to this day, tells you all you need to know about the impact what his star quality brought to American soccer. The man's an icon, plain and simple.

He was adored by many upon signing, and the crowds flocked in their thousands to catch a brief glimpse of the great Englishman running out in LA Galaxy off-white for the best part of five years - give or take a season-long affair to make himself feel pretty in Europe again with A.C. Milan.

Throughout this time, the league was transformed from a mere restart to a failed empire, and into a mecca for global superstars who seemed to *want to* make a difference by use of their stardom and remaining footballing ability.

Soon came other high-profile names in Thierry Henry, Didier Drogba, Ashley Cole, Sebastian Giovinco and Wayne Rooney to name a few - who all went on to proudly represent their respective clubs and generate the kind of buzz that had been started off by the Beckham move.

Together, they all helped to raise the playing ability of the league to the point where attention has turned to many of their developing prospects like any other producer. And that man Becks even went one better to start up his very own club (Inter Miami C.F.) in 2018, which suggests that this positive advancement has little sign of slowing.

Plus in 2013, one of the final clubs to be admitted into the MLS (before Inter) was one by the name of New York City FC (the future employers of Frank Lampard and David Villa among others); whose existence served to add to that bulging profile of the City Football Group we touched upon earlier, which in itself was intended to be primarily used as a continuous financing mechanism for its largest member.

In fact, speaking of its 'largest member' ...

~ 26 ~

'WINNING BY KO'
Building the 'City Centurions'

With their affiliates set up, additional money flows readied, an impressive club infrastructure in place, and even a fortuitous long-term lease set up for their stadium, it came time for the City hierarchy to focus solely upon improving the immediate fortunes for the Sky Blues on the pitch.

In case you hadn't figured it out, winning the English Premier League is not an easy thing to do. In fact, it's pretty bloody hard.

It's one thing for the season to be spread out across the year as a whole, but the entirety of its gruelling 38-game-season takes place between mid-August of one year and mid-May of the next. Not to mention the infamously packed mid-Winter schedule, and the odd European or cup tie thrown in the mix to test your squad's endurability and depth in quality.

So, to actually *win* the overall championship is a true test of consistency, relentlessness, passion and dedication to winning. And there is a very clear argument for suggesting that the famously 'invincible' Arsenal squad of 2003/04, did this better than any other side.

Having said that, many of their results ended in a draw without the sustained fearlessness to go on to get the win where it was 'unnecessary' to do so; as it was putting their untarnished record at risk. Fast forward to 2017/18, and City couldn't care less about being unbeaten, for their aim was to go higher than any other club had ever gone before. And in short, they wanted to win the Premier League title by achieving the highest points total ever achieved in the history of the competition; thus, putting to work the years of preparation which went into foreseeing their eventual sustained championship-winning side. But even by City's nouveau-sky-high standards, this was a big ask of their current squad, and a re-structure was required.

Forever immortalised in the *Amazon Prime* documentary depicting Manchester City as part of their *All or Nothing* series (which is brilliant, by the way), Pep didn't hold back in creating his all-conquering Sky-Blue machine, and he wasn't too proud to learn from some of his earlier misgivings in Manchester.

In the previous season's Champions League campaign, City were going relatively strong before coming up against a never-say-die AS Monaco side in the Round of 16. The red and white outfit spearheaded by the miraculously talented Kylian Mbappé (more on him, later on), took the world by storm that year.

But where most did little else but sit back and marvel at this fledgling group of potential superstars, for the game's elite, it was time to earmark some of these lads and stick them right atop their summer shopping list.

'How much? ... Yeah alright'

– Manchester City ... probably

The aforementioned Mbappé jumped ship for the oil-rich PSG the next year (more on that later on, as well), and that opened the floodgates for poor ol' Monaco to lose many of their younger stars to clubs whose ceilings were far higher than theirs. Two of whom were directly courted by the head honchos of the Etihad.

Beginning at the shallower end of City's formation, domineering left-back Benjamin Mendy appeared a sturdy, stable and long-term replacement for the then-struggling Gaël Clichy and Fabian Delph. A player who drew plaudits for the entirety of his *Ligue Un* and Champions League outings for the Southern France group, Mendy's game was driven by pace, fearlessness and a shrewd level of intelligence in order to make the correct decision in the final third; with his eventual £45 million price tag deemed reflective of these attributes on top of his limitless potential.

At the same time, City's investment into youth seemed to be paying off as they welcomed Ukrainian wide defender Oleksandr Zinchenko back from his brief loan spell in the Eredivisie with PSV Eindhoven. So, in one fell swoop, they managed to cement the left-sided hole in the back line with a European-experienced Mendy and a promising Zinchenko; whose respective ages of 23 and 20 stated the long-term intentions of their inclusion in the squad, and how the pecking table would be ordered between them.

Now, with no intention to disrespect Clichy or Delph, the insertion of Mendy and Zinchenko were solid improvements on them for that pure left-back berth, though it would be far more difficult for City to find a like-for-like replacement for another one of their stalwarts whose betrayal by Father Time was as hard-felt as anybody's.

As I alluded to earlier, David Silva's legacy at City cannot be understated. Though at the beginning of this season, his statistics in terms of physical sprightliness and box-to-box involvements had fallen by the wayside, signalling that it was time to think about recruiting a long-term successor capable of carrying on that play-making midfield mantle; an unenviable role if ever there was one.

Hence why City felt the need to tunnel-vision an offer tailored specifically towards Monaco's outstanding Portuguese attacking midfielder; who'd exhibited similar qualities to David's earlier years in Manchester.

His name? Bernardo ... *Silva* ... go figure!

Still only 23 years of age at the time of signing, his development was intended to be overseen by the sage-like Spaniard; before passing on the baton for Bernardo to carry the 'Silva' name. And assuming how well he's taken to the role thus far, it's fair to suggest that the club are in good shape for when the aftermath of David's retirement comes into view.

Once Monaco was invaded, City felt the need to make their right-back spot just as efficient as their left-back position was threatening to be, hence why no expense was spared in bringing *both* Kyle Walker and Danilo to fix that up.

The former had long held the full-back reponsibility at Tottenham Hotspur, and was widely regarded as one of the best right-backs in the league, and the latter, who was frustrated by a lack of game time at Real Madrid, looked a versatile proposition for the Citizens to aid their back line on either flank, though overall acting as understudy to the aforementioned Walker to provide enough depth in quality for cup competitions in particular. Imagine that, buying somebody of Danilo's calibre as *cover* for your existing options. Oh, how the other half live ...

Then, with the sides of the defence bulked up for the years to come, its midriff needed just as much attention. Over the years, fans watched through squinted eyes as the defensive walls of Martín Demichelis, Matija Nastasić and Eliaquim Mangala were erected in sky blue - a defence formed with more holes than a rusty colander ... one that was run over by a car ... repeatedly. So, just imagine the relief from the shoulders of all 'Cityzens' when Aymeric Laporte walked through the door.

Another added to the list of 'you don't really want to join Manchester United, do you?' signings, a mere £54 million was paid to Athletic Bilbao for the ball-playing central defender, who would be embedded under the limited captaincy of Vincent Kompany; with a view to hopefully taking over the Belgian's role one day. And again, *on current form*, he appears to be a more than worthy candidate for succeeding the now-Anderlecht manager in the near future.

Overall, City's rejuvenated back line saw a net spend of around £150 million; an invoice soaked up relatively easily by their Arab funding mechanism. Oh, hang on! They forgot the goalkeeper. Get your chequebook back open, Mansour, we aren't done yet!

In order to fully account for Pep's *Total Football / Tiki Taka* -esque transformation of Manchester City, a change was also needed in between the sticks in order to maximise his 'play out from the back' game plan. Of course, incumbent 'keeper Joe Hart was an outstanding shot-stopper, and deserves much of the acclaim which garners the initial successes enjoyed by the pre-Pep Manchester City, though his ball-playing and overall distribution qualities weren't of the quality necessary for his new manager's all-conquering style. For Guardiola, the opportunity to begin the attack starts from the very moment at which your side obtains possession; which can, at times, begin with the goalkeeper.

Therefore, it became crucial to his plans that his called-upon stopper was capable and confident enough to: break through enemy offensive lines, sweep up the danger, relieve some pressure from the defence, and feed the ball onto the further outfield men, or restart the play at the most opportune moment once the ball had arrived with them with a counter-attack in mind.

And with the greatest of respects to Joe Hart, who I admire greatly for how he came to flourish in a City shirt, his game stuttered when it came to adhering to Pep's tactics, hence why he was deemed surplus to requirements once Brazilian 'keeper Ederson was flown over from Benfica.

Eight years Hart's junior, brimming with confidence and an eye for a dribble, Ederson would become everything that Pep would envision in a goalkeeper. He's quick-witted, cheeky, very good with the ball at his feet and an undeniably good shot-stopper to top all that off. And I'm sure we'll see a very stellar career from the Brazilian if his development continues in the vein that it has done so far – much like his adjoining new teammates.

So, there you had it, a lavish yet miraculous transfer window for the Sky Blues where, almost in one fell swoop, their worryingly ageing squad were replaced by a young, talented and hungry hoard of individuals who were being managed by one of the most inspiring and innovative coaches of his generation.

Ergo, from hereon in, Pep's men were set to take on the English Premier League once again - a crown only earned once since their maiden triumph. And if any of the previous seasons were defined by some cross between a fairy tale story, or some promise as to what *may* lay ahead of them, then this 2017/18 season is an illustration of pure, unadulterated, dominance.

***

When you talk about being the most 'dominant' team in the league, then there are a number of factors which can amount to this title; all of which are subjective.

There's an argument to consider United's 2007-09 team as 'dominant' in regard to their consistency and triplet of titles during this period, but then the same label ought to don the Chelsea side who stormed away with the league twice in a row; amounting the league's most commanding ever points difference in the process.

However, this is a judgement made considering a *number* of seasons, and if we're talking about a single campaign, then the only real data which needs pulling together would include a club's league record, number of wins and ultimately, the amount of points they end up with for that year.

And, in keeping with these criteria, nobody has since recorded a more dominant league win than Pep Guardiola's fully evolved Manchester City. Not only did they establish the longest continuous run of wins with eighteen, they also went a club-record-breaking twenty-eight games unbeaten, and registered the highest number of home *and* away wins ever seen in a single Premier League season. On top of this, their goal-scoring records were abhorrent, their defensive steeliness was forged from *Wakanda* itself, and most miraculously of all, they became the first ever team to gross an eventual tally of 100 points when reaching the top.

So, to put all of this campaign's records into some data-based context, out of 38 top division games, a triple-figure points tally means winning at *least* 31 of those (with the other games being only draws to make up the required difference). In reality, they went one better with 32 wins, 4 draws and 2 losses.

Sure, it may not match Arsenal's aura of 'invincibility' given the *obscene* (!) level of losses on their record, but often in situations where the Gunners might have settled for a draw to preserve their 'we-no-lose' title, City would go for broke in order to get the win. And for me, that is the key difference between these two outfits.

For that single season, they had relentlessly sought after winning each and every game. There were very few 'scraps' throughout the year where they 'grinded out a result', and the vast majority of their outings were peppered with precise, free-flowing football that typified their way of playing; where a positive result became an expectable bi-product.

Plus, serving as an extra dusting of icing sugar to fall upon the cherry on top of the cake, much of their triumph is owed to the new crop of lads brought in that summer - who would only seek to get better under the guidance of their manager and more experienced teammates. And so it came to be as this side went from strength-to-strength to retain their Premier League title against an outstanding Liverpool team who'd pushed them right on until the final day of the 2018/19 season.

Therefore, in doing all of this, Pep had not only managed to smash many of the expectations which landed at his feet when first taking on the job, but he'd somehow managed to one-up his *own* incredible list of managerial achievements.

At first, he changed the game with his Cruyff-inspired Catalonian *tiki taka* patrons, then he followed it up with his equally impressive Bulls of Bavaria, and now he had the famous 'City Centurions' to add to the list. Another notch on the belt for what has been a rather glittering coaching career for the ex-Barca midfielder … which is nowhere near its completion!

All in all, Manchester City had ultimately done what they'd initially set out to do after their inaugural title win; to move away from that 'lucky' aspect which began to drown out their initial achievements, and asserting a long-term vision which was communicated to their haters in the most silencing of ways.

Yet still, despite doing *all* of this and as annoying it may sound to some, it wasn't exactly the purist's idea of what the game of football stands for.

The advent of the Premier League as a whole was introduced to, *yes*, bring additional resources and overseas interest into English football. A result of which saw an improvement in how the game was presented via its progressively sophisticated setup, and in how competitively and 'beautifully' it was played; given the volume of talents attracted from afar.

But away from the pitch (so to speak) as discussed at length already, the foreign ownership model was introduced in order to make the most out of the commercial opportunity presented by the league's re-brand. Indeed, this has provided an additional income stream for the league, as well as the many other positive benefits derived from having money flood into a previously untapped market (by relative means). Though it seemed to contradict the idea of maintaining a *competitive* league; where many different competitors had a fair-enough probability of claiming its ultimate prize.

Whatever your own stance on the matter, this intense influx of money into the league had shifted the balance of power in favour of those that were lucky enough to receive it.

Right from Edwards and Walker in the early '90s, through to Abramovich and Mansour decades later, the game we knew and loved for its relatability and innocence, had drifted further away into a form of elitism which has grown common in money-driven sports like Formula One; where a boringly consistent number of front-runners for the championship is all we had to look forward to come the campaign's finale.

And indeed, champions like Manchester United, Blackburn Rovers, Chelsea and Manchester City are all examples of the point raised. Though just when it seemed like our wonderful sport was doomed to be another fad for the top earners, a plucky little side from the Midlands were on hand to remind us all that football is indeed a *beautiful* game.

~ 27 ~

'WHAT JUST HAPPENED?!'

I thought that this was a rich man's game . . .

Like any team game, you can assemble the greatest team in the world on paper, but a number of external issues come into play by the time they pull on their robes and engage in battle. Hence why the sphere of sport is bereft with a number of key moments which challenge our understanding of what we believed to be possible before it takes place, and are capable of setting their very own precedents if significant enough to do so.

Take, for example, a number of the notable timeline ignition points detailed in this book so far ...

The public Clough and Revie rivalry was relatively new in its era, but has since become commonplace between competing managers in the age of social media and regular televisual engagement, the embryonic 'Total Football' concept went through its own evolution before being ultimately transformed into Guardiola's updated *tiki taka* format, and the Premier League invention ushered in this new, commercial outlook to an otherwise provincial game, which had its own timelines leading into international competition. And here, we have another ignition point in Leicester City's miraculous drive towards the most unlikely of Premier League crowns in the 2016/17 season.

While Manchester City were slowly cultivating their big-money side to obtain the league in a form of supremacy warranted by their exorbitant levels of spending, it looked as though we were moving into an era where your bank balance ultimately dictates the level of success that you're able to enjoy.

But this season was different. It was like a case of divine intervention where an omnibenevolent power sought to correct the imbalance of power running rife in the game, with the Foxes as its subject party.

As we look back on this campaign, we've arrived at the point where I'd usually write squeamishly about the absurd amounts of money being spent by the eventual champions. However, that's only on the basis that the club in question are genuine title contenders for the year ahead. Yeah … Leicester weren't that.

Under the screw-loose managerial style of Nigel Pearson, Leicester were not in great shape leading up to the previous season's final day, yet a mix of resilience and fortune preserved their immediate topflight future - one which wouldn't include Pearson at the helm. In his place, came ex-Chelsea manager Claudio Ranieri; a surprising appointment for all involved. Over the years, a broad variety of tasks had arrived at the Italian's desk. He had been Head Coach at Atlético Madrid before ushering in the Abramovich era at Chelsea, and more recently, he was 'head *ultra*' for Inter Milan and AS Monaco. And as can be deduced from his experiences to this point, Ranieri's comfort zone lay firmly within the upper echelons of continental football; where the club's fortune favours his more open, free-flowing attacking style - almost the antithesis of a Premier League relegation battle. Though luckily for him, his way of football was exactly what his new employer was looking for.

Having taken over at the club along with an Asian sports consortium in 2010, wealthy Thai businessman Vichai Srivaddhanaprabha had been there to oversee the club's ascent into the Premier League from the depths of the English Third Division.

Under his charm, the Foxes stayed within their means throughout their revolution, and over time, they were able to slowly develop into the type of squad which meshed in well with their hierarchy's mantra - understated, hard-working and effective. Though now, by recruiting Ranieri, it seemed to be a signal of intent that the club were ready to ascend into the upper heights of the league.

Generally, this would mean attempting to navigate away from a relegation battle, to the point where you land in a mid-table spot, or if the Lord hath shined His light upon thou, perhaps even a free top-half European space. Strikingly, Leicester went a bit *higher* than that, though their summer transfer activity wasn't very indicative of what would become of them.

Their most significant outlay was shy of £10 million for FSV Mainz striker Shinji Okazaki. A modest, hard-working striker during his time in Germany, his relentless enthusiasm and business on the front line embodied everything required to become a fan's favourite at the club. Having said that, and while he may court a favourable testimonial from fans in blue, City's most shrewd and important acquisitions came for those stationed behind the Japanese busy body; beginning with the modest £3 million cheque written to secure Stoke City's own Robert Huth.

As somebody who doesn't attract much of the credit for their forthcoming campaign, I deem Huth to be one of their most pivotal arrivals that summer. Having initially begun his Premier League career with Mourinho's Chelsea, his latter spell at Stoke solidified his calm and no-nonsense defensive reputation; which could now be brought to the Foxes on their journey to ascension. Similar to the signing of Robert Huth, the Bosman-induced acquisition of full-back Christian Fuchs was a wonderfully timed piece of business from Leicester City.

Supposedly, the experienced Austrian had been courted by a number of Premier League and overseas clubs during his final season in the Bundesliga with FC Schalke 04, though the draw of Ranieri's forward-thinking requirements of his full-backs proved pivotal to Fuchs' relocation to the East Midlands.

Ahead of the pure defensive area, Ranieri knew better than anybody the importance of employing somebody to marshal the lines between the defence and midfield. Lest we forget, he worked closely with Claude Makélélé at Chelsea and with his image lingering fresh in the memory, promising break-up man Daniel Amartey was drafted in from FC Copenhagen, though unfortunately for him, his inclusion in the squad was soon limited in light of who his new club had signed shortly after him.

Now, I'm going to go out on a limb here, but I believe that this deal should credit Leicester City with sorting out **one of the greatest overseas Premier League transfers of all time**.

Of course, I'm referring to the signing of N'Golo Kanté from SM Caen for £7.5 million, though I like to refer to it as 'the passing of the torch' moment for club and country. Much like the preceding Makélélé, Kanté is a combattive midfielder, who favours the sideways pass nearly as much as he does messing up the opposition's plans. Moreover, he is tenacious, always on full charge and never seems to seek to want to bask in the limelight for his own personal gain. Actually, he seems to revel the thought of providing for his more extroverted teammates to do what they do best, and Ranieri was all too happy to accommodate this.

Yet, in spite of adding Demarai Gray to their ranks after the promising winger outgrew his boots at Birmingham City, this season's attention and goal return lay firmly with the group of forwards he himself was fortunate-enough to join.

Only two seasons before, *Ligue Deux* side Le Havre received the princely sum of £275,000 from Leicester for Algerian wide-man Riyad Mahrez. Which, if we are to assume that the average Premier League ticket comes to about £30 (give or take a few coins), and that the usual attendance at the King Power Stadium in the Premier League would be anywhere between 30-32,000 people every other week, then the fee for Mahrez was near enough less than half of their single intake for a home fixture; excluding their merchandise sales, food concessions, VIP packages and televisual receipts.

Nothing short of remarkable business from the Leicester City hierarchy when you consider his attributes. On the face of it, Riyad Mahrez cuts a slender figure on the right wing, with a style reminiscent to that of Arjen Robben, only much less injured … and *fuller* in the … hair follicle department.

Nevertheless, the similarities emerge from the unstoppable element of their forward play. Much like the glistening-scalped Dutchman, Mahrez' game hinged heavily upon his ability to pace towards the defence, cut back onto his strong left foot and angle the trajectory of the ball to its intended home. And given his manager's precedent with famous wingers like Alessandro Del Piero and Robben himself, he really couldn't have hand-picked a better coach under whom to thrive.

The thing is though, even somebody like Arjen Robben needs a competent front line in order to bring the best out of him. Throughout his illustrious career, the Dutchman had somebody like Didier Drogba, Ruud van Nistelrooy or Robert Lewandowski next to him, and fortunately for Mahrez, Leicester had their own ... slightly less domineering version of an elite front man.

Whoever has been involved in the club's scouting and recruitment department throughout this time deserves a knighthood and a lifetime of pleasure. As mentioned, scouting N'Golo Kanté was a masterstroke, and Riyad Mahrez' cut-price investment was outstanding for sure, but the purchase of Fleetwood Town's Jamie Vardy is in a league of its own.

The story of Jamie Vardy is so uplifting, that it makes my heart all warm and fuzzy. It also helps to reaffirm the idea that pure talent and desire remain the pivotal mechanisms behind one's eventual success in the game's top competition.

However, to begin with, a combination of educational disinterest and general 'ne'er-do-well-ism' meant that elite-level football was not much of an afterthought in the striker's mind when he reached adulthood. As such, the glory of the bigger academy lifestyle didn't appear as much of an option to a young Jamie Vardy, and if his love of football were to remain ignited, it would be up to the striker himself to make the most out of whatever limited opportunities sprung up in front of him.

In keeping with this, his story begins in the English non-league setup with FC Halifax Town, where his aforementioned run-ins with the law led to: regular court appearances, an electronic tag and a series of time-honoured curfews which cut through a number of his first team evening commitments! Nevertheless, he obeyed his orders, appeared to have matured in his new profession and even attracted some interest from elsewhere once some grainy footage surfaced of his time with Halifax. I mean, he did score thirty goals in that single season with them, so maybe that explains Fleetwood Town's bid better than anything else.

Having said that, his questionable personal life meant that this was a move that would've been met with a stern 'your job is on the line if this doesn't work out' to whoever spotted Vardy *and* sanctioned the deal for him; not least due to the fact that Fleetwood had to smash their transfer record to make it happen!

Now, this could have gone one of two ways ...

a) Vardy would fall just as quickly as he rose, as he fails to shake off the demons of the past or;

b) He would prove the doubters wrong, repay the faith of his new employers and put his unfavourable record out of sight in search for the career he was aiming for.

Needless to say, an average of a goal scored every 1.2 games for Town suggests that the plucky lad came good, and it even helped to make sense of what must've been considered a rather hopeful release clause in his contract.

As we have seen before, release clauses generally attract a negative stigma; that of being imposed by a wantaway player or itchy-footed agent as a threshold to get a potential deal done. But in this case, Fleetwood rightly decided that if they were to put this amount of faith into buying Vardy (given that they weren't exactly the richest club to begin with), they were entitled to protect their investment via receiving a record-breaking sale amount in return. And by the time Srivaddhanaprabha's Championship side were in a position to meet that £1 million amount, I bet they were pretty content that they did.

Make no bones about it, this transfer was met with more scepticism than applause. For a club like Leicester today, that type of fee would be a nominal amount splashed willy-nilly on anybody with even an ounce of potential on display. But to fork out that amount of money back then for a *non-league player*, and task him with moving up three English divisions whilst continuing that rich vein of form against much better opposition, was a big, big ask. And in the early stages, Vardy himself had struggled to cope.

The defenders he became so used to coasting around and leaving for dead, were suddenly sunken further into their shape and were more difficult to break down.

So, it took him at least a full season to understand how this league plays, and what weapons in his arsenal were best equipped to deal with his new opponents. And in the following season, his improved IQ aided Leicester in laying siege to the Second Division and topping it for the majority of the campaign - eventually earning their way to the Premier League before scathing off that initial relegation battle and welcoming in Ranieri. Who himself, now had a fresh-faced Kanté, an eager-looking Mahrez and a fully compliable Vardy to work with.

They started this season the way they finished the last; where their intentions weren't centred upon negatively shutting out the opposition by preventing them from scoring, but more so to allow the game to progress in its most organic way and out-doing them at their own game.

They seemed to understand that, the minute you enter a game with a negative style against seemingly superior opposition, you have pretty much lost from the moment you've stepped onto the pitch. With this style, unless your counter-attacking abilities are '*A-1*', you are playing right into the hands of the team who need to see more of the ball if they are to carve out the attack and, more importantly, you're allowing them to dictate the pace at which the game is played. But, if you flip that on its head, and assert yourselves into the game; are first to every loose ball, don't give them enough time to steady themselves and get the crowd behind you, then you have set the stage for a top-level performance. In short, it sets up an upset.

So, the more games in which you're able to exhibit this way of thinking, the more it becomes a systematic style of work as opposed to a new improvement for a particular opponent. Thus, we have the story of Leicester - the ultimate example of team spirit and positivity against challenge and adversity.

Having fought off relegation a matter of months before, the Foxes were considered underdogs to repeat that feat; let alone daring to reach any higher. Correspondingly, the bookmakers had them as a laughable 5000-1 underdogs to win the Premier League title when their first win of the opening day took them to the top on goal difference!

But get this ... they *stayed there!*

As mentioned, much of their game coincided with not allowing their opponents to settle into their shape - even if it meant sacrificing theirs. The back four remained as consistent as ever in terms of selection, though they looked out for each other whenever outnumbered or in a dangerous situation. Plus, if the play reached the midfield area, the AAA-battery-powered N'Golo Kanté would be there to win the ball back and continue what became an explosive counter-attacking operation with Mahrez and Vardy leading the line.

Sure that's a rather *simple* way of looking at it, though when we team this with their powerful set-play formations, top-notch Fuchs deliverables from the wings, Mahrez' mazey runs in from the right flank, and Vardy's highly intelligent running in behind the back, you begin to understand why they were tough to catch.

And by the time their competitors realised what their game-plan looked like, it was too late to do anything about it. Leicester City took the competition by storm, ran towards the unlikeliest of triumphs ever recorded in the Premier League era (and perhaps throughout the annuls of English football as a whole), and Gary Lineker's clothes-less presentation of *Match of the Day* stands to represent how outlandish this whole thing was. Outlandish ... but brilliant. In fact, it was *beautiful.*

You know, I'd like to think that everybody became an honorary Leicester City fan this season, and their proliferation since that year has become a welcome destabilizer to the institutions at the top of Premier League football. But even more than that, the story of their top goal-scorer set of its own chain of positivity which very few have centred upon since it occurred. I guess that's what I'm here for!

The tale of Jamie Vardy's rise to glory does not end with his Premier League success, as his legacy seems to have had a profound effect upon the leagues he'd previously worked for.

On the one hand, he is Jamie Vardy: Premier League champion and record-setting goal-scorer, but on the other, he is Jamie Vardy: juvenile delinquent who developed from the lower leagues in a way that many deemed impossible. Too often do we hear of the broken careers for those who had had their hopes raised and dashed by a mis-leading topflight academy lifestyle, so what a joy it was to see a lesser league patron come good as an alternative to the mentioned journey. And, with the aspirational aspect aside (that's a lot of 'as's), his coming-of-age story thrusted some positive attention on his prior establishments … which had a more profound impact on some than others.

'Out of their league'

Back in the day, it was common practise to scour the lower leagues for diamonds in the rough and impose upon them the task to make the step up at higher level. Indeed, diamonds like Kevin Keegan, Denis Irwin and Lee Sharpe rose to the fore in such circumstances, before foreign influences lessened the desire to keep looking where they were used to looking.

As a result, the quality of lower league football began to plummet. The focus on England was towards the national team and the Premier League - where the former would regularly only consider players who were contracted to teams in the latter. So, to suddenly have a lad like Jamie Vardy win the Premier League less than five years after playing lower than the fifth tier of the English game, incited a new-found interest into going back to stock. Especially when you consider that his development isn't an isolated case.

Here are some examples ...

To the untrained eye, the visibility of Charlie Austin came when he was playing for the Saints in the Top Division, or perhaps with Burnley in the league below. But in light of Vardy's antics, a magnifier reveals his humble upbringing with Poole and Swindon Town - each of whom received some much-deserved recognition for breeding an elite-level striker.

On top of this, we've already mentioned Joe Hart's 'big break' at Shrewsbury Town which opened up the doors to City's position in goal, and players like West Ham's Michail Antonio and ex-Crystal Palace wide-man Yannick Bolasie became similar cases in point; with each of their stories being as uplifting and life-affirming as the last.

So, altogether, it helped to remind us that a non-league prospect could actually be good enough to obtain the greatest prize in the Premier League, provided we looked beyond their lack-of-star-academy CV to uncover their beneficial qualities. And with this boost in lower league interest, few went even further than that to actively improve the EFL's foundations with the aim of creating more stories like these. There was even a *Sky Sports* documentary serving to educate us all on the subject.

Salford City: A Case Study

Alright, even I'll admit it's a more than tenuous link to make between stories like Vardy, Hart *et al,* and the overtaking of a seventh tier football club by a group of Premier League legends, but both go hand-in-hand with bringing some much-required positive attention to the EFL's foundations.

Think about it: if you had your own distinguished playing career and were now looking for the right step up to the boardroom, you're better off investing your money into a long-term goal with a club which affords you the freedom to realise whatever you envision, as opposed to becoming some shareholder in a big brand like those you've been employed by. So, in my opinion, the pure dedication and intensity with which the Class of '92 have approached their takeover of lowly Salford City since 2014, somewhat showcases a desire to cultivate their very own positive stories from the lower leagues. And before you cynically discard this undertaking as some publicity stunt for the old boys to 'get some attention', here's what Gary Neville has to say to you:

> "We could have departed and said, 'let's just sit on the television and take money for the next 20 years' … [But] outside of all the noise we've heard in the last few years, ultimately it's *just noise* and **what we're doing on the ground speaks louder.**"

> – Gary Neville

You know, it's very easy for the media to clout a footballer in so much soot that you begin to forget who they are at their core. As presented, Gary Neville is a passionate right-back-cum-polished *Sky Sports* pundit. Paul Scholes attracts more positive fellow baller reviews than a 5* *Airbnb* villa. Nicky Butt and Phil Neville are as bubbly as they are well-respected in the game, and David Beckham is ... *the* David Beckham.

But if you peel that all away; all of that money, acclaim, fame and media attention, they're a simple group of hard-working, humble lads whose pubescent years in the modest neighbourhood of Salford helped to guide their forthcoming success. And now, they could hopefully become the driving forces behind their own team's success.

Prior to the takeover, the club experienced your typical hand-to-mouth existence for a non-league outfit; constantly recycling their nominal funds into wherever it needed to go with little room for self-interest or wider business initiatives. Therefore, having a number of rich and famous local lads returning to guide them to prosperity, was as divine an intervention as anything we've considered so far.

Similar to other clubs in the league, Salford was a fan-run club which, apart from a few who were able to kick a ball and the fewer who believed they were good enough to instruct them how to do so, was comprised of a group of stealthy, determined and passionate volunteers who kept the club running for the good of the cause. They weren't paid a salary, were rarely commended for their actions and yet worked tirelessly every match day (and free time in between) to ensure that their wonderful club remained afloat. Admirable, this certainly is. But professional, this is not.

Therefore, in this search for 'correctness' and 'order' to qualify for higher competition in the future, the Class of '92 were soon to be dealt with the various trials and tribulations that affect club owners; and some which may go beyond your average jurisdiction.

In fact, if ever there was a fitting metaphor for the state of the club at the time of the takeover, it's that quaint little clip of Neville examining their existing toilet facilities in their *'Class of 92: Out of Their League'* series by *Sky Sports*. Because as we know, all great stadium developments begin with the toilets. Right, Mr. Dein?

The bogs were crumbling to pieces. Bits of urinal all over the floor, the lights barely worked, and the door was caved in, but that was only the start of their worries! God forbid we arc our necks towards the boggy pitch, blocked drains or litter-laden stands. So, let's just say that there was *a lot* of work to do. Resultantly, they proposed to concede up to 50% of their stake in the club as an offering to a wealthy businessperson who could provide them with some additional financial acuity and commercial acumen to oversee their renovations.

Singaporean man, reveal yourself!

Hereafter, it was Peter Slim's investment and the Class' use of it which eventually led to the professionalisation of Salford City Football Club in their third season in charge. Though, just from a purely substantive point of view, the process of professionalising a football team is not an easy one, and only ever really comes into view once you're at tier 5 of the English pyramid or above.

In fact, there is a simply marvellous book written by Nige Tassell titled, *'The Bottom Corner: Hope, Glory and Non-League Football'* which offers a fabulous insight into a number of cases where non-league clubs have reached a similar state in their evolution, and have had to alter their current state of affairs in order to comply with where they were looking to be.

And if you want to find out more about these like-minded instances, then I implore you to snag yourselves a copy of this magnificent read as I cannot recommend it highly enough. Actually, Tassell himself dedicates a particular highlight to the new Salford hierarchy in his novel, which speaks to the idiosyncratic journey that they seemed to be going on.

As Nige details and I shall summarise, new stands were fitted to the stadium, an isolated commentary section was made for EFL freelancers, branding became synergistic throughout their new-look home, a range of amenities were available on the outskirts of its shell, a part-time work schedule was in place for security and community organisers on matchday, a club shop was set up and became fully operational, broadcast sponsorship was created on team merchandise, social media and other club apparel, and the squad became filled with a mix of higher-experienced pros and non-experienced youths to be fit for their new purpose.

Thus, the newly christened 'Peninsula Stadium' was open for business to welcome the bulging cohort of new 'Ammies' fans arriving to catch a glimpse of this historic transformation. And just in time to oversee a tremendously dramatic play-off journey before securing a spot in the English Fourth Division; headed up by the calm, composed and cashmere-donned frame of Graham Alexander.

The club are currently seated comfortably in the underbelly of the EFL League Two, and as I'm sure you'd agree, it's a simply miraculous transformation given how far they were made to trek. And I hear the toilets aren't in bad nick, either!

Only time will tell to see just *how well* the club will be able to do in the forthcoming years, but nevertheless, their story serves as a welcome reminder that, away from the suits, oil and lies of elite-level football, there are clubs below them that are finally receiving some recognitive trickle-down benefits for some of their previously unnoticed work. And I see little option but to attribute some of this development to what went on in Leicester's title-winning campaign.

***

Plus, *another* effect derived from Leicester's Cinderella story was that clubs of a similar ilk to them began to seem a more viable overseas investment than before.

As we know, the sport's wealth had already reached London and the North East in terms of commercial interest and angel investors, but Leicester had shone a particular light on the growing stature of clubs in the Midlands who, if operated correctly, were supposedly capable of writing some historical chapters of their own.

The chief case among which was Wolverhampton Wanderers ('Wolves') who would become one of the first direct beneficiaries of this evolution, though their example would highlight a decidedly different (yet incredibly crucial) aspect of how the modern football world operates. One which largely flies under the radar on the face of it all, until it often rears its ugly and intrusive head when we delve a little deeper; the football agent. Of them all, Jorge Mendes appears to be one of the 'good guys', whose star-studded client list pays homage to his professionalism and daringness to stand out from the crowd in a highly saturated industry. And most poignantly, one whose expansion was aided in great part by *FIFA's* alarmingly blasé tactic to regulate the industry that he serves.

~ 28 ~

'THE AGENT'S PLAYGROUND'

Let's make some money!

It may surprise some of you to learn that agency is not a term invented for football, in fact, it's an area of law which spreads into the realms of: real estate, dealerships, recruitment and wider sports representation, to name a few.

It surrounds this concept of a *fiduciary* relationship between an agent and their client; where the agent is obligated to prioritise the best interests of their client above everything else.

So, in footballing terms, if your client wants to move to another club, or would prefer not to engage in negotiations with another team and stay where they are, it is up to the agent to recognise these interests and act accordingly. Plus, outside of pure club-related matters, the agent is also enlisted to navigate the worlds of finance, commerce and wider business functioning to enact any ulterior interests of their player; ones for which their own lack of knowledge may leave untapped.

Correspondingly, the role of the football agent is a pivotal and largely *admirable* one; provided that it is conducted within its parameters and centres on respecting those fiduciary obligations. But when dealing with human beings, sometimes you come across people who like to obscure the law in their favour. Worse still, the overarching law of agency itself becomes muddied when morphed into the idiosyncratic world of sport, particularly in the amount of money that can be demanded for their services; and its unwelcome impact on the rules that were made to be respected.

You see, in most other businesses, agents or 'middle-men' are compensated on a pro-rata basis; which is often directly reflective of the deal that they brokered, or the original agreement they entered for acting on their client's behalf.

However, in football, the money involved can rise to very high levels and be attracted from all angles; all to the benefit of those who are shrewd enough to carve out the most personally beneficial route for access.

Let's think about it …

How many different business-related football deals require the use of a single agent or agency?

1. Well, if a prospective owner is looking to make an investment into a football team, who operates on the consortium's behalf to make their bid viable?
2. Then again, what if a club is looking for a long-term sponsor and want to get the deal done as smoothly as possible, who do they turn to? And;
3. When *Nike* or *Puma* come knocking at the doors of the game's brightest prospects, who's best placed to broker a deal for them?

<u>Answers here</u>: The agent. The agent. *The. Agent.*

In the most basic of terms, whenever a business deal needs to be concluded, footballing etiquette dictates than an agent need be present - a feeling which only grew as the game developed into a more commercial setting.

The inception of the Premier League and Champions League in particular, had represented a new-found boost in transfer market value which an agent could now fully exploit. Then, the year 2002 signified the introduction of the game's first ever transfer window.

'What? But I thought there were *always* transfer windows in place?' Nope. Prior to this date, all of your favourite players were at risk, and it was eventually seen as nonsensical for clubs to not have the security of preserving their players for at least a season or so.

Therefore, 'windows' were introduced as pockets of time per year within which all of this business could be concluded – one prior to the season starting in the summer, and one during the season in the winter as a 'top-up' of sorts.

The idea stuck and remains to this day, but to think that business simply begins and concludes solely within these periods, is a dramatic misunderstanding of how imposing time-specific windows began to influence the minds of those involved. After they were enforced, the agent's income became largely funnelled into these fast-paced business periods, and that only served to make it *even more* imperative to make them as fruitful as possible for them whenever they came around. And this sometimes means setting up a deal (in principal) outside of its parameters, with the view that they could eventually be concluded within them.

So, this whole illusion of 'sticking within your business period' in a bid to curtail the impact of not having them ... is exactly that; an *illusion*. As is the case with many of the regulations concerning the entire area of football agency. Now, in its earlier days, football agency wasn't anywhere near as fervent and pervasive as it is now – partly because there were several key restrictions upon anybody who wished to define themselves as one.

Back then, before paying an initial flat registration fee, the applicant needed to provide their credit score and existing banking and savings balances, to ensure that they were in a viable position to incur any job-related costs whilst registered. Another similar fee would then be required by both their local football association and to FIFA themselves in two different currencies - again, to prove proof of funds and quell any suspicions surrounding their intent to become an agent.

Then, all eligible pupils were subject to an aptitude test on: their knowledge of the game, the regulations surrounding it, and the deeper-rooted ideals behind the job they intend to perform; with a myriad of multiple-choice and scenario-based questions used to test them on their ability to improvise and call upon their revised knowledge. Which was basically a university-level exam to represent sports players ... debt 'n' all!

And once they pass (which requires an 80%-or-higher score on both sections of the exam), they were subject to a character-based evaluation from a representative of their local footballing authority.

This bit was like meeting the in-laws for the first time of somebody you've been dating for a few years; a relentless, personal barrage of impossible-to-answer questions to prove your innocence to those who love to question it.

But if you hold yourself in strong esteem, and navigate your way through their piercing stares and blood-curdling scepticism, then you finally get that 'agent' title; and are legally authorised to behave like one … unless you intended to broker international deals … then you would have to go through all of this again for each respective territory.

I need to lie down!

… oh yeah, and if you fail to go through any of these steps before engaging in the profession, or if you merely forget to enclose your earned registration number in any related documentation, you risk the wrath of the Court of Arbitration for Sport ('CAS') having cause to revoke your licence.

But for those with enough attention to detail to evade their scorn, you needed only concern yourself with the job at hand and the level of remuneration at your disposal. Which, using the FA as an example, was no more than 7% of a client's net income whilst the player was stationed in the UK.

Objectively, this is not much more than a welcome imposition which serves to protect the player from an agent whose implicit desires are to rinse their pockets dry. However, its resulting misappropriation is an almost *natural* consequence when you consider the stereotype it aims to constrain.

Whenever you enter into an area where money stuffs are involved, the savviest of inclusions are continuously looking to make the most they can, and because the money-makers in football are *so* vulnerable, it's become a hotbed for opportunists to worm their way into a position from which they can (at times) prey on that vulnerability; and reveal the restrictions themselves to be flawed.

Firstly, that whole 7% malarkey was a loophole in itself. The cap was focused solely on the *direct* commission earned by the agent from their client's wages i.e. that they could only earn a maximum of 7% from this *particular* income stream. So, I guess, in a time where this specific source was the sole birthplace for a player's income, then the restriction poses a relatively impregnable barrier to break. But bring this into the modern-day atmosphere, with all of these ulterior revenue streams being present, then it throws it up into the air.

Whether it's seeing Jesse Lingard endorse the new *Lynx: Chill* brand or the stubble-laden Liverpool players slap a bit of *Nivea* on their cheek, footballers have become inescapable branding figures via the game's modern updates; and are largely free to engage with these commissions provided that they don't directly conflict with their club's aligned business initiatives – be it an entire mature venture away from the game, or an endorsement made possible by how famous they've become while playing.

And remember, the agents responsible for enabling these demands are often front-and-centre when it comes to organising payment for their clients *and* themselves; which usually goes well beyond that initial 7% cap by throwing in something it had never previously considered.

Therefore, it has since proven an innovative way of using the game's new commercial setting, to circumvent the archaic restrictions on an agent's income. Ergo, there was no telling when this nouveau-riche agency finance stream was going to relent. So, naturally, change was afoot when there was a meeting announced between FIFA and various domestic associations; with the intent to resolve these irregularities.

And judging by the archival material available on the subject, the general consensus was that such disregard for the restrictions, were bred by the wealth of requirements needed to become an agent in the first place - a sort of 'do you know what I had to go through to get here?!' mentality.

Correspondingly, to encourage a much-needed transparency within this area, a radical step was taken by FIFA in 2015; to categorically remove all of its entry requirements for new applicants. Because as we all know, if you had a group of frivolous drivers on the road, then removing the obligation to take a driving test would be the perfect way to sort out their indiscretions (!) ...

Among the more pivotal associations to follow FIFA's 'instruction', the UK were one of the first to get rid of all those silly examinations, interviews and stringent background/credit checks. All in favour of a single £500 registration fee with a yearly £250 renewal. That's it. And to officialise their rejuvenated doctrine, the term 'agent' was done away with in favour of the title, 'intermediary'.

This means that if you or I wanted to become an FA-registered 'intermediary', we wouldn't have to be even remotely 'qualified' to become one; nor be subject to any of the older in-law tests. Instead, we need to only: be an adult, have a bank account set up, and relieve ourselves of £500. Then Bob shall be our uncle.

Hang on a second ...

For a moment, let's not be cynical as to how near-sighted this 'solution' proved to be (which it most definitely was), and look at this issue as level-headed and balanced a way as possible. As admittedly, there are other, more humanitarian benefits to the FA's new rules … or lack thereof.

Before the change, the selection process was inherently tailored toward the richer and more privileged edge of society. Where, for your everyday applicant, the fees were a monumental financial commitment to make, not to mention the timing issues with having to attend multiple interviews, sit exams and be submitted to a character check; all assumed during your full-time occupation; unless fortunate enough to have an accommodating schedule.

Therefore, I guess to relieve certain hard-pressed applicants of these restrictions, allows for a more diverse pool of potential 'intermediaries' to get involved; which could help to improve the overall morality of the applications flooding in – which is purely suggestive over how one's background implies they would behave in a setting like this … which is not an exact science.

However, we also need to remember, that the benefits presented by this new regime were completely indiscriminate. So, it really didn't matter whether you were a new applicant or an existing licensee, or indeed if you came from a modest background or one of innumerable means, *everybody* was intended to benefit from this; and that's precisely where the problem lies. In that not everybody can have the best intentions. Once allowed in, it was completely down to the discretion of the intermediaries to recognise the gift of the Football Association and reward them with the personal candour that their changes expected.

So, What Happened Next?

In short, the plan had completely backfired, and the game has been paying for it ever since. Such to the point that current FIFA president Gianni Infantino has been in fervent discussion with his committee, to come up with a policy aimed to reverse the amount of influence it has afforded some of those within the industry.

Chief among which are two high-profile examples. Both with international acclaim, a wardrobe full of *Gucci* and a client list to make your children cry. Though where one's success is clouted in a halo of pride and skill, the other is attracted by as much infamy as it has been by respect. So, let's start with *that* one.

Beginning as a wannabe businessman in his native Spain, the bullish nature for which Mino Raiola has since become famous, served him very well in his earlier years - constantly worming his way into meetings he wasn't invited to, and into one-on-one conversations with people he had no business approaching; in order to obtain a pathway towards the game's biggest stars.

Over time, he learned on the job, forged some rather fruitful working relationships and, at the time of writing, his portfolio includes the representation rights for Paul Pogba, Zlatan Ibrahimović, Matthijs de Ligt and Erling Braut Håland.

And what do all of these players have in common? Well, besides being outstanding professionals in their own right, each have been the subject of big-money moves with the game's elite during long, protracted, media-centric transfer negotiations - facilitated by their immoveable agent for obvious, money-making motives.

Ibrahimović has moved onto three different clubs over the past four years, each time receiving handsome registration packages for the English Premier League, Major League Soccer and Serie A. Both de Ligt and Håland engaged in a shameless flirting act between clubs like Manchester United, Manchester City and Real Madrid before opting for Juventus and Borussia Dortmund respectively ... both for an inflated fee, compared to any of their initial speculation.

And last but not least, the transfer saga surrounding Paul Pogba is still ongoing, with experts claiming that the recent rejuvenation of Manchester United could see the Frenchman continue in the North East but others, including Raiola himself, deem the player to 'not be [his team's] property', and persist with this DM-based relationship with Europe's best. Some shady stuff.

So sure, a deal concerning Raiola would often equal a deal involving a lot of money (for the benefit of himself *and* his client), but for employers and potential buyers, he's what you might call an 'unhealthy influence'. Like one of those kids around the corner that your parents forbid you from 'messing with'; because they're 'no good' for your future.

Suitably, he has proven to be an absolute mastermind at playing off bidders against each other; in an attempt to secure the most lucrative deal for all beneficiaries. Typically, this would be via wages, playing bonuses, signing-on fees and other playing-based incentives, though 'innovators' like him have since grown accustomed to asserting an 'agency fee' - which works in a very similar way to the mentioned bulk amount offered to their client when signing for a new club. Again, think of it like a 'Thank You' amount for their involvement in the deal ... or an unofficial 'bung' to facilitate it - but that's hearsay and hereby inadmissible in court.

This agency fee is adjacent to the agreement and therefore does not fall directly under the salary cap imposed by FIFA. Instead, it's an ulterior arrangement made at the discretion of the agent and other associated parties, to decide on a fair-enough fee for their services. And generally, the amount isn't wholly indicative of how involved / integral the agent has proven themselves to be to this process, but instead on how sought-after their client is, and correspondingly, how imperative it becomes to keep their agent happy with the process.

So, when you have as extensive a top-drawer portfolio as Raiola's, his agency fees can amount to an ungodly sum and have, at times, proved a stumbling block in some of his negotiations. It's no wonder then, that he's earned himself a fair few enemies among those in contention for his clients' services.

In fact, no less than the great Sir Alex Ferguson recalls a number of fallouts with the super-agent when dealing with him during his long, successful tenure as manager of Manchester United. Though that's not to suggest that his own testimonials are reflective of his industry as a whole, because on the flipside, another super-agent has attracted a juxtaposing level of positive reviews from his admirers. Not just for his amorous style, but also for his willingness to test the waters, and revolutionise his role in a way that no other agent has ever dared to do before him.

'I like Jorge Mendes!' – pretty much everyone

His *Gestifute* agency ranks among the most reputable in the world, and follows their star attraction in being the pillar of consistency and properness within the industry. Moreover,

Mendes himself actively denounces the wider interpretation of those within his field, and assures that his business does all it can to preserve the fiduciary duty of their role above all else. Though he couldn't quite figure out why this duty need only be applied to a single player as a client and could not work for a club

He was of the firm belief that, provided he acted with contempt for a breach of the rules and with total confidence in the actions of his client, he preserved just as much standing in representing a club as he did any footballer, just from the opposite end of the table. He decided it was time to investigate, and his alignment with Wolverhampton Wanderers soon formed once there appeared very few hurdles for doing so.

Wolves are a club with a topsy-turvy history. Back in the days with Steve Bull leading the line, the West Midlands outfit were a fine institution with a certain level continental success to boast. But then you fast forward to around thirty years later, and they've succumbed to a double, successive relegation from the Premier League right down to League One; with very little sign of a meaningful rebirth on the horizon for them.

Nevertheless, their fall did little to discourage interest from potential buyers focused on restoring their reputation. And as we know, interested parties sometimes come in the form of an investor whose background is as little to do with football as mine is to do with pole-dancing (alright, that was one time!). So, the announced decision to become buddies with one of the game's biggest *internal* businessmen was a real shock to the system - one that every 'Wolf' is thankful for; considering that Mendes' allegiance included having dibs on much of his client base.

But wait, isn't this a conflict of interest?

Well, yes, though this is where Mendes' true savviness (as a *businessman*) shines through.

You see, he never actually *signed* an agreement with Wolves to officialise his connection with the club. Instead, it was a mere understanding between himself and the club's hierarchy to establish a precedent of bringing in Mendes' clients on a quasi-exclusive basis. And it was this precise informality which protected a formal investigation into his setup with them by the EFL in 2018.

Hence why his pairing with Fosun International (the new Wanderers' ownership group from two years before) has enjoyed its most fruitful relations since being given the full green light. A growth which also owes a lot of its development to head coach, Nuno Espírito Santo – also a Mendes client.

As it stands, the club's registration books include some very notable names indeed; most of which are either direct Mendes associates or were intrigued at the thought of being part of his informal Midlands revolution.

Not least midfield fulcrum Leander Dendoncker, Portuguese wonderkid Rúben Neves, explosive winger Adama Traoré, and prolific front man Raúl Jiménez. They even escaped a CAS trial to bring in longstanding Portugal national stopper Rui Patrício on a compensatory package. Major moves! Altogether resulting in a stable top-half Premier League side capable of mixing it with the big boys, and provided that this trajectory continues, the sky's the limit for the West Midlands side. Having said that, there's no getting away from the fact that those within his position were exerting an exceedingly large influence on the game. I mean, even though *his* involvement in the Premier League has turned out to be a largely wholesome and beneficial one, it's a set-up that you wouldn't usually expect given the connotations behind it. And this is the issue, really.

Whether good or bad, agents were beginning to obtain an unhealthy level of influence in world football - something which was arguably bred from *FIFA's* initial deregulation of the industry and has since been *re-addressed* at a European level by *UEFA* in a bid to correct the problems it had caused. So, go on then, let's see if they could stitch up this wound … but bear in mind, that the problem grew to be far less controllable than what we've considered here.

Far. Less. Controllable

~ 29 ~

'LET'S TRY THIS AGAIN'
Correcting the In-Correctable

Increases in player power and pervasive third-party influence had led to an intense over-inflation of the world football transfer market.

We mentioned a little earlier how the standpoint of a player's contract can affect their value over its course, though the actual figure itself is a state of constant negotiation which takes into consideration a myriad of factors, some of which don't even have much to do with football!

Beginning with the ones that do, you have: current ability, presumed potential ability, experience on the international stage, first team inclusion, European competition experience, in-game statistics, positional versatility and other perceived 'human' attributes that make you a better player, e.g. your evident levels of determination, work rate and physicality.

But by these assumptions, the game's most valuable player would be the biggest, most physical, fastest and positive player who has years of experience under his belt. However, this is only a *section* of a valuation recipe, and the other constituents have already been discussed at length so perceive this as nothing other than a helpful reminder.

Let's begin with the most basic and visual of them all - the player's face … or for the purpose of legal interpretation, their 'image'. It works in a similar way to a sport like Formula One (though not as intrinsically considered), where a driver brings with them to a team all of their personal sponsors to feed back into their constructor's kitty to improve the welfare of the car, and it's a similar circumstance with popular footballers; though things often tend to develop *after* signing, as opposed to being considerations *at the time* of signing.

Here, a player can sign career-long agreements which actively enacts an affiliation with a well-known brand or, in the cases of Ronaldinho, David Beckham and Cristiano Ronaldo, develop their *own* brands which can feed back into the retail and extra-curricular efforts of their club. Plus, as most evident with the *'Galactico'* policy, you have the excitement and expected financial return from a player's reputation – which makes up for much of the outlay required to bring them in.

Accordingly, football is in this constant cycle of funnelling in and branching out new forms of financial revenue; to reach heights vaster and more impactful than their last. Plus, with commercial advancements, wider economic inflation and third-party motive thrown into the mix, the transfer market transformed into a hedonistic exploit to see just how high a club was willing to go.

And it's a search which encourages an imbalance of power in favour of those who have a greater amount of resources to hand, and against those who now have to contend with the very same market that their misuse has inflated … but not on *UEFA's* watch … apparently!

Remarkably soon after the Abu Dhabi Group's announcement to take over Manchester City Football Club, talks progressed behind closed doors at the *UEFA* headquarters (as the primary arm responsible for regulating European teams) to exert a policy aimed at preserving the competitive aspect of their sport.

So, among others to come, City's then-new financial position was of great cause for concern in terms of anti-competitiveness, and this new policy by *UEFA* (previously discussed between themselves and *FIFA* – yes, I know it's confusing) was directed towards big spenders like them to ensure that they weren't spending *too* much. And the same would apply for clubs who aren't nouveau-riche like City, but are able to draw upon their prestige and existing financial position to exert the same effect - like a Barcelona or a Manchester United.

In theory, it was an anti-discriminatory balancer for the world of football commerce, which looked to restrain the levels of spending across Europe's major players to (hopefully) encourage them to live within their means and level out the playing field a bit; a policy aptly titled as 'Financial Fair Play' ('FFP'). The phrase 'hmm, good luck with that!' comes to mind.

Strangely, and despite being technically enacted in 2011, it was right up until their world became practically uncontrollable years later, that FFP began to be used as a *retrospective* mechanism. Its aim was to ensure that the purely *organic* sections of a club's financial policy were as balanced as ideally possible. In so far as that whatever a club's hierarchy were putting *into* the club, were being fairly balanced (to a certain, *undisclosed*, percentage point) against what they were getting *out* of the club. This would then, ideally, prevent a club operating in a disproportionate manner by extensive use of a financial backing which isn't bestowed upon their competitors.

Alongside this, an obligation has since been placed upon clubs to wilfully submit financial accounts to *UEFA* for regular housekeeping and/or specific investigation purposes - a failure or misappropriation of which will amount to a breach and resultant financial and/or competition-based penalties from the body.

Now, as a stand-alone principal, the imposition of FFP could have been disastrous for clubs who had been operating outside of its guidelines to begin with. To be told how you can spend your money can throw your entire recruitment out of whack if you're caught completely unawares by it - especially for those who have just been blessed with some new money in their pockets and are now effectively being told to ignore it

But that's the thing, by looking into the concept you begin to realise that, it's not about *what amount* you spend; it's more a case of *how* you spend it and *when*. So, from the get-go, FFP was never a well-defined principal, and its malleable instructions were left too open to interpretation to ever be taken as seriously as intended.

Time for another scenario:

Let's imagine for a second that I have walked away from my computer, massaged myself to get the blood circulated back to my gluteus maximus, popped on my snazziest Topman suit, and was suddenly installed as Manchester City's new

Director of Football; or indeed a similar role at any other well-resourced topflight football team.

Once settled, I'm ready and willing to go out and enter into top-level negotiations and, more encouragingly, am backed by a cash-hungry owner who wants nothing but to build a fantasy squad. As far as I can see, I am in a dream-like position with very few hurdles that could stop whatever I have planned.

So, when a governing body throws something like FFP into the pot, the last thing I'm going to do is just take it on the chest (at pure face value), instead, I would (as I'm sure you'll appreciate) look into the possibility of going beyond its black-and-white restrictions to enact my original plans; provided that it's done in a way which is beneficial for my own intentions, and doesn't affect the authorities *too* badly on my way through.

Not to mention the fact that I'm most likely going to be backed by a group of highly skilled legal and commercial executives; who could prove themselves to be savvy and intelligent enough to hopefully get around any issues which may arise.

Therefore, considering all of the resources at my disposal, I'm going to press on with my goal of making the best team possible for Manchester City. And with that goal in mind, let's assume that my mission is to launch an expensive bid to sign both Cristiano Ronaldo and Lionel Messi at the club's earliest convenience. Yes, it's a fanciful scenario, but my point is on the way. You see, this whole restriction business is limited to specific time periods - usually where a club's finances are scrutinised during a single transfer window or over successive ones.

So, the first thing I'd be thinking is: how much is Ronaldo going to cost me to begin with and; will his exorbitant fee mean that I have to hold off on buying Messi for the time being? It is *Ronaldo* we're talking about here, so let's assume that his fee will blow all potential player sales out the window as we do not possess similar quality to command a fee like his as a makeweight, thus we will operate in a deficit following his purchase and even more so if we tried to buy Messi straight after - perhaps to the point where it would attract unwanted attention from the FFP rozzers. So, what to do now?

Well, to begin with, the media will lead you to believe that transfers are simple transactions involving one-off fees and singular additional components - when the reality couldn't be any more different. For it's a rather complicated beast.

Granted, a transfer agreement will denote a single overall fee (the figure of which is often leaked to the media unless kept undisclosed), but the payment of it would often involve a structure which more so suits the buyer than any other party. And the higher the amount, the more likely it is that it'll be paid in a more convoluted instalment strategy, than a one-time payment.

Right off the bat, this is one of the easiest ways to circumvent the regulations; as you may *agree* to the purchase of a player for a specific transfer window, but then the fee only has a *financial impact* one or two windows down the line - spreading this commitment across a number of years which is just as favourable to the buyer, as it appears to their regulator.

And the craziest thing is, I used this whimsical example with Cristiano Ronaldo and Lionel Messi moving to a club as infinitely resourced and well-backed as Manchester

City, but the fact of the matter is that something similar to this *has already happened,* and has had a fair few knock-on effects in that of itself; both for the integrity of the FFP regulation and for a *hyperinflation* force upon the global transfer market.

So, stand up if you will, for Neymar and Mbappé are right around the corner, though as a mere peasant, please refrain from looking them directly in the eye. Yes, that means you too!

***

The story of Paris Saint-Germain's 21st century glow-up is remarkably similar to that of Manchester City. Though unlike their North-East relative, PSG held a much healthier domestic acclaim long before a bid was lodged for them.

This time, it was the Qatar Sports Investment (QSI) Group who took the plunge and transformed *Les Parisians* into the world's second state-owned football club after City. Though given the state of affairs in either club, both sets of investors had very different urgent plans for their new project.

For the 'noisy neighbours' in Manchester, it was more about achieving domestic success before trying their luck on the international stage, while for those in the French capital, it was a case of solidifying their position as the front-runner in *every* subsequent French League campaign after the takeover, *and* launching a daring challenge upon the established order in the *UEFA* Champions League.

As such, their transfer policy was front and centre of whatever they aimed to achieve. Though you would think, having completed the union during the tail end of 2011 (after the FFP regulations were put into order), that they might want to calm down a little before plunging into their bottomless bank balance. And well, considering that the next five seasons amounted to an average net spend of £60 million on transfers alone, I doubt that the message really sunk in. But even then, few could have imagined that they would follow through with their Neymar and Mbappé idea – a proposal which practically mirrors my Messi-Ronaldo example.

Beginning with the illustrious former, Neymar emerged from Barcelona's famous 'MSN' partnership with Lionel Messi and Luis Suárez, to become one of the most recognisable and sought-after forwards in the world.

However, considering the proud Camp Nou politics which run rife behind the scenes, even a player as fantastically capable and exciting as Neymar cannot be the 'main man' so long as Lionel Messi remains. And even if he lingered at the club beyond the Argentine's retirement, the vicious and straight-speaking Spanish media probably wouldn't have let any potential for comparison slip their inky quill.

Therefore, with his feet growing itchy and a move to centre-stage looking all but inevitable, PSG became the front-runner to use the Neymar deal as the ultimate signal of intent for their continental intentions, though Barca weren't willing to let their star go on the cheap. And that's putting it *lightly* …

After all, he was still well within a five-year deal (with around two full seasons left to go on it), and the only fee that would appease the Catalonian giants would be the stupid release clause they stuck in his contract to begin with.

So, how much money are we talkin'?

Well, the Brazilian's bail was set to a highly intimidating figure of €250 million. And personally, I doubt whether this was purposely included with the intention of actually bringing in that much money. Instead, I see it as nothing other than a deterrent to ward off any 'looky-loos' who may gather at the mere thought of luring him away. So, I suspect that they were as surprised as anybody when PSG came armed with a proposal, especially in this new constrained financial environment.

We can all agree, I'm sure, that his fee was a rather big one to commit to. A quarter of a billion pounds! That's a *billion* … with a *b*! Putting that into perspective given their prior transfer activity, and that's the equivalent of around 5 Edinson Cavanis, more than 8 Lucas Mouras, or about 20 Zlatan Ibrahimovićs!

Recognising this, PSG were not in the position to sell off much of their mentioned stock in order to finance the Neymar deal in line with behaving 'fairly'. Instead, it was time to get savvy in how they arranged the deal, so as to *appear* compliant despite inherently not being.

Now, this is highly presumptuous and I'm not trying to insist that the two clubs colluded together to get this deal done in light of the regulations, but what I am saying is that it was in both of their best interests to ensure that it was done, and they probably wouldn't have been able to escape *UEFA's* gaze unless they'd organised a mutually beneficial settlement between them.

Even to this day, it's currently undisclosed just *how* they were able to get around the government's financial instruction (and further investigation is pending on the matter), but it's widely believed that the instalment loophole was very much at play.

And even then, PSG hadn't established themselves in continental competition prior to Neymar joining, so they could always fall back on that 'longing for competitiveness' argument to re-settle the authorities. Plus, I'm sure *FIFA* and *UEFA* would be fine in casting blind eye to Neymar's deal provided that it was an isolated incident.

Well ...

You know, I'm not entirely sure what the most proper way is for saying 'taking the p***', so here's my attempt: Paris Saint-Germain's signing of Neymar under the FFP cloud was one thing, but their actions the following window with being linked for an equally big-money move for Monaco's Kylian Mbappé was ... taking the p***.

Take it from me, I spend a lot of my spare time watching football; whether that be a live game, a full re-run, highlights, my favourite moments, classic matches - the lot. And even with my shamelessly high wealth of personal experience, I've never seen anybody quite like Kylian Mbappé.

Lionel Messi broke onto the scene in a way befitting of his immense talent, as did Cristiano Ronaldo, and I consider myself blessed to have been born in their era. Though as the lights were beginning to dim on their time at centre-stage, I grew anxious in anticipation to see what the next wave of starlets would bring. More specifically, who would be good enough to hold the baton left by the two of them? Would it be Neymar? Perhaps. Raheem Sterling? There's definitely a case for him too. But in my opinion, I suspect our next regular Ballon D'Or nominee (and probably *FIFA's* future sweetheart) will be Mbappé. Evidently untainted by persistent comparisons with Thierry Henry and Nicolas Anelka before him, the youngster's humility has provided a solid foundation for any comparative ability to thrive on its own. And despite his relative inexperience, Mbappé has already shown certain hallmarks that a top-tier career is in the offing for him.

Explosively quick, highly intelligent and wonderfully fleet-footed, his coming to prominence grew in that precocious AS Monaco squad before it was pillaged by Pep's City, though his most influential outings appeared in a *Les Bleus* shirt, and on the grandest stage of them all.

Even now, almost two years after the French tasted gold, I remain in awe of Kylian Mbappé's display at the 2018 World Cup. You know, the competition as a whole goes down as the best during my lifetime as far as excitement, football aesthetics and controversy are concerned, yet there were only two teams for which I would move heaven and earth to ensure that I'd watch their full games - England and France.

England for patriotism's sake, and France to catch a glimpse of their forward line. And each appearance only seemed to further glorify my opinion of the teenage Kylian as their primary focal point, as he simply possesses a certain *je-ne-sais-quoi* that you wouldn't expect from somebody of his age. Usually, a young striker would run blindly forward without looking back or considering what to do when they arrive at their destination; with aforethought generally blessing those who have some form of experience to call upon. Yet Mbappé was able to envision what to do with the ball, *long* before racing towards that advanced position and making it a reality.

Then, after reaching the goalmouth, younger players tend to assess the goalkeeper's movement to provide some sort of data to dictate where their shot should go. Though the Frenchman seemed to instinctively know how the state of play would affect the 'keeper's position; and launch the ball effectively into the free space to the side of them. It was so fluid. So *natural* to watch.

And like I've mentioned already, the utter *modesty* of the guy just makes me want to give him a cuddle! In every interview I've watched with him, he presents himself as a top-level talent without the braggadocio of being one. He's well-spoken, fully understands the blessings that arrive with his level of ability and seems ever focused on obtaining the career that he looks destined to achieve. A career which required a high calibre move to give him a greater wealth of opportunity than that what would have been presented to him in Monaco.

And fortunately for him, with Real Madrid and even Manchester City priced out of a move for him, the ambitious QSI representatives couldn't get to the south coast quickly enough to give him that precise opportunity. As far as pricing goes, his fee wasn't *quite* up there with Neymar's (who'd arrived the season before), but it was pretty darn close … at around €150 million.

Alright, that's nearly €100 million away from the Brazilian's, but being seven years his junior, the relative difference between the two transactions is more nominal than what appears to the naked eye. And if anybody recognised this more seriously than any other, it was the originators of the very doctrine aiming to curtail this behaviour; *UEFA*.

Think of it this way:

Whenever a governor enacts a new policy, they want one of two things to happen: to see a widespread, *prima facie* acceptance of the rule, or in the event that you have little option but to correct an abuser, you'd like the opportunity to impose a significant sanction upon them to deter any future cases.

In this instance, Paris Saint-Germain's headline-grabbing deal for Neymar had set alarm bells ringing in Switzerland - a bit like waving that first piece of cloth in the eye of the bull - you may get away with that first one, but now that the bull's alert, you have to do something different if you are to evade its rage on the second occasion. Unfortunately for *UEFA*, this wasn't PSG's first time at the rodeo, and at least this time they weren't intent upon *totally* insulting the regulator's intelligence by doing the same thing again, but they had another trick up their sleeve for evading the FFP regulation. This time (rather wittingly) by masquerading the transfer deal under the guise of a loan agreement (with an obligation to buy).

This one's so simple that it's almost comical.

The loan itself was structured in a way which is largely undisclosed to the media (*quelle surprise!*), but the general consensus is this: the deal was predicated on Mbappé joining PSG at the earliest opportunity on a loan agreement until the end of that season, where the Parisians would pay 100% of his existent wage contract at AS Monaco for the privilege, and offer up around €40-50 million as a down-payment for Mbappé's release amount; to appease the Southerners enough that they would expect to receive the remaining amount upon the end of the loan.

In the meantime, the club could proactively balance the books by letting a few players leave, in anticipation of eventually sealing the Mbappé deal permanently the following window – something which they have made themselves 'obligated' to do under the original loan agreement. Basically, it was a bit like getting down on one knee, only there's a contract in place so you can't change your mind. So, marriage ... pretty much.

Ergo, It doesn't come as much of a surprise that, at the beginning of the 2019/20 season, the club recouped around €90 million worth of player sales from many of their squad members e.g. Giovanni Lo Celso to Real Betis and Moussa Diaby to Bayer Leverkusen; neither of whom were considered immediate first-teamers for the Parisians. But would bring them enough time, resource and respite to conclude their primary arrangement.

Overall, they behaved very tactically here, and have so far rebuffed any immediate sanction from their governors for acting unlawfully. And in most recent times, speculation has suggested a move away for both Neymar and Mbappé at some point before their contracts end ... so we may *never* get to the bottom of it all.

But what's more certain is that, if Neymar's deal was like sticking the proverbial middle finger up at *UEFA* and their silly new concept to combat *FIFA's* near-sightedness, then Mbappé's move was raising the accompanying index digit to ram home the point.

And their fragrant misappropriation of the authorities' intent behind behaving 'fairly' in the financial sense, serves as a damning indictment for a proposal which has since incurred more failures than it has successes.

But let's be fair here ...

Thus far, I have only really considered the foundation of this regulation given the empirical data which suggests that the elite will look to circumvent its restrictions whenever possible. Though the *other* fact is, that the deterrent has been successful for a number of higher profile clubs at the same time - one of which in particular has been the direct beneficiary of both the record-breaking deals that fell undercover to the rule, as well as the live-within-your-means-and-invest policy that it aimed to encourage. You may have heard of them, they're called 'Liverpool Football Club'.

Because remember, where one club is paying that unhealthy amount for players, it transpires into a very healthy amount for the recipients – and this is the 'domino effect' in its most delightful form.

~ 30 ~

'KLOPP'S MERSEYSIDE REVOLUTION'
Du wirst nie alleine laufen

Jürgen Klopp was definitely one of the most sought-after managers of his time when linked with the vacant Liverpool seat in 2015. And his all-out 'pressing' style shown in previous stints with Eintracht Frankfurt and Borussia Dortmund, identified well with the proud hordes of 'Kopites' funnelling into the Anfield Stadium every other week.

So, spirits were high upon his unveiling, which in itself came under a much more stable Liverpool environment than had been seen so far in the Premier League era … and they were thrusted *even higher* given how he'd dealt with the initial hurdles dealt to him that summer of taking charge. The club were threatening to spiral into a downward descent following the departure of Brendan Rodgers, which looked all but certain following the announcement that Steven Gerrard would be leaving the club; shortly after Raheem Sterling's City switch was finalised. Not the most ideal of starts for the new man in charge.

Undoubtedly, Gerrard ranks as one of the most loyal servants to ever don the red of Liverpool Football Club ... and also one of the most technically gifted to do so.

Sure, the Anfield clan have been fortunate to breed some of the greatest British players ever employed on these shores, but Gerrard's age-defying qualities thrust him nearer to the top than most. Allowing his shaven head, pimpled face and excitable running patterns, you'd suspect that he'd been there for years when he broke onto the scene. He began as a powerful, stocky and imposing midfielder and developed into a cultured, dependable and quite beautiful attacking midfielder.

Moreover, he was of the rare breed who looked just as capable of creating a goal-scoring opportunity as he was to finish them off. And most of all, each outing displayed his unrelenting dedication for the club he loved; altogether culminating in a fine fifteen-year elite-level playing career, which may have been even more distinguished had the Lords of time afforded him an opportunity to be managed by someone like Klopp.

Nevertheless, reality saw Gerrard move onto a swansong showing with the LA Galaxy in the MLS (presumably so as to retain his heralded status on Merseyside), and the club were potentially left in another state of limbo with his departure. Though mercifully, their bright-toothed new manager had considered that, and aimed to act in a manner which responded to the end of one era with the birth of another.

Correspondingly, he saw fit to transform the club's transfer policy; which now strayed away from short-term moves into the world of aforethought - a requisite for all potentially successful teams. Hereafter, the Reds promptly began shipping out those for whom a long-lasting first team involvement couldn't be foreseen. Alas, joining Gerrard and Sterling out the door were a number of lads who were either beyond their best at the club or weren't yielding anywhere near the return that came to be expected of their new coach.

Glen Johnson, given his form of late, looked quite fortunate to join a respectable Premier League defence at Stoke City under Mark Hughes. Sebastián Coates looked like a fish out of water and has only really *now* looked at his pay grade in the *Liga NOS* with Sporting Lisbon. I'd be surprised if Javi Manquillo lasted much longer at Newcastle under somebody as traditional as Steve Bruce (unless Ashley has his way with him before anything happens), Iago Aspas and Rickie Lambert looked like impulsive transfers who soon went to more comfortable surroundings, and receiving almost ten million quid for Fabio Borini was a bare-faced act of grand larceny on their part.

A thoroughly efficient 'fire sale' if ever there were one, and with that out of the way, it was time to go shopping. But remember, think: long-term, good value and sustainability. For that is how this new Liverpool shall operate, and indeed, how most sensible top-level clubs are supposed to be operated.

Needless to say, their influx that summer was outstanding, and even more so when you consider that the club only recorded a net transfer spend of just shy of £20 million. One of their first and, for me, among their greatest transfers ever was the nominal acquisition of James Milner once his contract had run down at Manchester City.

A highly versatile, yet endearingly 'boring' employee to whomever he has served, Milner possesses one of the most comprehensive Premier League CV's to date. Right from the academy at Leeds United to the bright lights at Anfield, his work ethic and natural ability have together forged an indomitable career spanning a term almost as long as Steven Gerrard's!

And in a time made unstable by the Scouser's leaving party, Milner brought talent, league experience, industry, integrity and stability to Liverpool's midfield setup - and even transformed into a bit of a full-back whenever the team required. A wonderfully astute pick-up for the club in this world of big-money signings … and a welcome addition to a long list of outstanding 'Bosman' moves.

Then, with that 'experience' checkpoint crossed off, Klopp set about securing the signatures of those who would bulk out two other key areas - 'youth' and 'excitement'; the 'longer term' stuff.

This began with the signings of Joe Gomez and Nathaniel Clyne from Charlton and Southampton respectively. Though where the latter's career has petered out through injury and the emergence of the club's own Melwood-trained prospects, Gomez' pace, reading of the game and love for the tackle has proven himself to be a worthy adversary for many of the league's top forwards, since he became comfortable in the Reds' back line.

Following him, came the dual signings of two lads who could not be more different - one of which may go down as one of the more pivotal learning curves in Liverpool's new recruitment direction under Klopp, and the other who served as a reminder for his intended direction. Beginning unconventionally with the latter (just because I can), he managed to pinch Roberto Firmino from under the wandering eyes of Manchester United - a no.10 Johan Cruyff-esque deploy who has formed the linchpin of

Liverpool's attacking behaviour since arriving. Whilst the purchase of the former Christian Benteke for an eye-watering £32.5 million, was a great example of how reverting to what's recognisable sometimes can negatively bypass your original vision.

Firmino embodied what Klopp wanted for his own Total Football-inspired 'false forward' - he was tricky, intelligent, technically gifted and spotted the gap with which to penetrate the defence when a normal layman would declare it filled; therefore, the ideal man to have behind a mobile centre-forward who could keep the attacking momentum going.

Christian Benteke was not that guy. He's a target man. Granted, he enjoyed a very good campaign at Aston Villa the season before, but flourished purely when acting as the focal point of an attack focused on getting the ball crossed above the defenders and onto his head. But that's not the direction that Liverpool were looking to go into and, if anything, was the antithesis of Klopp's free-flowing preference.

It therefore comes as no surprise that the ex-in-form Belgian only lasted a single season in front of the Kop, though away from his unsuitability in the Liverpool line-up, his sale displayed the club's innate business acumen to succeed in this new supposed 'FFP-focused' world. Margins became important and only smart investments were made after this. And a mere £5 million loss was a small price to pay for what could have been a terrible transaction for the Reds. After this, they didn't look back.

The next season saw the departing Benteke joined by Martin Škrtel, Mario Balotelli and a number of other lads who didn't fit the mould of a focused, driven 'Jürgen Klopp player', and in their place came Sadio Mané, Georginio Wijnaldum and

Joël Matip; all for an accumulative fee which was less than what Manchester United paid for Ángel Di María. And this is what I mean when I say that Liverpool operated in a much more intelligent manner than what they had been accustomed to.

Though nothing presents their new-found intelligence better, then how they responded to that quarter-billion Neymar transfer; for which the side-effects just so happened to directly benefit them more immediately than any other bystander.

O efeito domino

This is where we need to look at that Neymar transfer in a wider context, in order to fully comprehend its effects.

Naturally, though the financial windfall attracted by the Brazilian was a pretty pay-day for the Catalonians, it left a pretty large gap in their squad which now needed to be filled. There were stories circulating around the rumour mill that they were looking to bring in Antoine Griezmann from Atlético Madrid, or even Eden Hazard from Chelsea at the time to replace him.

But, seeing how they had just lost one of their most creative outlets and those aforementioned targets seemed too tied down to be prized away at the time, Barca were made to look elsewhere; a search which brought them to Anfield's own Brazilian superstar.

In case you hadn't noticed, I'm referring to Philippe Coutinho - whose once promising career as a Southern American starlet looked in danger of faltering in Italy, before a well-timed call from Brendan Rodgers re-organised his career in the appropriate direction. But unfortunately for him, it appears like his Liverpool venture may prove to be his finest hour. For he wasn't a like-for-like replacement for the departing Neymar in terms of comparable attributes, and yet the exuberant fee associated with his arrival suggested to the fans that this was a reasonable expectation.

Ergo, he was operating on the backfoot from the moment that Barcelona had declared their intentions to sign him. Where, upon officially relocating, he'd either: challenge with the incumbent players for their midfield spots (contestants included Andrés Iniesta, Ivan Rakitić and Sergio Busquets) or be played out of position to fulfil the gap directly voided by Neymar - none of which would do much in terms of promoting squad harmony or bringing the best out of their latest recruit.

Nevertheless, Barca persisted with the deal, and Liverpool used the situation to maximise their return on Coutinho - which eventually brought in over nine figures to supplement their impending vision.

So, when you look at all this given what we know now, you can infer that Liverpool knew that Neymar's deal had hyperinflated the market, and were sure to benefit in the greatest way possible. All the while using this bubbled amount to supplement purchases for whoever else they wanted to bring in; which could now practically be whoever they wanted. And it didn't stop there!

Another remarkable sale from this time falls far under the radar but deserves some uncovering. Mamadou Sakho, who'd originally joined as a promising young'un from Paris Saint-German, proved competent in terms of his positional play and aerial ability, but fell short with the ball at his feet - an absolute 'no-no' to Klopp. So, with his muscular behind plonked firmly in the discard pile, a number of mid-tier Premier League clubs came circling around, though Liverpool remained resolute in their valuation ... of a player ... that they deemed surplus to requirements. The nerve.

But whatever the reason, it was this exact nerve which bagged them a cool £25 million for Sakho when a free-spending Crystal Palace came calling. Therefore, they'd managed to raise around £150 million for two of their players when one could argue that this figure would've been halved if not for the facilitating Neymar transfer.

Now, it was pivotal that Liverpool didn't themselves fall into the big-spending trap akin to the ones they had set to earn the money in the first place. Like I said, it was time to *invest* their earnings in the most effective and sustainable ways possible. And if ever you're thinking on what 'good investments' look like; read on ...

They began by stripping Arsenal's midfield of Alex Oxlade-Chamberlain; an industrious, hard-working and bright midfielder built in the mould of Klopp's *'gegenpress'* system. For those who are unaware of what this tactic is, the term *gegen* in German translates into 'against' in English - and the overall term is coined for a team that is tactically set up to squeeze the creativity out of the opposition; by relentlessly closing down their play before it's able to develop.

Granted, that just sounds like a normal 'press' system but the *gegenpress* has been typically attached to sides who defend from the front - where the front-man is deployed as a pressing forward to squeeze some insecurity into the defence, and the wingers specifically man-mark their full-backs and track their movements in an attempt to springboard the attack in the opposite direction once possession is earned. Ergo, busy-minded midfielders like 'the

Ox' are pivotal to a set-up like this and, when fit, he is a competent figure at the heart of their midfield.

Then in came a nippy Scottish left back called Andrew Robertson; a stand-out performer in an inconsistent Hull side who were relegated before the Reds stopped by. And at £8 million, you'd struggle to find a better modern-day bargain than this fella.

Playing with that tenacity that derives from a hard time in the early years of your career, Hull was Robertson's 'big break' moment; one which took him from the periphery of Scottish football, and into the top-flight fray in the most visible competition in the world. While a registered 'Tiger', his tendency to get forward and whip a ball in often left his centre-backs isolated against the stronger opposition. But that doesn't mean that he should be made to fit the mould of a club whose standard is beneath his evident quality, if anything, he just needed to find a surrounding which could ultimately benefit from his first-choice game plan. And that was Liverpool.

Funnily enough, Liverpool were *almost* there in establishing their key centre-back pairing for the next few seasons, though internal troubles would see their key target escape their grasp right until the 2018 January window.

suave voice you know, I was an intern for a global sports agency ('Wasserman Media Group') during the summer of 2017 *normal voice*, where I was fortunate enough to work closely with the team's agents, one of whom had Virgil van Dijk on his books; the archetypal centre-back for the modern age. He's confident, integral to the defence, happy to bring the ball forward, talented enough to link up the play and imposing enough to ensure that his teammates understand what is expected of them. Also, the man had the vision of a lighthouse - which can only be a positive for the side so long as he had players good enough to ping it to.

He already had Sadio Mané and Roberto Firmino ahead of him, but the right side of the forward line was lacking an out-and-out winger. Divock Origi and Adam Lallana did all they could to plug that gap, but Klopp had his sights set on somebody in particular to take on that role. Remember a while ago, where we looked at how City's de Bruyne purchase had highlighted some glaring issues with Chelsea's loan policy? Well, here's another dreadful mistake.

Initially arriving from a promising FC Basel side in 2014, a young Egyptian by the name of Mohamed Salah found his game time exorbitantly limited at The Bridge. Well, when I say 'limited', it was shrunk to the size of a *Baby GAP* sweater.

From acting as Basel's primary exploit over nearly fifty outings across two seasons in mainland Europe (across both domestic and continental competitions), Salah became a spare bench-player in his only season in London - registering fourteen appearances with over three-quarters of his airtime beginning on the side-lines.

So, discontent with his false start and playing up to Chelsea's tendency to loan rather than play, the nippy forward was farmed out to ACF Fiorentina before a pivotal relocation to Rome was made permanent. And over sixty games and thirty strikes later only seek to highlight the gravity of yet *another* Chelsea mistake. One that they would be reminded of on home turf ... again. Mohammed Salah was completely imperious during his time in Italy, and the phrase 'practise makes perfect' springs to mind when assessing his attacking decisions.

Much like Mahrez and Robben before him, his deployment on the right wing served mainly to maximise the effectiveness of his left foot. To turn a defender, angle towards the penalty area, open up his body and finesse the ball to the far side of the 'keeper, was his preferred way of conducting business.

Technically, he was what you call a 'typical' right-winger, with an 'atypical' scoring rate for the league that he was in. More often than not, a Serie A wide-man's proficiency is more dictated by their team play and assists record than their own personal scoring tally - one which is often fobbed off to the side's 'natural' striker as the focal point of their formation.

So, when you consider these variables, Salah was quickly becoming a winger whose attributes were better aligned with the Premier League than most other domestic tournaments, and few teams were as understanding and well-resourced to act upon this fact than Liverpool.

A base €42 million offer was enough to attract the Egyptian to Merseyside, and his new number 11 shirt and freedom afforded by the manager, had completely revitalised their attacking trio. Which, when you look at everything in as macrocosmically a manner as we've attempted to in this book, is yet another modern-day adaptation of *Totaalvoetbal*. 'Oh God, here he goes again' … *yes!* Here I go again! Whether we like to admit it or not, we owe a lot of our current 'best tactical innovations' to the greatest one ever trialled.

The first sign of this is how Roberto Firmino has since approached his role in the heart of Liverpool's attacking line. For all of his mobility and nimble energies, he isn't the most gifted, hard-headed goal-scorers to ever don the famous 'number nine' jersey. In fact, in this sort of controversial Berbatov-esque way of operating, his game is more focused on supplying his teammates than having his teammates supply him. He's a *creator*.

Instead of being an advanced forward, he is a *'False Nine'* - deployed in that further region but expected to sit back, link up the play, thread the ball through to his inverted wingers and press high up the pitch in order to protect the midfield.

Hence why his scoring output has become a 'meme' of sorts; in that it falls far behind many of his respective frontmen. But once you remove this stigma and home in on his specific qualities, then he must rank as one of the most creative, selfless and talented assist-makers in the world right now. And a few additional seasons at the top may louden his speech at the table of all-time playmakers. But that's yet to be seen.

For now, we can only assess the career of Firmino and his Liverpool teammates in the context of what they've been able to achieve so far. And as things stand, they threaten to become the latest all-conquering dynasties to ever be thrusted onto the world stage ... much like the Total Footballers before them.

And back-to-back Champions League finals (with a deserved win on the second attempt), plus a near-centurion figure to achieve their first ever Premier League title is testament to what Klopp has built. Dynamic wing-play, full player culpability, a team spirit to intoxicate an elephant and a variety of attacking options that'll leave you dizzier than a *Thorpe Park* ride. Truly mesmerising. True, many of their domestic competitors had fallen away for various other idiosyncratic reasoning during their winning 2019/20 campaign, but that shouldn't detract from the fact that Liverpool have achieved a decidedly *dominant* topflight win compared to their nearest battlers. Finishing over 20 points ahead of Manchester City in this year, and even adding another ten onto that against that other part of Manchester, is a phenomenal achievement. And if they get things right and continue on the trajectory that they're currently threatening to embark upon, then the Reds finally appear to be regaining their past glory by moving into the 21st century.

Though mind you, there are a few things that they need to contend with before we can even engage in that conversation.

In fact, there are a number of transcendent issues that we will all need to contend with moving forward …

~ CONCLUSION ~

'Looking into the Crystal Foot-ball

... see what I did there?!

Thus far, the majority of this novel has been an exercise of looking *back* at some of the most momentous occasions in the world of football - and anally linking together the bits and pieces to best describe how we got from Point A, to point B.

But now that we're at point B, let's have a look at where we could be going in the future; off the basis of some of the instances which have happened up until this point, and various speculative issues which could impact where we're headed.

The Potential Impacts of Covid-19

For many of us, 2020 was supposed to be the year that we all would look back on as one that we approached in the most positive of ways. A new decade! A new number formation. I mean it even *sounded* nice to hear!

So surely, this is when we change our appearance, our eating habits, spending tendencies, link up with our families, bring a lovely partner home to meet them and live happily on a beach in Kavos? No. Instead, we have had to bind together against something which completely transcends the world of football, and indeed any sport … or any*thing*.

<u>DISCLAIMER</u>:

Before I go on, I implore you now to please consider my narrative in the way in which it was intended. By not going into detail over the tragedies resulting from the virus, it in no way communicates my stance on the matter from my own personal perspective.

It has been a terrible time to live through and one in which I am incredibly fortunate to state that I haven't been massively affected by. But to the millions of people around the world who have: suffered from the virus, experienced its economic impact or worse still, are dealing with the aftermath of a loved one who has succumbed to it, there aren't enough words available to express my deepest sympathy and condolences to you.

I can't pretend that I'm able to fully comprehend what you have had to go through, but I do my best to be as sympathetic and thoughtful to it as I can possibly be. And in this context, it's my job to communicate some of the other significant issues in the context of the sport which governs the journey of this book, and it will be of the greatest disrespect on my part if it were to come across in any other way. The first official ban on sporting events resulting from the attempts to constrain the reach of Covid-19, began in

Italy in mid-February 2020; where they were declared as the worst-hit territory away from its country of origin. As reported, it was briefly contained to the Lombardy region in the north of the country, though a lack of quick action and border restrictions allowed its impact to accelerate toward mainland Italy - affecting its most densely populated areas such as Rome, Naples and Milan.

During this early stage, it was considered almost *illogical* to target many of the day-to-day actions of their civilians in an attempt to strangle the virus e.g. prohibiting travel or congregations of a certain number of people; with the simple reason being that it would disrupt the areas integral to the country's economy, without truly understanding the severity of the situation, nor the best way to prevent the side-effects of establishing such preventative measures. With hindsight as our guide, this would prove to be a truly destructive and near-sighted way of tackling a much broader issue.

Instead, things began by restricting the levels of attendance permitted in gatherings which were mainly ticket-controlled – like football matches, though there was never a proposal for the government to provide any aid to the clubs who'd miss out on the ticket revenue, as it was only meant to be a short-term measure.

As we now know, the postponement of *Serie A* and *Serie B* fixtures in Italy were to be the tip of the iceberg, with cases of Covid-19 cropping up throughout the core of Western Europe - with France, Spain and the UK soon following in their footsteps.

Strangely enough, I was readying another notch on my 'how many football matches can I go to' belt, before the news had 'affected' me. One week, I'm booking myself into a modest hotel in Nice after arranging return flights over the 13th-14th March weekend, with the intent to travel to AS Monaco's Stade de Louis II stadium for an eye-level view of their mid-table *Ligue Un* clash with AS Saint-Etienne.

In the next, the match is postponed (along with the league schedule as a whole) for an indefinite period, and we progress even further into the world of uncertainty.

For whatever reason, perhaps the commercial ramifications of a delay in schedule, the Premier League and *UEFA* competitions were the last to follow their neighbours' examples - with many Europa League matches being played behind closed doors, and EPL authorities gathering to discuss the best ways of finishing the season; both of which are even more glaring examples of not truly understanding what we were dealing with here.

Either way, they eventually got their act together, and an indefinite waiting period was also put on their games. Soon thereafter, a global ban was imposed on all domestic football competitions with other sports taking a similar step.

The inaugural Australian Grand Prix for the Formula One 2020 season was postponed, all boxing events (including a potential trilogy finale between Deontay Wilder and Tyson Fury) was put on the back burner, and expectedly, the international football European Championships and wider Summer Olympics were rearranged for the following year.

That's a lot of stoppages. And all within an era where sport is so closely linked with its commercial and financial funnel. And some have proven to be far more dependent on this stability than others ... and to catastrophic effect.

Too often, all of the focus tends to be on the elites in any sport; especially in the footballing hemisphere. And it's a crying shame that the troubles of the lower leagues act as footnotes for the 'bigger story'. In fact, this season serves as another indictment of what could so easily happen to lower clubs; that don't benefit from the levels of commercial attention and investment enjoyed by larger clubs, when times get tougher.

In this case, times couldn't be harder for those associated with Bury FC or Wigan Athletic FC. Exploring the details of Bury's demise is a very dim undertaking, and the striking fall from grace for the Latics is one which still confuses me.

Anybody anywhere in the world can 'fall in love' with a club as visible and 'great' as a Liverpool, Manchester United or Real Madrid. Yet smaller clubs like Bury and Wigan form the linchpin of their local communities and become deeply embedded within their fans' lives; where anything that affects their club directly affects them.

And very unfortunately, both had fallen victim to poor ownership and related financial mismanagement - factors which could have been prevented and even reversed if fortunes were different. But this virus, and its destabilizing effect on a once dependable and structured money funnel, had plunged them into a depth from which they could not emerge.

I sincerely feel for this pair of clubs and indeed any other whose similar experiences haven't made their way to the mainstream media yet. But either way, let's hope there's a more positive twist of events whenever these institutions resurface ... if they ever do. And most importantly of all, let's hope that we can (as a society) band together in the face of this adversity in order to emerge more united and knowledgeable than ever before.

From one tough-to-discuss topic to another, but for very different reasons indeed. For the record, I rarely ever engage in much political discussion *en masse* as it's become a smorgasbord of unfiltered opinion with little substance or reason. But what I will say is that I'm in the apparent minority who voted 'remain', so you could probably predict my feelings towards the outcome of the EU referendum, and its expected side-effects; not least for a game which has benefited so handsomely from the creation of the European Union.

Upon leaving, various existing community agreements will need to be revised or scrapped altogether in order to coincide with the winning '*Brexit*' campaign. One of which will concern how easily accessible the UK shores are to European football players – both for 'regular' *and* Bosman deals. So, take away membership to the Union, and there's a possibility that these opportunities will be greatly limited.

As of now, everything appears 'up in the air' as to what these developments will look like in practise (with the mentioned pandemic crisis re-organising the government's priorities), but if they evolve in the way in which many of us expect, then the consequences could have very diverse effects for the welfare of British football, and indeed for the countries who remain in the Union; and no longer have the English league behemoth as a direct competitor for their primary targets in the transfer market.

Firstly, if the United Kingdom leaves the EU and its football-related principals behind, then that means players are no longer freely able to relocate to the UK and register for one of their football teams. Instead, they will have to be granted a 'work permit' by their home authorities in order to sanction the move - one which is granted based on a number of factors, including: how many first team appearances the player has made, whether or not they've been considered on an international level, how old they are, and how much money they're supposedly being sold for.

As such, there will either be a decreased likelihood of many targets clearing these performance-based hurdles placed in front of them, and it may even impose a greater financial burden upon the buying clubs who wish to sign them.

Worse still, we've already made the argument for the benefits of having foreign competition brought in, and English football is at risk of losing that continental influence which has since benefited them so greatly - not to mention the managers and coaches whose legacies are ensconced within the game's tactical archives.

But on the flip side, without this outsider competition, there is greater capacity and reason for clubs to look from within their own ranks as opposed to going for a foreign alternative. Which, in a league that has attracted negative headlines for its lack of focus on domestic talent, may be a welcome arrangement for budding academy starlets and local players thinking of trying out at their favourite clubs.

Having said that, simply having a *larger* crop of talent to work with doesn't necessarily correlate with a *more talented* crop at the end of it; as there are a wealth of variables to consider for a player's success, which ultimately doesn't lead to a 'there are more, so there will be more' level of efficiency.

Adding onto this, simply adding more domestic players to the mix doesn't guarantee that a newcomer (who may have been phased out in an era with a greater level of competition), is of the calibre required to make sense of this change. And in fact, over a period of time, the level of national output might localise to a median point at which this new group of talent has become accustomed to - which can be better or worse compared to who the country has produced so far.

So, it's an argument but a very faint one. And like I say, I completely disagree with the motive behind moving away from the Union in the first place, so I struggle to stay impartial when discussing this. Sure, there are cases for and against our inclusion in the EU from an economic viewpoint, but from a pure footballing aspect, I feel as though this would enable other member territories to benefit from their continued membership, to a point where the UK's progressively home-grown batch may not be able to catch up for a very long time.

Plus, there's this idea that domestic clubs might improve slightly with mainland Europe not having to worry as much about the UK pinching one of their fledgling stars (as they have done so frequently in the past), and even that seems to be a very long-term concept for them leaving the Union's territorial membership for the time being. Plus, who's not to say that these powerful clubs in the UK wouldn't be able to (in some way) develop a legal loophole which puts us back at square one - thereby rendering the entire motion obsolete but without the potential for a recount?

Yeah ... *not* a fan!

Football has not been short of its advances in technology over the years, and some of its more substantial in-game developments have happened in my own millennial lifetime.

Beginning off the field, a vault chocked full of scientific jargon and scary mathematical equations introduce you to the world of sports science and nutrition; altogether forced through progressively sophisticated and intuitive sports technology and software.

Back in the eras nearer to the beginning of this web's timeline, your typical pre-match meal might have consisted of … well … whatever you wanted to eat. Provided you stuck to the major carbohydrate food group, you could eat as much as you liked before a game kicked off, and perhaps even a slice of orange if you were lucky to find one lying around. Then, Wenger (a notable name among a select few) went against the grain to make things slightly more appropriate for an elite sportsperson.

He was one of the very few managers in the early '90s to have enforced a strict, bespoke dietary regimen on each of his players; all depending on whatever the medical tests and muscle-related software reports could tell him about them. We all know Ian Wright wasn't too fond of this 'no-seasoning, no problem' attitude, but mix this in with a few vitamin supplements, protein drinks and iron tablets, and perhaps the ex-Palace man wishes that his previous managers had kept up with the Joneses a lot sooner!

Sam Allardyce was also a major voice for this area, where a lot of his sports science focused on a player's stamina and durability, and even Don Revie long before him opted for a more rural 'tell me what you see, and write a dossier' tactic to analysing his opposition.

Nowadays, sports physiotherapy experts and opposition analysts have made these jobs a lot easier - all through the mediums of a few clicks of a mouse and a concurring 'hmmm' or 'aah' when looking at whatever code appears in front of them.

Some *players* have even gone further than this in order to bring some forward-thinking scientific outlook into their personal lives and have welcomed their own eating and training formulas for extending their careers. Though where a lot of this is an optional idea for those who wish to go that extra mile, the game itself has undergone its own development in order to portray that modern image. The most recent addition of which proving to be one of its most controversial to date.

'Video Assistant Refereeing' ('VAR') has received a mixed reception since its introduction. As a concept, it allows a referee's pivotal decisions to be reviewed by an independent panel to ensure that the correct one was made. So, in theory, it works perfectly fine in affording the officials some much-needed respite whenever they're forced to make a controversial decision. But in reality, a lot of work is needed in order to make it … less … conspicuous than it's proven to be so far.

Of course, we are commenting during its infancy and are sure to see some much-needed improvements in the way in which VAR is handled in future, though I sincerely hope that a good amount of focus is angled toward its effect on game momentum, lack of rule clarity and overall mis-communication to the crowd. If so, then we're on to a winner, and I suspect it may become commonplace to the lower leagues once we get a grip on how best to operate it higher up.

Once that's sorted, I personally believe that the sky's the limit for technology to have a greater role in the overall officiating of a football match; namely, with the offside rule (which may be changed altogether), and the gizmos provided to the referee in order to communicate his thought process in as clear a way as possible; perhaps like they're able to do in rugby.

After all, *their logic is undeniable* … and if you understand that reference, then hit me up on Twitter so we can be friends.

Just one more game ... I promise!

In its simplest description, 'E-Sports' are digitised versions of organised sport, which are elegantly packed into a disk before being displayed by a complex set of electrical impulses and LED screening to engage the user.

It's ... erm ... it's a *game*. Really, it's a game.

Since moving into the era where kids would rather stay inside than go outdoors, much of that thought process is owed to a games console. Be it a spawn of *Nintendo*, *Xbox* or *PlayStation*, it's believed that almost 9 in 10 children have confessed to spending their spare time immersed in a world which doesn't resemble their own.

Personally, I've always been a fan of the *FIFA* franchise (but for a brief, yet meaningless affair with the *PES* community), and the commercial world has since enveloped the game much like it had done to the very organisation which bears its name. Hehe ... that rhymed. I'm so great.

Nowadays, playing a video game isn't *just* a simple pastime for those who are willing to take it seriously enough. Therefore, for those dedicated 'gamers' out there, the emergence of streaming platforms like *YouTube* and *Twitch* have afforded a modern-day opportunity to be completely self-employed - where 'streamers' film and edit their antics on screen for the next generation to swoon over. And I'll admit, I'm a big fat *swooner*!

Even to this day, at my big age of twenty-three, I struggle to fall asleep without my daily fix of *YouTube* content; which more often than not involves somebody my age or younger playing a game that I can't be bothered to play myself. I'm not entirely sure why this is the way that it is, and

I'm sure the aforementioned advancements in science and psychology might help to explain some of it, but for the time being, I shall watch *KSI* and *The Sidemen* until my heart's content!

However, in terms of breaking the mould on the *actual* footballing side, a sign of things to come might just have been presented by a certain Spencer Owen - my personal choice for one of *YouTube's* most innovative and ground-breaking producers.

Since arriving on the platform with global football brand *Copa90*, Owen has managed to create a dynasty which centres around his love of football, and a desire to merge together the world in which his name was made, and the other which gives it meaning.

Operating in this dual-purpose manner has since seen a number of effective collaborations for his charity-focused 'Wembley Cup' events, right up until the creation of 'Hashtag United'; an amateur sports outfit which currently sits in the ninth tier of English football with a following that would threaten a side seven or eight divisions higher than where they are!

Now, at this stage, it would be very irresponsible for me to declare that a team like Hashtag are capable of rocking the big-boy boat anytime soon. But to think that some dude with a camera in front of him was even able to create a team in the first place, is a sign that we are entering into a new age of digital entrepreneurism; where the rewards and rigour are capable of rocking most boats ... and *buying* a few!

A Message from the Author

As this is my first ever novel, most of my time has been spent mulling over particular turns of phrases just to ensure that it's readable and 'proper'. But in my final address to you, I want this to be as unfiltered as possible. So, if you spot: a typo, a misuse of grammar, or even a swear word, well then that's just a darn shame.

Ever since I was a kid, football has been something of a guiding star in my life. I suffered from obesity from a very young age, and all of the adorning mental struggles that came with it. Other children made fun of me, I was bullied at school, and there even came a time where I didn't want to look in the mirror; for fear of not liking whatever disgusting figure was staring back. And it was through football, as a goalkeeper (go figure!), that I was finally able to connect with my peers on a level which transcended my appearance.

Between the sticks, I went from being an outcast to part of a *team*; where other kids were *on my side* and *listened* to what I had to say! It was something I'd never experienced before, and without it, I don't know what else would've been strong enough to pull me out of that negative cycle that I was trapped in.

As soon as I put my 'keeper's gloves on, I no longer had to be the 'me' that I didn't like. Instead, I could be Edwin van der Sar, or Iker Casillas, or whoever else I'd been watching the night before a game - shout out to my dad for paying for Sky Sports all these years, too!

As a whole, football has allowed me to feel like I *belonged* somewhere, and it's a childhood love which has since blossomed into a teenage anchor and an adult obsession - one that you've just read about, and I hope you've enjoyed.

Thank you.

Check Out my Other Content.

Twitter: @ammandev
Instagram: @ammandev
Linkedin: 'Dev Bajwa'
YouTube Channel: 'Dev Bajwa'

Printed in Great Britain
by Amazon